# Torch Singing

# ETHNOGRAPHIC ALTERNATIVES BOOK SERIES

**Series Editors**
**Carolyn Ellis and Arthur P. Bochner**
(both at the University of South Florida)

*Ethnographic Alternatives* emphasizes experimental forms of qualitative writing that blur the boundaries between social sciences and humanities and experiment with novel forms of expressing lived experience, including literary, poetic, autobiographical, multivoiced, conversational, critical, visual, performative, and coconstructed representations. Emphasis should be on expressing concrete lived experience through narrative modes of writing.

**Books in the Series:**

Volume 1, *Composing Ethnography: Alternative Forms of Qualitative Writing*, Carolyn Ellis and Arthur P. Bochner, editors

Volume 2, *Opportunity House: Ethnographic Stories of Mental Retardation*, Michael V. Angrosino

Volume 3, *Kaleidoscope Notes: Writing Women's Music and Organizational Culture*, Stacy Holman Jones

Volume 4, *Fiction and Social Research: By Fire or Ice*, Anna Banks and Stephen P. Banks, editors

Volume 5, *Reading Auschwitz*, Mary Lagerwey

Volume 6, *Life Online: Researching Real Experience in Virtual Space*, Annette N. Markham

Volume 7, *Writing the New Ethnography*, H. L. Goodall Jr.

Volume 8, *Between Gay and Straight: Understanding Friendship Beyond Sexual Orientation*, Lisa Tillmann-Healy

Volume 9, *Ethnographically Speaking: Autoethnography, Literature, and Aesthetics*, Arthur P. Bochner and Carolyn Ellis, editors

Volume 10, *Karaoke Nights: An Ethnographic Rhapsody*, Rob Drew

Volume 11, *Standing Ovation: Performing Social Science Research About Cancer*, Ross Gray and Christina Sinding

Volume 12, *The Time at Darwin's Reef: Poetic Explorations in Anthropology and History*, Ivan Brady

Volume 13, *The Ethnographic I: A Methodological Novel about Autoethnography*, Carolyn Ellis

Volume 14, *In Search of Naunny's Grave: Age, Class, Gender, and Ethnicity in an American Family*, Nick Trujillo

Volume 15, *A Methodology of the Heart: Evoking Academic Daily Life*, Ronald J. Pelias

Volume 16, *Travels with Ernest: Crossing the Literary/Sociological Divide*, Laurel Richardson and Ernest Lockridge

# Torch Singing

## Performing Resistance and Desire from Billie Holiday to Edith Piaf

STACY HOLMAN JONES

A Division of
ROWMAN & LITTLEFIELD PUBLISHERS, INC.
*Lanham • New York • Toronto • Plymouth, UK*

ALTAMIRA PRESS
A division of Rowman & Littlefield Publishers, Inc.
A wholly owned subsidiary of The Rowman & Littlefield Publishing Group, Inc.
4501 Forbes Boulevard, Suite 200, Lanham, MD 20706
www.altamirapress.com

Estover Road, Plymouth PL6 7PY, United Kingdom



British Library Cataloguing in Publication Information Available

**Library of Congress Cataloging-in-Publication Data**

Holman Jones, Stacy Linn, 1966–
Torch singing : performing resistance and desire from Billie Holiday to Edith Piaf / Stacy Holman Jones.
p. cm. — (Ethnographic alternatives book series)
Includes bibliographical references (p. ) and index.
ISBN-13: 978-0-7591-0658-1 (cloth : alk. paper)
ISBN-10: 0-7591-0658-4 (cloth : alk. paper)
ISBN-13: 978-0-7591-0659-8 (pbk. : alk. paper)
ISBN-10: 0-7591-0659-2 (pbk. : alk. paper)
1. Popular music—Social aspects—History—20th century. 2. Love songs—Social aspects—History—20th century. 3. Women in music. 4. Desire in music. 5. Women singers. I. Title.
ML3918.P67H65 2007
782.42164082—dc22

2007005531

Printed in the United States of America

# Contents

# Acknowledgments

This book was many years in the making and touched by many minds, hands, and hearts. I am particularly grateful to my mentors and teachers at the University of Texas, including Joni Jones, Lynn Miller, Paul Gray, Dana Cloud, Katie Stewart, Stacy Wolf, and Ann Daly. Deanna Shoemaker, a colleague at Texas, was a keen reader, enthusiastic critic, and remarkable inspiration for this work. I am also indebted to my mentors and colleagues at the University of South Florida, particularly Carolyn Ellis and Art Bochner.

I would also like to thank the many friends and family who have encouraged and supported this work, often in the form of accompanying me to yet another nightclub or concert hall to experience torch singing firsthand and to talk through the night about what transpired. Don Jones is by far the most adventurous and dedicated of these souls, though in good company with Georgine Hodgkinson, Eric Norton, Brenna Curtis, Dianne Lee, Melissa and Joe Skidmore, Kim and Curtis Nickerson, Denise Baker, and Nicole Roberts. My parents, Mary and Dean Holman, along with my sister, Jodi, and much of our extended family were patient and supportive listeners.

This work is dedicated to my beautiful son, Noah, and the memory of my grandmother Bernice Holman. Noah, you are a constant source of wonder and inspiration. And Grandma, you will always be my best reader.

# 1

# Interpreter of Lies

Listening to the female singing voice is a . . . complicated phenomenon. Visually, the character singing is the passive object of our gaze. But, aurally, she is resonant; her musical speech drowns out everything in range, and we sit as passive objects, battered by that voice.

—*Carolyn Abbate, "Opera; Or, the Envoicing of Women"*[1]

[She] pushes certain notes so they almost go flat. I'm not sure this is tasteful. And yet I wait for it to happen, and I might even stop the record and put the needle back to hear that note again—the doubtful note—because the world is alive with recognitions and quickenings when I have established a relation to such accidents, when I am not the victim of what I hear, but its willing accessory.

—*Wayne Koestenbaum,* The Queen's Throat[2]

Love's signs . . . are deceptive signs which can be addressed to us only by concealing what they express: the origin of unknown worlds, of unknown actions and thoughts which give them a meaning . . . . The interpreter of love's signs is necessarily the interpreter of lies. [Her] fate is expressed in the motto: to love without being loved.

—*Gilles Deleuze,* Proust and Signs[3]

---

In this text, I imagine myself an interpreter of love's signs, of the torch singer's refrain: to love without being loved. In this text, I ask whether loving without being loved is the torch singer's *destiny*—an unalterable (dis)course; source and means of her destruction, her ruin. I ask whether another interpretation is imaginable—the torch singer as naysayer, as critic, as the voice of resistive and radical possibilities. I wonder whether I can hear concealed thought and action and untold delight sung under the cover of a torch tune.

In this text, I imagine that torch singing is a complicated phenomenon—more than a woman voicing the familiar tune of her own (and other women's) victimhood. I hear a woman singing "My Man," the quintessential torch song:

It cost me a lot
But there's one thing
That I've got
It's my man. . . .
Two or three girls has he
That he likes as well as me.
But I love him!
I don't know why I should,
He isn't good
He isn't true
He beats me too,
What can I do? . . .
Oh my man I love him so
He'll never know
All my life is just despair
But I don't care. . . .
What's the difference if I say
I'll go away
When I know I'll come back
On my knees someday
For whatever my man is
I am his forever more.[4]

I hear scores of women singing this song over and over again. I could see these singers and hear their song passively, purely the objects of my musical affection. I could turn away from my own reflection and the images of other women. I could assume torch singing is apolitical, inconsequential in the discourses of politics. I could also choose to believe that the radical potential of performance is not an either/or proposition—that musical politics exists along a continuum from overt protest to covert commentary. I could ask whether performances whose critique is sounded furtively—underneath and within lyrics that batter down women's voices—can be easily ignored or dismissed. If it is possible for a singer to critique the lyrics she sings, I could hear how torch singing claims the composing voice to sound the first notes of resistance, of change. I could understand why so many women are singing "My Man." And if I can imagine these things, I can't wait to see—and hear—what happens.

I begin again, imagining myself a careful listener, waiting for the accident to happen—an embellished phrase, a muted laugh, a doubtful note, a fulsome pause, a wink and a sigh. At the scene of these accidents, I am alive with recognitions and quickenings, no longer the victim in (and of) a sad story and a violent, wanting narrative. I am a willing accessory. I become witness to another story, privy to hidden—though not silent—ironies, indiscretions, and interruptions voiced inside sweet and sleepy melodies.

I imagine, too, that I am not the passive spectator battered by a voice, but an active contributor to a boisterous musical dialogue. In the space between music and language, torch singing is an invitation, an opening to desire. I move with the music and an audience, remaking myself in the electricity of emotion and connection. In the distance between key signatures and the arc of a lyric, torch singing is a becoming, a provocation to participate that doesn't erase antagonisms and contradictions. I speak inside the music, adding my voice to a cacophony that sounds the promise of possibility within a standardized form. I envision points of contact that complicate the easy opposition of spectators and performers, emotion and intellect, action and passivity, love and politics. Instead of hearing love's signs as a woman's violent mistake—as her willing deception and passive fate—I hear an opening for critique; an active search for hope. I hear music for torching, deeply inside history and alive with unforeseen pleasures.

I imagine a text that performs like the music I listen to—a narrative that moves and changes with each repetition of a note, a line, and a song. I create collages of ideas and fragments of feeling that evoke the voices and politics of torch. I assemble these collages and fragments as I experience them—here and now, there and then, within and outside the music. Like my listening, my interpretations are iterative and itinerant, full of gaps and pauses and fits and starts. Like the multiple verses on torch singing, my interpretations are layered compositions that can be played on several frequencies. One recounts my experience and understanding of torch singing. Another plays back the music as I hear it—sometimes in a rush, sometimes slowly, note for note. Another traces the contours of my desire for performers, stories, performances, fleeting moments. Another adds to and talks back to discourses on torch singing in a delayed transcript of asides and footnotes. Listening to these multiple, layered narratives presents a complicated phenomenon. It requires an active imagination, a feel for when to interrupt one story to tell and hear another, and a willingness to open up spaces of pleasure and critique within a standardized form. If I am the interpreter of love's signs—the interpreter of lies—this text is a deception of my own imagination. But this text, like torch singing, makes no sound without an audience. It needs a witness to see her own reflection and the images of women. It needs a listener to hear the voices of critique. It needs an accessory willing to join the dialogue. Imagine a text that asks you to imagine your own interpretations and make your own improvisations, variations on the theme.

## WITNESSES

1. Carolyn Abbate, "Opera; Or, the Envoicing of Women," in *Musicology and Difference: Gender and Sexuality in Music Scholarship*, ed. Ruth A. Solie, 254 (Berkeley, CA: University of California Press, 1993).

2. Wayne Koestenbaum, *The Queen's Throat: Opera, Homosexuality, and the Mystery of Desire* (New York: Poseidon, 1993), 21.

3. Gilles Deleuze, *Proust and Signs*, trans. Richard Howard (New York: Braziller, 1972), 9.

4. Albert Willemetz and Charles Jacques, lyrics for "My Man," trans. Channing Pollock, music by Maurice Yvain, in *The Great American Torch Song*, 114 (Miami: Warner Bros. Publications, 1996).

2

# The Scene of Desire

The metacommunicative . . . extrapersonal address may . . . be aimed at a vacant chair or at a space that is not occupied. In such cases, we can often infer that some absent member is being addressed, or else some figure of the past.

—*Albert E. Scheflen,* How Behavior Means[1]

She would place her right palm over her heart. This gesture is . . . generally recognized, even when it occurs without comment, as an indicator of sincerity.

—*Scheflen,* How Behavior Means[2]

Sometimes in my mind I imagine myself physically handing somebody in the audience a key. Once they have the key, I feel that they will follow me anywhere.

—*Patricia Barber, quoted in Friedman*[3]

All political action takes forms that are designed to obscure their intentions or to take cover behind an apparent meaning. . . . Precisely because such political action is studiously designed to be anonymous or to disclaim its purpose, infrapolitics requires more than a little interpretation. Things are not as they seem.

—*James C. Scott,* Domination and the Arts of Resistance[4]

Alice is seeing red. The theater is voluptuous and desperate in crimson curtains and candy apple carpets. She was early tonight and had to stand in the rain until the house was open. Once inside, she walks slowly, carefully avoiding the near run that the others use to stake out tables in front of the stage. Instead, Alice scans the room and chooses a table to the left of center, in front of the piano. She pulls out the red vinyl chair in front of her and another next to her and sits down to wait. A waitress nods at Alice. No, she doesn't want to place a drink order, thank you, but is informed that there is a two-drink minimum all the same. Alice says, "I'll wait until my husband arrives."

The singer paces barefoot in the dressing room, her dinner growing cold. The airplanes and hotels and promotional appearances and packaged meals and wake-up calls and untouched cocktails and questions and turn downs and lobby sales—all of it—make her behave like a caged animal. The only thing that keeps her here is the anticipation of being on stage, the music, the audience. On stage, she is *playing*. Open, vulnerable, and exposed? Yes, and *alive*.

Alice watches the crowd rush and burst into the room. She looks into the faces of men and women—some older than her, almost all of them white—and wonders if they see her. Wonders, too, if they will take the two remaining chairs at her table and sit with their backs to her. She watches for his face—a man, yes, but not her husband. She'd asked him to come because she knew he would like the music. She was sure he would feel moved as she was the first time she saw the singer perform. Sure, too, that in the singer's voice they would hear their stories speak together, that an understanding and perhaps an explanation would pass between them. Alice looks at the empty chair beside her and imagines all of these things.

The crowd is growing steadily larger, their talk rising up from white tablecloths and glasses of champagne. Ushers move in and around the tables down front, asking, "Is this seat available? How about that one?" and pairing couples into small groups of strangers. An usher asks Alice if the seat next to her is available. Alice shakes her head. He asks about the two seats opposite her. "Yes," she admits, "those seats are available." Then Alice asks, "May I take a picture before the show begins?" She holds up a disposable camera in a cardboard box and shrugs. She says, "I know photography is prohibited during the show, but I've never been to this historic venue" (Bimbo's 365 Club, Home of Dolphina, the Girl in the Fish Bowl, since 1931).

The usher says, "You'll have to talk to the house manager. I'll send her over."

The house manager arrives with a smile, asking, "What can I do for you?"

Alice says, "I wonder whether I might take a picture before the show begins? I'd really like to have a photo of a place with such history. I won't take any others after the music starts."

The house manager looks out at the crowd. She says, "I don't think now is a good time. If the other patrons see you taking a photo, they might get the wrong idea, and, well, we can't have that."

"I understand. It's just that I'm writing a book about these kinds of places and the performances they stage—a book about torch singing to be exact—and a photo of this venue would be great to include."

The house manager looks out at the crowd again. "I *am* sorry. Maybe you could come back, when the club is closed, and take your photos then?"

"It wouldn't be the same without the people here, without the anticipation."

"I'm sorry," she repeats, then disappears into the crowd.

The steady stream of people has dwindled to a few late arrivals, here and there. Alice searches their faces, but doesn't see the man she is waiting for. It is almost time for the show to begin. She stares at the ceiling and wills him to walk into the red room. Alice lowers her eyes and looks at the empty chair next to her and knows that tonight she will be alone with the music.

The lights dim and the applause begins. The singer takes the stage, but it is dark and Alice cannot see her. But she hears the singer's fingers on the piano. The first few notes send the applause to a fever pitch and the lights come up. The singer is barefoot and dressed in black. She sits at the piano and plays, then sings, "Just for a thrill . . ."[5]

Alice takes notes while the singer performs. She watches the singer bend over the keys, hair falling over her face. She sees the singer listen to her bass player and drummer, hands behind her back. She hears the singer hum and call out over their solos, the pleasure of the music deep in her throat. She closes her eyes, throws her head back, wide open. She puts her hand over her heart and beats out the music. Her graceful fingers tap at throat and voice. Alice looks at her own fingers grasping the pen, white with effort. She sees dark ink mottled and bleeding into a glowing napkin. And when the singer returns her fingers to the keys, Alice reaches for her own heart and closes her eyes. She sees the empty chair and tries to imagine that the man who is not her husband is sitting next to her. Even in her thoughts the chair remains empty. All Alice can see is the singer with her hand over her heart, though this time her fingers are curved and each time she moves them to tap out the beat she beckons Alice to her, to the piano and the music and the nakedness of the sound in her throat. And Alice says, "*Yes.*"

The solo complete, the theme reasserts itself and Alice opens her eyes. She sets to work noticing, noting. The singer has Edith Piaf's hands, flying in the air, hovering over the music and words, fleshing out the story. She has Sarah Vaughan's range and daring in the piano, racing up and over and through the scale, tone on tone. She has Billie Holiday's voice, full of the promise of emptiness. She has Lena Horne's subtle feel for melody and Barbra Streisand's appreciation for drama. And the singer winks like k. d. lang, singing "She's a Lady," words intact, range complicit with the male narrator so that the singer and the song's possibilities are incisively opaque.

And the singer has something else: an intellectualism that makes Alice smile as if an inside joke has passed between them. When the singer says she likes "French philosophy" and "deconstructive obscurity,"[6] Alice answers that she, too, likes Jean Baudrillard and Roland Barthes and Julia Kristeva. Alice says she remembers Baudrillard saying something about our deepest desire: the desire to give responsibility for our own desire to someone, some*body* else.[7] She thinks Baudrillard called this desire an "ironic investment in the other," a strategy of expulsion—of "philosophers and people in power"; of the "obligation of being responsible."[8] Alice knows something of the desire to be irresponsible and indecisive, to turn over her desire to someone or something else—the empty chair, the singer, the music, French philosophy. She wonders about the irony of this desire—irony as a play of opposites, of contradictions, of connections to and separations from subjects and emotions, of an irreverent style. The irony she wonders about is a desire to know oneself by abandonment to the other and at the same time talking back to those who would tell us how to be responsible lovers. It is an explosion of ideas and categories from the inside out, from behind and below and around the beat. And Alice wonders about being here, thinking of Baudrillard and listening to the singer and desiring her in and through the music—all the while knowing that this is an illusion and still seeing some hope and humor in this abandonment. . . . And then, in an instant, a flash, an opening, Alice understands that *this* is the art of torch singing. It is a remaking of the torch song—that sentimental ballad of unrequited love, victimhood, and the pleasure of pain. Alice understands that *this* is what her story is about. The torch song speaks to Alice and talks back to itself and love and victimhood. The torch singer says look closer, read between the lines. Lean in and listen to the backbeat, variations on a theme. Things are not as they seem.

Alice is seeing red. The music speaks to her in the public space of intimacy; the singer calls to her—beckons her—into herself and out into the world.[9] Alice takes the key. She blinks and looks around. She sees the others here, with her, listening and desiring and moving. And Alice follows.

## AND FOLLOWS . . .

1. Albert E. Scheflen, *How Behavior Means* (Garden City, NY: Anchor, 1974), 130.

2. Scheflen, *How Behavior Means*, 132.

3. Patricia Barber, quoted in Michael Friedman, "Patricia Barber on 'Modern Cool,'" *All about Jazz*, November 1998, www.allaboutjazz.com/iviews/pbarber.htm (accessed April 12, 2001).

4. James C. Scott, *Domination and the Arts of Resistance: Hidden Transcripts* (New Haven, CT: Yale University Press, 1990), 200.

5. Lilla Hardin Armstrong and Don Raye, lyrics for "Just for a Thrill," Todd and Sharon Peach website, n.d., www.thepeaches.com/music/randb/JustForaThrill.txt (accessed June 3, 2005).

6. Patricia Barber, "Company," *Modern Cool*, Premonition Records, 1998.

7. Jean Baudrillard, *Selected Writings*, ed. with an introduction by Mark Poster (Stanford, CA: Stanford University Press, 1988), 215.

8. Baudrillard, *Selected Writings*, 215.

9. Will Friedwald, *Jazz Singing: America's Great Voices from Bessie Smith to Bebop and Beyond* (New York: Da Capo, 1996), 126. This line is drawn from Friedwald's discussion of Billie Holiday. He writes, "Billie Holiday's art is the kind that takes you deeper inside yourself and ultimately out again."

# 3

# Sing Me a Torch Song

Such is the anxious desire of the book. It is tenacious too, and parasitic, loving and breathing through a thousand mouths that leave a thousand imprints on our skin, a marine monster, a polyp.

—*Jacques Derrida,* Writing and Difference[1]

The sounds of pain, lust, ecstasy, fear, what one might call inarticulate articulacy: the sounds, for example, of tears and laughter; the sounds made by soul singers around and between their notes, vocal noises that seem expressive of their deepest feelings because we hear them as if they've escaped from a body that the mind—language—can no longer control.

—*Simon Frith, "The Body Electric"*[2]

---

**WRITING**

The singer wakes when she wants. She is not on the road and relishes her time at home. She listens to music and drinks coffee and listens to more music. Maybe she goes out for groceries or dinner with friends; maybe she takes in a concert or two. She does some serious daydreaming. She sits and waits. She is writing, playing around with rhythm and melody, making tricky musical puzzles play underneath easy lyrics.

At home, away from the road, she reads that her work is about desire and loss and contemporary culture. She reads that she is *frighteningly intimate, deep in the distance.*[3] She reads that her songwriting is ironic and agrees, not because her work would be lost without it, but because the form demands it.[4] She knows, too, that the irony in her work is not romantic—it's not self-righteous superiority masquerading as humility.[5] Her work is humbled by what it critiques; it reaches for the kind of irony Kenneth Burke wrote about—yes, she's read Burke. What is that line? Here: "True irony, humble irony, is based upon a sense of fundamental kinship with the enemy, one *needs* him, is *indebted* to him, is not merely outside him as an observer but contains him from within. . . . True irony-and-humility . . . [is] simultaneously both outside . . . and within" us.[6]

Maybe she should have told the interviewer this, so later when she is asked why she is doing standards now, she could say that at this point in her career, singing standards won't cast her as only or simply a ballad singer or put her material in opposition to her musicianship. That she is ready to do standards because she can get some distance from the songs, so she won't be seen as a gold digger or the victim of romance in the age of feminism.[7] That when she sings these songs, it's clear they are *performances*, not unadulterated confessions or markers of some fixed, fastened identity. Or maybe she just should have said she is ready to record standards because she knows how to perform the ironic possibilities of her material—the "inevitability" of victimhood as a strategic moment of reversal.[8]

The singer thinks and reads and listens to music and sits and waits. And the singer writes.

### BATHROBE[9]

I am writing, too, and I enjoy being home, drinking coffee, and listening to music. I like wearing my pajamas most of the day. I believe I have better ideas when I'm wearing my bathrobe. I have long thought this, though I admit feeling a pang of pleasure when I read Madeline Grumet's tribute to her bathrobe as a costume for her writing self, her dramatis persona.[10] I take her words and refashion them to fit my own robed image: *My robe is a red cocoon. After a while words fly out of it.*[11] I do not like sitting and waiting, though that is part of wearing a robe all day and hoping for words to come. It is part of what I do. I am a writer, but not of songs. I am an ethnographer, a teacher, and, sometimes, a performer. I am a woman, a feminist, a music lover—though I am a terrible singer, even out of my bathrobe and in the shower. I am not a Deadhead or a folkie or an opera queen. I am a . . . well, there's not really a word for my kind. I rifle through jazz and blues and pop/rock sections, looking for my music. I cruise the vocalists. I listen to show tunes and sound tracks on the in-store headphones. I am after the ballads, the woman-done-wrong songs, the doormat lyrics, the weepy violins: "Stormy Weather," "Mean to Me," "The Way We Were," "My Man." I love these songs, even though I know they're bad for me—bad for women.[12] I love them like the woman who loves the man who leaves her—who beats her, too—what can I do? I carry a torch for these songs. I am a torcher.

And I am Alice, though Alice is also someone else, a character in a story I am writing about torch singing. I need Alice in this story because she is both me and not me, just as the woman in a torch song is both the woman performing the song and someone else. I chose Alice because, like me and the woman in a torch song and like the singer, Alice ran into texts—into books and poetry and song—in order to find herself.[13] In order to find what gender and bodies, desire and language, might be and might become.[14] I need the empty chair and the man who is not my husband and philosophy in this story, too, because they are characters who want to have a say in and about torch singing. I am telling you this story because I have long loved torch singers and because I believe that these women—these singers of suffering—are telling their listeners to look at them and to look at themselves and to see a different sort of understanding and set of possibilities. I also believe this story is another chapter in the tale of how artists and audiences use music as an everyday form of resistance, an evocation of how lived experience and politics intersect to "exercise some power over, or create some space within, the institutions and social relationships that dominate our lives."[15] This story is a fiction and an auto/biography, an analysis and an argument, an irony and a literal rendition, a scrapbook and a fan letter. It is, above all, a torch song. And in my robe, in writing, I believe I can sing.

## PAYING YOUR DUES

I find Tammy Weis on an Internet search for "torch," and am transported to her homepage and a head shot meant to recall the 1930s—black evening gown, opera-length gloves, red lipstick, long blond hair rolled and waved, a microphone like a tiny skyscraper clutched in her hand. Announcing her arrival is a disc jockey and music critic who proclaims, "If velvet had a sound, it would sound like

Tammy Weis." I see that she's scheduled to play on Saturday at Starbucks as part of an International Jazz Festival in Vancouver. I wonder why this jazz diva is playing at Starbucks and not on the festival stage, but it is, after all, a large and international festival. I drive from Seattle to Vancouver Saturday morning and arrive just in time to catch the performance. I pick up a program for the festival's activities and attempt to look up the performance in the program, but there is no mention. Weis's name does not appear in the program. Anywhere.

The Starbucks is small—only a counter and three tables. Where will the stage be? I wait in line with the other customers and when I reach the register, I ask when Weis is scheduled to go on—it's now noon and there's no sign of a performance about to happen. The cashier looks confused. She asks me to wait while she finds the manager because he's the person who usually books these kinds of things. When the manager appears, he tells me that they have no performances scheduled today. He doesn't know anything about Tammy Weis. I am disappointed. I leave the Starbucks and decide to take in some of the shows happening on the outdoor stages. It is a beautiful, sunny day in Vancouver and I want to take advantage of it.

As I'm walking up Water Street in Vancouver's Gas Town, I see Weis's photo outside The Comedy Store. There's a barker outside inviting passersby into the venue, and I ask him what time Weis is going on. He says 2 p.m. I look at my watch. It's 1:45. I go inside.

The Comedy Store is a stark contrast to the bright day. I go downstairs, into a space dark and cool to the touch. There are only a handful of people here—the barker; a bartender; a waitress; a man caressing (not smoking, just caressing) a cigar at a table along the back wall; a woman I recognize from the website photo as Weis who says, "Check, check," into a dead microphone; and a man wrestling to plug an electric keyboard into an outlet in the lighting system. I shrug and pull out a chair.

The waitress comes by and asks if I want a drink. I ask for a soda. A man and a woman with two young children come in and sit at a table beside me. They ask the waitress what's going on here and are informed that Tammy Weis is set to perform in a few minutes. The man and woman debate about whether to stay while the children wiggle and squirm. They decide to get back outside. They leave and I wait.

Once the keyboard is plugged in and the microphone is working, the show can begin. She wants to start by singing "Take the A Train" for us and she does. She also sings "It's Only a Paper Moon," "Route 66," "Summertime," and "Somewhere Over the Rainbow." She is a proficient singer, her voice rising up and over the piano, carrying the lyrics with her. Nearly all of the arrangements are up-tempo, making even the saddest of her selections feel optimistic; a celebration, rather than a lament. She smiles out at the crowd—all five of us—and hurtles herself into the performance. Though she's very understated—very still—save the staccato snapping of her fingers and her occasional calls of appreciation to the keyboard player. I think of Billie Holiday's sparse delivery—a cock of the head in time with a chord change, a slow blink, a limp-wristed snap of fingers made with a hand that seemed tethered to her waist. Weis has a semblance of this style, though on her it beats in front of the music, pulling the melody and lyrics along. When she discovers her sunglasses still perched on her head during "Fly Me to the Moon," she coolly removes them and places them on the stool next to her, though her face betrays the flush of embarrassment. She is working hard, and the effort shows in her smile. Toward the end of the hour-long set, Weis announces the release of her new record, *Legacy*. It is a tribute to her mother, who loved to sing these songs but never got the chance to record them. So Weis lives out her mother's dream, singing in a Vancouver basement room to the waitress, the bartender and the barker, the man caressing a cigar, the keyboard player, and me, paying her dues.

## BEGINNINGS AND CONTEXTS

Beginnings are like this—learning about genre and theory and technique and then putting your own spin on things. Putting things in context. Discovering your *sound*. Working in dark, cool spaces looking for the light of day. These are points of departure strikingly similar for the torch singer and the woman who wants to write about her work. My point of departure is tied up with the elusive practice of torch singing—is it a genre of music? A style of performance? A type of narrative? The signature material of certain performers?[16]

How is the torch song situated in history? In story? When did the torch song and torch singing become "popular" music? How is torch singing connected to performers, venues, and listeners? Connected to culture and politics? Billie Holiday said she found her sound by listening to recordings of Bessie Smith and Louis Armstrong and then feeling her way through the music.[17] I begin by listening to standards and standard bearers, too; I look for the torch song in the dictionary:

> torch′ song′ (tôrch sông). A sentimental song of unrequited love (the name comes from the phrase to "carry a torch" for someone), a popular feature of jazz singers and in nightclub acts [1925–30].[18]

A few clues here. The term *torch song* entered the U.S. lexicon during the mid-1920s—age of European immigration and mass migration of men and women from country to city, from the south to the north and west; time of increasing racial and class stratification and cultivation of a mass-consumption society; era of the automobile and Fordism, the banker and the broker, and the New! Shorter! 54-hour workweek.[19] The moment big business declared defacto victory over communitarian goals.

Fresh on the heels of women's suffrage, the emergence of feminism's "new woman" and later the "flapper" signified a shift in gender relations—a rejection of overt patriarchal rule and emergence of a "free-thinking, economically independent product of higher education."[20] This shift was far from complete or without its price: the new woman of the 1890s and the flapper of the 1920s were both accused of aping the achievements and characteristics of men—going to work, voting, cultivating masculine bodies by dieting and cutting their hair, frequenting illegal speakeasies and cocktail bars (and smoking and drinking there!), and relaxing their moral standards by engaging in premarital sex and practicing birth control.[21]

Women's newfound social, legal, and financial independence was also strictly circumscribed. Although a woman in the United States could vote, own her own property, and keep her own earnings, her husband still possessed legal and sexual rights over her. In addition, her education and entry into the workforce were largely limited to domestic, clerical, and factory work, the wages for which barely enabled a single woman to subsist.[22] These "opportunities" resulted not from the demands of feminists, but rather as a response to the needs of business and commerce for "docile, well-educated, and cheap" labor.[23]

The 1920s and 1930s were also times when codes of racial and ethnic segregation and exclusion were strengthened and formalized; this segregation and exclusion was underscored by the "absence" of the Depression. As Michael Denning notes:

> The depression was a curious crisis, marked not by upheaval, civil war, or *coups d'état*, but by an absence: the absence of work. . . . The quintessential depression stories were stories of downward mobility, of stockbrokers leaping to their deaths: it was a crash, the comeuppance of the established classes. . . . But for working-class black and ethnic Americans, the depression was summed up in the common joke Billie Holiday tells: "By the time Mom and I had got together and found us a place of our own in Harlem the depression was on. At least so we heard tell. A depression was nothing new to us, we'd always had it."[24]

Holiday's "joke" turns on the ways in which people of color and the poor were subject to an absence of economic, social, and political opportunity long before (and after) the period between the wars.[25] However, this absence should not be read as an empty, vacuous silence. For people of color and the poor, the absence of any real change in their daily lives during the Depression was voiced in bread lines and on shop floors, as well as on street corners and in dance halls and jazz clubs. The absence of the Depression also gave rise to distinctive forms of expression, including, broadly, two sorts of cultural creativity.

## FRONT-STAGE AND BACKSTAGE CREATIVITY

First, there is the sort of cultural creativity fueled by an active and organized "public culture" that transected race and ethnicity, class, and political affiliation in aesthetic work depicting the lives and political and social allegiances of the working class.[26] Denning terms this cultural work the "Popular Front"—a fusion of the antifascist, labor, and leftist movements in and through creative production.[27] Examples include the writing of Langston Hughes, Leo Huberman, and Ralph Ellison; Jacob Lawrence's paintings and illustrations; theater productions including *The Cradle Will Rock* and *Pins and Needles*; and Paul Robeson's "Ballad for Americans" and Billie Holiday's "Strange Fruit."[28] Within this popular entertainment for the masses, these artists made direct and satirical comment on issues of work and labor, racial inequality and genocide, and international politics.

But confining cultural production to *front-stage* theater, literature, film, and music would miss a large element of cultural labor of the time—the *backstage* work created by writers, painters, filmmakers, and musicians who were not activists nor considered themselves "political artists."[29] This creative work features a politics of the everyday and the elaboration and creation of hidden and radical discourses. In conversations, storytelling, folklore, jokes, and songs, as well as in spaces and "stages" controlled by the powerful, a resistant and active political culture was created, though "almost always in disguised forms."[30] Underground and undercover, this backstage cultural work engaged a "critique of power spoken behind the back of the dominant."[31] Such critiques constitute "hidden transcripts," a "disguised resistance" that is the "silent partner of a loud form of public resistance."[32] Here, silence becomes something larger, something different than absence. It is a strategic opening; a wink and a nod speaking loudly of what cannot be said in oppressive spaces and places.[33]

Thus, where some front-stage creative work was *loud* in the sense that it announced its resistive intentions, there was also a hidden—though not *silent*—backstage resistance in the cultural work of the 1920s and 1930s. This work is exemplified in the singing of Billie Holiday, and later Lena Horne and Sarah Vaughan (and many others)—torch singers who turned love songs into subtle but public protests. Understanding how Holiday and the others refashioned their love songs into hidden transcripts means understanding something of torch as a musical and commercial innovation, standard club fare, and critical commentary.

## A STORY OF A TORCH

The torch song is a story, a narrative sung primarily by jazz singers and nightclub performers. As a musical form, torch singing developed in the United States during the Tin Pan Alley era of music publishing. Although the term was coined some time during the 1920s, its meaning is hard to pinpoint. Some writers attribute the creation of "torch" to describe particular performers—most notably Libby Holman and Helen Morgan.[34] Other writers reserve the term to signify the subject matter of the piece and the gender of the performer. Here, a torch song is "a tale of unrequited love, almost invariably sung by a female personage who has either not yet acquired or has lost her man. In the latter case, the dastardly fellow has fled, probably never to return. In the former case, the singer expresses the desire to solidify the love relationship in a more or less concrete fashion."[35]

The earliest torch song is generally believed to be Francis Carco's "Mon Homme," adapted by Jacques Charles for the French chanteuse Mistinguett. In her revue titled *Paris qui Jazz*, which opened during the winter of 1920 at

Casino de Paris, Mistinguett sang, "My only joy and happiness on this earth/Is my man."[36]

"Mon Homme" was an immense hit with audiences and became Mistinguett's signature tune. In the United States, Fanny Brice debuted a translated "My Man" in the 1921 edition of the Ziegfeld Follies. The English translation includes the lines:

Two or three girls has he
That he likes as well as me.
But I love him!
I don't know why I should,
He isn't good
He isn't true
He beats me too,
What can I do?[37]

Brice's rendition of "My Man" became an instant success, and the song would be performed and recorded by countless performers.[38] In addition to becoming the quintessential torch song—*the* narrative about middle-class, heterosexual heartbreak, subject of endless interpretations and iterations and repetitions—"My Man" supplied the musical formula for the Tin Pan Alley ballad.

### Songs of Innovation and Commerce

Aspiring composers and lyricists had been congregating in New York's theater district since the early 1900s when the advent of vaudeville stages created an enormous need for sentimental ballads.[39] In the early 1920s, sheet music publication companies clustered in New York's Union Square began contracting with these independent songwriters, making it almost impossible for composers to publish their music elsewhere.[40] Taking advantage of this monopoly, publishing houses hired composers and lyricists as employees who composed on company premises. The term *Tin Pan Alley*, coined by Monroe Rosenfield, describes the "sound of the partly muffled pianos upon which employees, under the constraint of continual production, composed songs with an inevitably standardised format."[41]

Tin Pan Alley composers drew on European art and popular music; the French chanson; and African American ragtime, blues, jazz, and swing to structure their new creations. From English parlor songs, the torch song inherits its obsession with romance and true love.[42] From the chanson, the torch song assumes a textual (rather than melodic) primacy and an emphasis on imagery designed to arouse intense emotion in both performer and audience.[43] From African American–inspired ragtime, blues, jazz, and swing, the torch song derives a rhythmic complexity—performances that play around and against the beat—and the "blue note," which involves using the voice to enrich the musical sound by "dirtying" the tone with bends, growls, and rasps.[44] Drawing together these diverse musical structures and traditions, the torch song played a significant role in revolutionizing the business of American popular song.

The torch song's compact form aided the industrialization of musical production and worked to create a vigorous system of supply and demand. The 32-bar AABA form required few lyrics and featured melodic repetition, which helped "drill the song into the mind of the listener and to create an immediate identification with the song."[45] In addition, Tin Pan Alley's innovation signaled a shift from 12-bar blues and ballad form—a series of verses answered by a short refrain—to a shorter chorus-based format.[46] These miniature sound stories became the means for creating a dramatic mood or evoking melancholic feelings.[47]

Tin Pan Alley composers' preference for the more immediate and confrontational lyrical form—expressing love in the second person (I love *you*) rather than the third person (I love *her*)—combined with use of the microphone and amplification, made an "intimate" and "conversational" style of singing possible and desirable.[48] By the time Brice performed "My Man" on the Ziegfeld stage, sales of Tin Pan Alley phonograph records often surpassed sheet music revenues (though singers and musicians were paid, on average, just five dollars to twelve dollars per side).[49] And with the proliferation of jukeboxes in post–Depression era cafés and "juke joints," the torch song was performed and heard by an increasingly large and diverse audience.

More than making music intimate and accessible, technological developments meant that the love story and emotional lessons of white, middle-class, heterosexual romance were heard by individuals with "other" social, historical, and economic experiences and circumstances. Popular ballads not only depicted heterosexual romance and marriage as an ideal, but also offered up music as a means to build and maintain such relationships.[50] Even within the narratives of failed romance depicted in the torch song, heterosexual love is dramatized and idealized.

As middle-class, heterosexual balladry, generic discourses often *distinguish* torch songs from music that references poverty and race and ethnicity, and/or celebrates homosexual, bisexual, and transsexual desire. For example, Marlene Dietrich's gender-bending performance in the film *Morocco*[51] is characterized as a cabaret performance that subverts normalizing gender identities, even while she sings the French chanson "Quand L'amour est Mort" ("When Love Dies"), a distinctly torchy ballad.[52] The same marshalling of generic boundaries occurs in the case of Bessie Smith and Ma Rainey, women who both sang of the oppression and consequences of poverty,[53] as well as in the work of Rainey and Ethel Waters, who openly sang of "homosexual love's superiority to heterosexuality."[54] As African American *blues* singers (and *not* popular or torch singers), Smith, Rainey, and Waters are given the task of "more frankly express[ing] a wider variety of female sensibilities" than were addressed by popular singers.[55] Here, generic classifications work to reserve popular song for the *mainstream* (heterosexual, white, middle-class listeners and performers) and to exclude *difference* (performers and listeners who are homosexual, bisexual, or transsexual; people of color; and/or poor) as peculiar to blues or cabaret.[56] Such classifications also elide the torch song's musical influences. Why make such musical, social, and political distinctions? Understanding these distinctions is bound up with how European cabaret was imported to the United States and proliferated on minstrel, vaudeville, and Broadway stages, as well as in jazz and swing concert venues.

### Standard Club Fare

The cabaret tradition began in 1880s Paris with Rodolphe Salis's artist's salon Chat Noir. The Chat Noir featured readings of original poetry, political commentary, dialogues, puppetry, dance, and vocal performance all centering on satire and parody of middle-class values and culture. Cabaret transgressed theatrical convention by directly addressing audience members and thus involving them in the performance.[57] The politically inspired French chansons came to serve as cabaret's most powerful "weapon for criticism and protest" because they captured an audience's "daily history" and publicly voiced "their reactions to contemporary events."[58] The *singer* was important to cabaret because he or she created its essential form: a relationship between audience and performer marked by "intimacy and hostility, the nodal points of participation and provocation."[59]

In the 1920s, cabaret was imported to America and refigured into minstrel shows and vaudeville and Broadway musical revues. These shows drew on cabaret's vernacular subject matter, satirical traditions, and variety-show format. And like cabaret, minstrel and vaudeville shows both featured singers, though in vaudeville the chanson of the cabaret tradition was tamely christened the "singer of sentimental ballads."[60] Still, the satirical and confrontational power of the cabaret chanson could be felt on these stages. For example, Eric Lott's discussion of the lyrics of "Jim Crow," a popular minstrel number, highlights the critical potential of minstrel singing: "This is hardly the stuff of which revolutions are made; it was easy enough to patronize such happy-go-lucky bravado. . . . Like most of the potentially subversive moments of early minstrelsy, they are qualified by 'darky' dialect. . . . But in the mouth of the very figure who had begun to make the question of national unity an issue, such lyrics could be dangerous, even if it was understood that the singer need not be taken seriously."[61] As Lott's comments indicate, minstrelsy questioned the nature of national unity and with it the doing of class, race, and ethnicity (as well as gender and sexuality) within the frame of cabaret performance style and form.

While the cabaret tradition of satire and explicit politics as imported to minstrel, vaudeville, and Broadway stages may have lost some of its toothiness, the critical impulse of the form still strongly registered with audiences and performers. These performances do not so much directly confront the issues of racial/ethnic, gender, and labor power relations as "show a *peeking through* of coexisting, alternative levels of reference."[62]

Along with the popularity of vaudeville and Broadway musical revues, the 1920s and '30s also saw the rise of swing bands and jazz ensembles. Again, owing to the cabaret tradition, swing and jazz bands often featured a singer who would perform a single vocal chorus in the midst of an instrumental arrangement. During the 1920s, these singers were almost exclusively men, including Louis Armstrong and Bing Crosby; however, in the 1930s, a transition occurred. When Mildred Bailey, Lee Wiley, and Connee Boswell—the "three white goddesses"—took the stage, the age of the girl singer began.[63] Music scholar Will Friedwald writes, "White goddesses were as essential to the big-band era as brass, reed, and rhythm sections. They decorated the fronts of swing bands like the figureheads on a ship, and no bandleader who wanted to fill dance halls or sell records dared go on the road without one."[64]

Not all bands employed white goddesses, however. African American performers including Ella Fitzgerald, Hazel Scott, and Ruth Etting fronted jazz bands, and Billie Holiday and Lena Horne traveled with Artie Shaw and Charlie Barnet's all-white orchestras, respectively. Further, the icon of the white goddess symbolizes a rhetoric of assimilation in jazz singing that exists alongside and apart from the ethnic and racial tension of cabaret, minstrelsy, and vaudeville performance. Such accounts of the evolution and meanings of jazz (as well as other musical forms and styles) subordinate and sublimate racial and ethnic difference and power relationships, which in turn mask the political potential of the music. Such accounts signify an emphasis on assimilation and "color blindness" in New Deal America that worked to obscure African American influences on jazz aesthetics by enclosing "jazz and jazz musicians securely within the orbit of white, European culture."[65]

As in minstrel and vaudeville performance, the complexities and contradictions of color-blind music were not lost on its practitioners, and, indeed, informed the ways performers set about transgressing the lyrical limitations and assimilation of jazz and swing generally and of Tin Pan Alley balladry in particular, most notably at Barney Josephson's Café Society.[66]

**Voices, Ballads, and Politics**

Café Society opened in 1930 as a jazz cabaret designed to combine political satire with African American jazz and swing. Josephson equated the venue's presentation of comedians, small ensembles, and singers more with agitprop[67] than nightclub entertainment. Café Society was also the first integrated New York nightclub outside Harlem. It was at Café Society that Holiday, and later Horne and Vaughan, matured as singers and experimented with "political" material. Holiday first performed "Strange Fruit," an anti-lynching anthem and her signature song, on the Café Society stage. She sang, "Southern trees bear a strange fruit/Blood on the leaves and blood at the root."[68] While "Strange Fruit" is a ballad, it paints a landscape of murder and oppression, rather than a story of unrequited love. However, where many music scholars and fans contrast Holiday's singing of the political "Strange Fruit" with her rendition of Tin Pan Alley love songs,[69] Denning asserts that

Holiday's performances of "The Man I Love" or "Gloomy Sunday" employ cabaret techniques and a blues aesthetic (without strictly adopting a blues *form*).[70] Combined with the slower tempo of "Strange Fruit" and the intimacy of the jazz combo, Holiday's love songs say, "love too is a pastoral scene that yields a bitter crop."[71]

In her own analysis of Holiday's love songs, Angela Davis echoes Denning's position, adding that Holiday uses her *voice*—her timing, phrasing, and timbre; her ability to walk the line between speech and song—to push "the ideological content of the song to the surface, subjecting to a process of demystification the portrayal of women" and race relations.[72] Holiday uses song—even the commercial Tin Pan Alley ballad—as a catalyst for creating social and political consciousness.[73] In bringing cabaret's theatricality and blues phrasing and melodies to torch songs, Holiday revises and reshapes the standard narrative to fit her performance style and political agenda. She uses her voice to encourage audiences to examine the social contradictions embodied and enacted in their own lives and to adopt a critical stance toward these contradictions and relations.[74] She uses her performance to create a hidden transcript.

Holiday's performance of ballads illustrates the ways in which songs of unrequited love become *torch singing*—product of the Great Depression and the years between world wars; the resistive politics of backstage cultural creativity; the mass production of American music and the marshalling of generic boundaries to mark off performances of "difference"; the importation of cabaret and popularity of minstrel, vaudeville, and Broadway revues; and the rise of swing and jazz amidst a New Deal rhetoric of assimilation. Not all ballads are torch songs; not all vocalists are torch singers. Torch *singing* is a *performance*, the embodiment of a relationship of intimacy and hostility that is both provocative and participatory.

But I cannot understand torch singing apart from torch singers, the women who sing these songs. Everybody knows that torch singers are "fallen angels," "damaged divas," "tragic victims," "tortured sound-angels," "suicide queens," "ethereal sonic documentarians of our romantic dark sides."[75] Don't they? Can torch singers be self-conscious about the radical possibilities of their art? Can they be stars *and* create performances that move audiences to hear a critique, rather than settle for a "thrill over cocktails"?[76]

## ONE SAD SONG

The singer records "Just for a Thrill" for her album of standards. She sings, "You made my love one sad song . . . You just led me along."[77] The cut is one of her favorites and she begins most evenings of the new tour singing it earnestly, sparsely, not wanting to overwhelm the lyric. A hush falls over the audience. They are riveted to her voice and they follow her, breathless. They let her lead them along, even if it is just for a thrill.

Alice is seeing red and blue and shades of gray. She visits coffee shops and restaurants, supper clubs and nightspots, community theaters and opera houses, following the music. She fixes ticket stubs and bar napkins and postcards into her scrapbook. She listens to the music, pressing close to hear what happens beneath and beyond lyric and melody. She puts her hand over her heart and taps out a critique. She sits and waits, and after a while the words come. And Alice writes.

## MORE CLUES

1. Jacques Derrida, *Writing and Difference*, trans. Alan Bass (Chicago: University of Chicago Press, 1978), 298.

2. Simon Frith, "The Body Electric," *Critical Quarterly* 37, no. 2 (1995): 2.

3. Janet Seiz, "An Interview with the 'Queen of Cool'—Patricia Barber," *Jazz Review*, May 2000, www.jazzreview.com, par. 3 and 4 (accessed April 15, 2001).

4. Seiz, "An Interview with the 'Queen of Cool,'" par. 32.

5. Kenneth Burke, *A Grammar of Motives* (1945; Berkeley: University of California Press, 1969), 512. Citations are to the 1969 edition.

6. Burke, *Grammar of Motives*, 514–15.

7. Concerns not of Barber but of Barbra Streisand. See Anne Edwards, *Streisand: A Biography* (Boston: Little, Brown, 1997), 361, and Susannah McCorkle, "'I Swear I Won't Call No Copper If I'm Beat Up by My Poppa,'" *New York Times Magazine*, January 9, 1994, 33.

8. Burke, *Grammar of Motives*, 517.

9. Portions of this section appear in revised form in Stacy Holman Jones, "Emotional Space: Performing the Resistive Possibilities of Torch Singing," *Qualitative Inquiry* 8, no. 6 (2002): 738–39.

10. Madeline R. Grumet, "Scholae Personae: Masks for Meaning," in *Pedagogy: The Question of Impersonation*, ed. Jane Gallop, 37 (Bloomington: Indiana University Press, 1995).

11. Grumet, "Scholae Personae," 37. Grumet's bathrobe is green. She writes, "It is a green cocoon. After a while words fly out of it."

12. Stacy Wolf, in *A Problem Like Maria: Gender and Sexuality in the American Musical* (Ann Arbor: University of Michigan Press, 2002), vii, writes, "How can it be that so many women who were raised on musicals or became fans of musicals once they were exposed to them in college or during visits to New York City or through film versions—how can it be that so many of them adore musicals even as they consider themselves feminists and/or identify as lesbian?"

13. I am borrowing from Kathy Acker, "Seeing Gender," *Critical Quarterly* 37, no. 4 (1995): 81, who writes, "When I was a girl, I ran into books. Like Alice in Lewis Carroll's *Through the Looking Glass*. . . . I was asking 'Who am I'? Alice falls, as I do when I read this book, into a mirror-world, a text world, and there is presented with five poems and songs. New texts as opposed to the songs and lullabies she remembers. These five texts try to teach her who she is."

14. Acker, "Seeing Gender," 84, writes, "Like Alice, I suspect that the body . . . might not be co-equivalent with materiality, that my body might be deeply connected to, if not be, language."

15. Robin D. G. Kelley, *Race Rebels: Culture, Politics, and the Black Working Class* (New York: Free Press, 1994), 9–10.

16. Definitions offered by Charles Hamm, *Yesterdays: Popular Song in America* (New York: Norton, 1979), 329; Michael A. Gonzales, "Torch Song Soliloquy: One Man's Poetic Tribute to Ladies Who Sing the Blues," *Mode*, February 1998, 52; Allen Forte, *The American Popular Ballad of the Golden Era, 1924–1950* (Princeton, NJ: Princeton University Press, 1995), 238; and Ronald L. Davis, *A History of Music in American Life*, vol. 3, *The Modern Era, 1920–Present* (Huntington, NY: Krieger, 1981), 329, respectively.

17. Billie Holiday, *Lady Sings the Blues*, with William Dufty (1956; New York: Penguin, 1992), 39. Citations are to the 1992 edition.

18. Philip D. Morehead, "Torch Song," with Anne MacNeil, in *The New American Dictionary of Music* (New York: Dutton, 1991).

19. Michael Denning, *The Cultural Front: The Laboring of American Culture in the Twentieth Century* (London: Verso, 1997), 27.

20. Valerie Bryson, *Feminist Political Theory: An Introduction* (New York: Paragon House, 1992), 85.

21. George E. Mowry, *The Urban Nation, 1920–1960* (New York: Hill, 1965), 23–24, 27.

22. Bryson, *Feminist Political Theory*, 84.

23. David Rubenstein, *Before the Suffragettes: Women's Emancipation in the 1890s* (Brighton: Harvestor, 1986), x.

24. Denning, *Cultural Front*, 243–44.

25. Reynolds Farley and Walter R. Allen, *The Color Line and the Quality of Life in America* (New York: Sage Foundation, 1987), 189 and 209.

26. Denning, *Cultural Front*, 9. This work included music, literature, theater, visual art, and film.

27. Denning, *Cultural Front*, 3.

28. I mention these works to illustrate the proliferation of "political" cultural production during the 1920s and '30s. See Denning, *Cultural Front*, and Kelley, *Race Rebels*, who both consider how this cultural work functioned to create national and international solidarity around communist, antifascist, anti-imperialist, and antiracist political goals.

29. Denning, *Cultural Front*, 333.

30. Kelley, *Race Rebels*, 8.

31. James C. Scott, *Domination and the Arts of Resistance: Hidden Transcripts* (New Haven, CT: Yale University Press, 1990), xii.

32. Scott, *Domination*, 199.

33. Dana L. Cloud, "The Null Persona: Race and the Rhetoric of Silence in the Uprising of '34," *Rhetoric & Public Affairs* 2, no. 2 (1999): 178.

34. See R. Davis, *History of Music*, 329, and Marjorie Farnsworth, *The Ziegfeld Follies* (New York: Bonanza, 1956), 110, respectively.

35. A. Forte, *American Popular Ballad*, 238–39.

36. Translation by David Bret, *The Mistinguett Legend* (London: Robson, 1990), 90.

37. Albert Willemetz and Charles Jacques, lyrics for "My Man," trans. Channing Pollock, music by Maurice Yvain, in *The Great American Torch Song*, 114 (Miami: Warner Bros. Publications, 1996).

38. "My Man" was performed and/or recorded by performers including—but by no means limited to—Alice Faye, Helen Forrest, Billie Holiday, Sarah Vaughan, Dinah Washington, Ella Fitzgerald, Pearl Bailey, Shirley Bassey, Carmen McRae, Dinah Shore, Peggy Lee, Barbra Streisand, and Abbey Lincoln.

39. David Lee Joyner, *American Popular Music* (Madison, WI: Brown & Benchmark, 1993), 7.

40. John Moore, "'The Hieroglyphics of Love': The Torch Singers and Interpretation," *Popular Music* 8, no. 1 (1989): 31.

41. William G. Hyland, *The Song Is Ended: Songwriters and American Music, 1900–1950* (New York: Oxford University Press, 1995), 5.

42. Joyner, *American Popular Music*, 12.

43. Marcelle Clements, "Sighing, a French Sound Endures," *New York Times*, October 18, 1998, AR2.

44. Joyner, *American Popular Music*, 43.

45. Joyner, *American Popular Music*, 13.

46. Joyner, *American Popular Music*, 13.

47. Denning, *Cultural Front*, 300–301.

48. Jim Bedoian, liner notes, *The First Torch Singers*, vol. 1, *The Twenties*, Take Two Records, 1992, 1. See also Joyner, *American Popular Music*, 13, 15.

49. Brian Priestley, *Jazz on Record: A History* (London: Elm Tree, 1988), 56.

50. William Howard Kenney, *Recorded Music in American Life: The Phonograph and Popular Memory, 1890–1945* (New York: Oxford University Press, 1999), 105.

51. Dietrich wears a tuxedo and seductively sings to the men *and* the women in the audience. At the close of the number, she kisses a female audience member.

52. Peter Jelavich, *Berlin Cabaret* (Cambridge, MA: Harvard University Press, 1993), 193. See also Allison M. Kibler, *Rank Ladies: Gender and Cultural Hierarchy in American Vaudeville* (Chapel Hill: University of North Carolina Press, 1999), 169.

53. Angela Y. Davis, *Blues Legacies and Black Feminism: Gertrude "Ma" Rainey, Bessie Smith, and Billie Holiday* (New York: Pantheon, 1998), 104.

54. Kenney, *Recorded Music*, 107.

55. Kenney, *Recorded Music*, 106. See also A. Davis, *Blues Legacies*, 40. Representations of Holiday's bisexuality provide an interesting example of how a popular singer's material—her biographers maintained that she was *not* a blues singer—is *not* read as signaling or signifying her sexual preferences. Holiday's sexual experiences and preferences remain firmly outside of her material and performances on stage, reserved instead for subtle allusions or outright outings in biographies and autobiographies. See, for example, Farah Jasmine Griffin, *If You Can't Be Free, Be a Mystery: In Search of Billie Holiday* (New York: Free Press, 2001), 53. Griffin notes, "Though she does not explicitly say [she is bisexual] in the text [of her autobiography *Lady Sings the Blues*] itself, she does imply it. She notes fighting off advances from lesbians during one of her prison stints, but when she acknowledges accepting the favors of another, she doesn't admit or deny involvement." See also Donald Clarke, *Wishing on the Moon: The Life and Times of Billie Holiday* (New York: Viking, 1994), 345–48. On the issue of Holiday's sexual preference, Clarke quotes musician Carl Drinkard at length. Drinkard notes Holiday's bisexual reputation, but takes great pains to assert that Holiday *primarily* desired men. Clarke notes, "Carl found it hard to describe how Lady did it, but she could act the way the girls expected her to act, lead them to believe that she was going to take them home with her. . . . But sure enough, when the quartet got to the Sherman Hotel, Carl

unlocked Lady's door and was about to hand her the key . . . wondering whether the girls would come with him to his room if Lady didn't queer the whole thing. 'And this time, Lady pulled me by the wrist into her room and said, "Good night girls," and slammed the door.'" In *Billie Holiday* (Boston: Northeastern University Press, 1995), 174, Stuart Nicholson is more straightforward about Holiday's sexual preference. Of her relationship with Tallulah Bankhead, he writes, "[Holiday's] 'dearest friend' was Tallulah Bankhead. . . . Indeed, several musicians claim that Billie made no secret about her lesbian relationship with 'Lula' and, more sensationally, a brief, explosive affair with Marlene Dietrich." However, none of these authors assert that Holiday's performance of love songs referenced or expressed her bisexual "tendencies" or desires.

56. Such marshalling of generic boundaries is not peculiar to torch singing, nor is it peculiar to the music of the 1920s and '30s. For example, see bell hooks, "Gangsta Culture—Sexism and Misogyny: Who Will Take the Rap?" in *Outlaw Culture: Resisting Representations*, 122 (New York: Routledge, 1994), who writes, "Mainstream white culture is not at all concerned about black male sexism and misogyny, particularly when it is mainly unleashed against black women and children. It *is* concerned when young white consumers utilize black vernacular popular culture to disrupt bourgeois values. . . . It is much easier to attack gangsta rap than to confront the culture that produces that need."

57. Lisa Appignanesi, *The Cabaret*, 2nd ed. (New York: Grove, 1984), 72.

58. Appignanesi, *Cabaret*, 9.

59. Appignanesi, *Cabaret*, 12.

60. Eric Lott, *Love and Theft: Blackface Minstrelsy and the American Working Class* (New York: Oxford University Press, 1993), 7.

61. Lott, *Love and Theft*, 24. See also W. T. Lhamon Jr., *Raising Cain: Blackface Performance from Jim Crow to Hip Hop* (Cambridge, MA: Harvard University Press, 1998), 139.

62. Lhamon, *Raising Cain*, 142.

63. Will Friedwald, *Jazz Singing: America's Great Voices from Bessie Smith to Bebop and Beyond* (New York: Da Capo, 1996), 69.

64. Friedwald, *Jazz Singing*, 68.

65. Jon Panish, *The Color of Jazz: Race and Representation in Postwar American Culture* (Jackson: University of Mississippi Press, 1997), 10.

66. This story of Café Society as the union of cabaret's politics and blues aesthetics is told by Denning, *Cultural Front*, 323–61.

67. Denning, *Cultural Front*, 57, defines *agitprop* as "the contraction of *agitation* and *propaganda* in political jargon—the name for a variety of forms of directly political art: topical songs and poems, street theater, manifestos, works of journalistic and documentary immediacy."

68. Lyrics for "Strange Fruit," by Lewis Allen (Abel Meerpool), quoted in David Margolick, *Strange Fruit: Billie Holiday, Café Society, and an Early Cry for Civil Rights*, foreword by Hilton Als (Philadelphia: Running Press, 2000), 15.

69. See, for example, Michael Brooks, liner notes, *Billie Holiday—The Legacy (1933–58)*, Columbia/Legacy, 1991. For an extended discussion of Holiday's performance of "Strange Fruit," see chapter 4 in this volume, "The Way You Haunt My Dreams."

70. Denning, *Cultural Front*, 343–45.

71. Denning, *Cultural Front*, 344.

72. A. Davis, *Blues Legacies*, 170.

73. A. Davis, *Blues Legacies*, 170.

74. A. Davis, *Blues Legacies*, 179–80.

75. Adjectives that Gonzales, "Torch Song Soliloquy," uses in the space of a three-page magazine article on torch singing and torch singers.

76. Denning, *Cultural Front*, 324.

77. Lilla Hardin Armstrong and Don Raye, lyrics for "Just for a Thrill," Todd and Sharon Peach website, n.d., www.thepeaches.com/music/randb/JustForaThrill.txt (accessed June 3, 2005).

4

# The Way You Haunt My Dreams

Stars are a case of appearance—all we know of them is what we see and hear before us.

—*Richard Dyer,* Heavenly Bodies[1]

Intimacy builds worlds; it creates spaces and usurps places meant for other kinds of relation. Its potential failure to stabilize closeness always haunts its persistent activity, making the very attachments deemed to buttress "a life" seem in a state of constant if latent vulnerability.

—*Lauren Berlant, "Intimacy"*[2]

To be haunted is tied to historical and social effects. To be haunted is to experience the glue of the "If I you were me and I were you" logic come undone.

—*Avery Gordon,* Ghostly Matters[3]

---

## WRITING CELLULOID DREAMS

Alice dreams she is writing—writing about torch singers. Ink from her pen, words pressed into cocktail napkins and drink coasters, bleeds and spreads onto the computer screen. Fingers trail behind thought, behind feeling. Hearing voices and following, Alice peers into the dim white before her for what is unseen and unheard, until now. The black cursor, heartbeat of the machine, pushes into her pulse, presses the record button. An image blinks into frayed focus before her. Movement now, a film behind closed eyelids.

Opening Shot: *The singer at home, eating breakfast, answering phone calls, getting the mail. Tense meeting with manager, who's trying to persuade her to do a short tour in Europe. The singer stalls, then finally agrees. Announces that she's going to take a shower and leaves the scene. Cut to preshow ritual shots from West Coast tour—warm-ups, pacing, laughing with band members, more pacing. Splice with footage of a hometown club gig, where the singer is relaxed, enjoying herself—where she really connects with the crowd. Bleed into a montage of the singer and other women—singers too—one appearing and fading into the next. Lips, eyes, mouths, voices. Between these appearances and vanishings, moments of uncanny connection.*

*Voice-Over Introduction by Respected Male Musician:* The most consequential artists—the most consequential visionaries who either change the course of music or set standards to which others aspire—do not make compromises. These days, we seem to have an abundance of such visionaries, including the singer.[4]

She is a superb piano player and arranger.[5] Her voice is one of the most emotionally flexible voices ever: with the slightest adjustment, she can convey heartache, lust, self-deprecation, cheekiness, empathy, cockiness, flirtiness.[6] Her sound gives people chills.[7]

Her music embodies the passion of jazz, a curious learning that cuts into your flesh, leaving a scar, a longing never satisfied, a wound of feeling hard to live with.[8] She packs so much meaning into seemingly simple gestures, transparent textures, and haunting melodicism that she forces the listener to reconsider the standards by which he or she gauges the jazz improviser's art.[9]

*Testimony of Unidentified Woman:* There was a time when I could listen only to the singer, only to her voice. I would lie in bed at night, surrounded by the dark beauty and sorrow of the music, my fingers spelling out melodies on tear-stained sheets. I would lie in bed, listening and weeping and waiting.[10]

*Respected Male Musician:* Waiting for what?

*Unidentified Woman:* I'm not sure. I felt she understood something about me, about my desires and my fears. And I felt, somehow, that she was waiting, too, yearning for something yet to come.

> *Respected Male Musician:* This blending of the singer's raw emotion with the hunger of her audience for intense vicarious expression may be the most indelible aspect of her style.
>
> *Unidentified Woman:* No. She just sings. To me. To me, she just *sings.*

Alice wakes, and for a moment believes the film is hers, a made thing inside the force of an apparition. Too soon, though, she knows it is gone. She gets up and looks for a pen and a piece of paper, determined to begin, again.

## BEGINNINGS

It is Streisand's voice I hear first. I am eight years old. I sit with my ear pinned to the stereo cabinet and she sings to me in a whisper. I try to get even closer to her voice, to take it inside my head and press out the din of my little sister's laughter and my mother's singing. I have attached myself to the stereo in a feverish desire to unlock the secret my mother and sister know, the secret they taunt me with: the beat. What is it? They say they feel it. Feel it where? They tap their toes, snap their fingers, and slap their thighs. They say they hear it. Hear it how? My mother sings; my sister giggles. I've tried Tom Jones and Johnny Mathis and Elvis, but the beat escapes me. And then "The Way We Were" fills my ear, fills my body, and I hear the beat in the most unlikely of sounds, in the most unlikely of voices.

"The *beat*?" I wail. "Well, yeah, I hear *that*... but what about the other sound?"

My sister stops giggling. "*What*?" she whines, nervous the joke has backfired. She looks at my mother. "What does she hear?"

My mother looks at me.

I shrug. "I don't know. Something . . . something in her voice."

"Heartbreak," my mother says, "pure heartbreak." She joins Barbra for the chorus.

"What's heartbreak?" my sister demands. "Mom, what's heartbreak!" She follows my mother into the kitchen, her questions bouncing off my mother's voice and falling around her dancing feet. I return my ear to the speaker, to the beat and the heartbreak and the love potion that is Streisand's voice.

## KISS

I try to decide when I fell for torch singers. I wonder when I fell first and hardest for Billie Holiday. I try to fix the moment in my own story— to say, *here my desire began.*[11]And then it hits me. It wasn't a moment at all, but a presence, an encounter.

I am in the library, casually flipping through a book on jazz singers, and there you are, smiling, determined. I stop and stare. Your lips are painted, lacquered, *made up*. They are compositions. I imagine them speaking, smiling, cringing, singing, moving over teeth and tongue. I take down another book, Robert O'Meally's *The Many Faces of Billie Holiday*,[12] and I see a thousand mouths, a thousand masks, and a thousand stories. I take these stories—your lips—to the circulation desk, and then home. I put on my one Holiday record and stare at each photo all over again, lip-synching your pout, your grin, your open-throated wail. I paint my own lips and press them into notebook paper, trying to write your sound. I place these traces of myself between the pages of the book, pinning my lips to yours in a textual kiss.

## FACTS

Before long, I wanted to know more—not about the songs, but about the voices on record. I wanted to know the stories of the women pictured on the covers of *All or Nothing at All*, *La Vie en Rose*, *Stormy Weather*, *All Time Favorites*, *My Name Is Barbra*, and *Absolute Torch and Twang*.[13] And so I read critics' profiles, biographic snapshots, encyclopedic portraits, eagerly recording the facts:

*Holiday, Billie.* Adopted name of Eleanora Fagan McKay, 1915–1959. U.S. jazz singer, also known as "Lady Day," born in Philadelphia, Pennsylvania. Holiday taught herself to sing in her early teens and made her debut in Harlem clubs. She had a singular voice steeped in aching emotion and fueled by an uncanny sense of swing. After being signed by Columbia Records' John Hammond in 1933 for her debut record, she became a star on the New York club scene. Her postwar work for the Decca label gave her popular acclaim. Songs she made her own include "Strange Fruit" and "I Cover the Waterfront." Her story, however, is a tragic one. As a result of her impoverished upbringing and constant bouts with drug abuse, her career was marked by a series of exaggerated peaks and valleys. In July 1959 she collapsed, and on July 17, died in a hospital of a kidney ailment.[14]

*Piaf, Edith.* Adopted name of Edith Gassion, 1915–1963. Parisian singer born into desperate poverty. After being deserted by her mother, Piaf sang in the streets with her father until a Paris cabaret owner discovered her. Her dramatic singing style and anguished voice appealed to French audiences and by the outbreak of World War II, she had become a star. She used her star status to criticize Hitler and smuggle French prisoners of war out of German camps. After the war, her reputation spread internationally and she appeared in New York City, singing at Carnegie Hall, where she was celebrated for her performances of "Milord" and "La Vie en Rose." In her private life, Piaf was as tormented as the heroines of her songs were, though the title and lyric of her famous "Je Ne Regrette Rien" ("I regret nothing") best expressed her attitude toward life. She collapsed in 1959, but came back to sing with renewed vigor, even though her physical condition was visibly deteriorating. She died in Paris on October 11, 1963.[15]

*Horne, Lena Mary Calhoun.* 1917– . U.S. singer and actress born in Brooklyn, New York. Horne is a dynamic performer and one of the great beauties of twentieth-century America. She began performing at age six and made her professional debut in Harlem's Cotton Club chorus line at sixteen. She sang with the Noble Sissle Orchestra (1935–1936) and Charlie Barnet's Big Band (1940–1941), but it was her movie career, with roles in *Cabin in the Sky, Words and Music,* and *Stormy Weather,* that made her a star. Though in the 1940s and '50s, her film roles were all guest shots that were easily removable—without spoiling the plot—for the benefit of southern-state distributors. Her live recording *At the Waldorf-Astoria* in 1957 was the best-selling release by a woman in RCA/Victor's history. In May 1981, she opened on Broadway in her own autobiographical show, *Lena Horne: The Lady and Her Music,* which received a New York Critics' Special Award and two Grammys. She continues to perform and record.[16]

*Vaughan, Sarah Lois.* 1924–1990. U.S. jazz singer born in Newark, New Jersey. As a child, Vaughan sang in her church choir and became church organist at twelve. In 1942, her singing talents won the amateur contest at Harlem's Apollo Theater. Soon after, she was invited to join Earl Hines's big band as female vocalist and second pianist. She also toured and recorded with Billy Eckstine before going solo. She had operatic range and control, which she often emphasized in a grand way, juxtaposing phrases sung in a soft and warm tone with others in a harsh, nasal vibrato or throaty growl. Her chops and style were imitated by nearly every singer who followed her. While contracted to Columbia Records from 1949 to 1954, Vaughan became an international star. Though she disavowed being strictly a jazz singer until her death on April 3, 1990, she was a singer of sheer, consistent brilliance.[17]

*Streisand, Barbra* (Barbara Joan). 1942– . U.S. actress, singer, and film producer from Brooklyn, New York. As a child, she sang for fun, but was set on being a stage actress and film star. Her dreams came true when she was cast on Broadway in *I Can Get It for You Wholesale* in 1961. She became a film star in *Funny Girl*, which earned her an Oscar for Best Actress for 1968. By 1969, when she came to the set to make *Hello, Dolly!* she had developed a reputation as a meddlesome perfectionist who wanted control over every aspect of the films in which she appeared. In 1983, she scripted, directed, wrote the score for, and starred in *Yentl*, her masterwork. She went on to direct *The Prince of Tides* (1991) and *The Mirror Has Two Faces* (1996). In the mid-1990s, Streisand returned to the stage after a nearly twenty-year hiatus, giving concerts in Las Vegas and Europe. Although critical reviews were mixed, these concerts proved that she had not lost her phenomenal vocal range or her unusual talent for blending sweetness and strength. Her Las Vegas "farewell" concert "Timeless" on December 31, 1999, set an all-time sales record for one-day ticket sales for a single event.[18]

*lang, k. d.* 1961– . Adopted name of Kathryn Dawn Lang, born in Consort, Alberta, Canada. She prefers the lower case appearance of her name because "it's generic and . . . it's a name, not a sexuality."[19] lang became a skilled pianist and guitarist in her youth and eked out a living performing classical and avant-garde music before turning to country on her independent debut, 1984's *A Truly Western Experience*. Her major label debut, *Angel with a Lariat* (1987), was praised by critics, but many country radio stations refused to play it, prejudiced by lang's spiky hair, vegetarian stance, and ambiguous sexuality (she would later come out in a 1992 interview with *Advocate* magazine). In 1988, she gained a breakthrough with the lush *Shadowland* and achieved international success with 1992's *Ingénue*. Her sensual and deep voice enjoyed great crossover success and generated a Grammy Award–winning single, "Constant Craving."[20] Subsequent releases evidence a genre-bending array of material, from urbane adult pop (*Ingénue*) to a touch of disco (1997's *Even Cowgirls Get the Blues*) to sophisticated torch (1997's *Drag*). In 2005, lang released *Hymns of the 49th Parallel*, a tribute to Canadian songwriting the *New York Times* deemed "entrancing."

Why these women? Why not Ella Fitzgerald, Aretha Franklin, or Diana Krall? Isn't Piaf too tragic? Vaughan too much a jazz singer? Horne too much a movie star? Streisand too insincere? lang too queer? Isn't Holiday too easy, too overexposed? Why not? Because these are *my* torch singers—women whose stories and voices speak to me, say something to and about the movement of my desires, my experience. Why not devote my search for knowledge, correspondences, explanations, and surges of emotion to other singers? Better singers? Perhaps such devotions are not entirely chosen.[21]

## I DO

In *The Queen's Throat,* Wayne Koestenbaum searches his love of opera for clues about his sexuality. He looks, too, for clues within the practice of opera "queens"—their desperate, addictive love for their divas, and the ways this fervent fandom and the sounding of desire confine and confound the opera singer as star attraction. He becomes a "pure receiver," a "phantom, a haunting . . . sick to find himself through singers."[22]

Am I sick to find myself through torch singers? And if I am, what does this say about me? About the women I love to listen to? What does searching for the missing person of the torch singer mean for the fan and for the star? What does this search mean for the writer, the ethnographer, and the performer? Is my infatuation with torch singers too eager? Too easy? Does my desire trivialize the performer and seal me off from any real engagement with the music, with the voices and stories on record?[23] At a conference, after I've spoken lovingly of my torch singers, someone in the audience asks if I understand the degree to which my writing about torch singing is invested in my hearing of performances made—moments that were live and alive—long before I was born. If I understand how much of this story—their stories—I am making into my own. I am aware of the fantasies built up around these women's voices and bodies. I realize how peculiar my passions are—peculiar to my own hearing and reading and love-struck fandom. Don't I? I *do.*[24]

## RECORDS

This weekend, like every weekend for a month, I drive to the local antique mall. I flip through stacks of records, looking for you. The smell of vinyl penetrates the thick plastic casings that Dealer Nineteen has lovingly wrapped around the images and voices of Judy Garland, Julie London, and Dinah Washington and there you are—Sarah, throwing a sly smile over your shoulder—and Lena, eyes half closed and lips parted. I pull away a plastic cover and let the record slide into my hands. The vinyl makes a mirror and I examine my own expression of delight at having discovered you here, together.

I pay for the records and ask the cashier if he would mind playing them for me. I tell him I don't have a record player at home.

He says, "Sure," and takes the records from me. "They're mine. I'm Dealer Nineteen. I love these old records."

"How can you part with them?"

"I have to sell these so I can buy more—so I can support my habit." The vinyl flashes as he turns, then positions the record over the turntable. The hiss and scratch of the needle gives way to Vaughan's lilting voice. As she sings "My Funny Valentine," people staring through Depression-era glass and flipping through musty copies of *Life* magazine stop to listen. They look toward the ceiling, toward the invisible proscenium of her sound.

"Did you ever see Sarah on stage?"

"No."

"Her live performances were breathtaking. Her control, her swing, her vibrato—simply amazing. Just hearing her begin low and sweet on 'Valentine' gives me chills. One note, and I'm gone."

And then we put on "Stormy Weather." Horne begins, "Don't know why . . . there's no sun up in the sky,"[25] and we smile. Dealer Nineteen says, "I love her light touch, her optimism. Don't you?"

We listen, Dealer Nineteen and I, thrilling at each run of the scale, each delicate hush. The needle works the grooves of our desire.

### HEAT

I am too late. I want to see k. d. lang from the reserved seats, but the close-ups of her are sold out. And so I bring a blanket and wait for her on the lawn. It is well over 100 degrees and I am sweating, leaking everywhere. I mist my face with a squirt bottle full of water, trying to stay cool. I wait. I mist. And then I see the people in the reserved seats stand and applaud. I look to the stage and see a tiny lang leap from the wings and run for the microphone. I stand with the others on the lawn and cheer. She sings, "Overflowing with possibility . . . pull me under . . ."[26] and I am drenched.

I leave my place on the lawn and move toward the reserved seats. I stop and wait, and when the usher looks away, I rush down the stairs toward the stage. k. d. comes into focus—moving, singing, and glistening in the sun. I look back over my shoulder and see the usher coming toward me. I try to blend in with the reserved customers, to disguise my transgression. I turn all of my attention on k. d. I put my arms in the air and sing, "Can't you see me standing here. . . . Hoping for the depths of blindness?"[27] I feel the usher's arm on my shoulder, and I turn myself in.

"I just wanted to get a closer look," I say. "I'm a huge fan. *Please.*"

"No."

"Please? What can it hurt?"

The usher stands firm.

"Okay. I'm sorry. I'll go."

The usher escorts me back to the lawn. I sit on my blanket and listen to k. d. sing her story, my story—our story. I mist myself with water, but it is too late. I am ablaze.

## DESIRE

My torch singers are constructions, productions of my desire.[28] They are "cases of appearance";[29] all I know of them[30] is what I see and hear on stage and record, in photographs and handwriting, through star publicity and stage names—Lady Day; The Sparrow; Sassy; The Chocolate Chanteuse; The Voice; The Lesbian, Feminist, Vegetarian, Canadian. My torch singers are stars, complicated women singing complex autobiographies that wind together personal narratives, star personae, and musical characters.[31] These women create—perform—a storied life in which the lines demarcating the "real" person from the star persona from the character in song are often blurry and indistinct, complex and ambiguous.[32] They experiment with and in "fictional bodies" that, while maintaining a certain image and star quality, shift and change both inside and outside the concert hall.[33] There is a pleasure to be had—for a singer and her listeners—in that uncertain space between and among songs, selves, and performance.[34] It is a space that invites performances that challenge the status quo, if not wholesale or completely, then incrementally, partially.[35] This is the radical potential of torch singing: to create stories and selves that "give rise to the creation of new . . . possibilities in performance."[36]

## BIND

The ways a torch singer enacts the pleasures and possibilities of a performative double negative[37]—a performance in which she is both *not* performing her self but also *not not* performing herself—aren't always hopeful, full of freedom. If the lines demarcating three performative selves—the woman, the singer, and the woman in the song—are blurry, yet distinct for popular music stars, such distinctions are collapsed for a torch singer in predictable, if interesting, ways: if the torch singer is singing autobiographically (even though she rarely writes her own material), then the star image we see and love is rendered powerless in her performance; she is unable to overcome the victim messages in the song. Though we—her fans—love her in spite (or is it because?) of this.[38] If, however, the torch singer distances herself from her material, her performance is wholly unsatisfying—she's become too full of her (star) self to give us what we want: her *real* self.[39] We wish she'd get back to what she does best: living her material.

And the torch singer's "fictional body" becomes a material enactment not of a carefully constructed and manipulated performance persona, but instead the *enfleshment* of a weak and vulnerable character-as-self: "He beats me too, what can I do?"[40] And while such weakness and vulnerability does not—cannot—hide within the "safe" space of fictional representation (including performances),[41] the *ease* with which character collapses into star persona collapses into woman inscribes the violence of exchanging texts for bodies and bodies for texts. Thus, the multiple and ambiguous identities that arise out of the double negatives of performance that are, for some popular musicians, so full of possibilities, become a series of performative double—triple—binds for torch singers.

### FANFARE

I am the singer's biggest fan. I don't think she's lost her voice or that she's become a caricature of her former self. I love her because no matter how much the critics put her down, she keeps on singing.[42] She knows her real audience will always accept and forgive her. Though sometimes you are afraid to listen to her, to hear the need and suffocated desire in her voice.[44] All the tragedy and happiness of her life is echoed in every word she sings.[45] Yet she is strong in her suffering. She's survived automobile accidents, attempted suicides, drug cures, comas, insanities, blindness.[46] She's suffered death of the heart.[47] And if she burns her candle at both ends, it still burns exceedingly bright.[48] *She* is the knife-edge between irony and hurt,[49] and *I* am her biggest fan.

### SINGING THE DREAM

The singer is the highest paid female entertainer—black or white—of her generation.[50] She transcends genre, achieves "crossover" hits, appears in film and on television, tours Europe, sells out Carnegie Hall. She takes control. She sets her own terms, writes her own ticket, produces her own spectacles, buys the rights, has the last word.[51] She takes easily to extravagance—sequined dresses and motorcycles and antique lamps and paintings and silverware and sports cars and furniture and diamond-and-jade Cartier clocks.[52] Not bad for an ugly girl with a weak voice.[53] And marriages? Of course, there are the marriages, not to mention the long list of lovers. Why not? Doesn't the singer deserve her success? Her happiness? Her excesses? She knows success comes with a price, and that happiness and excess don't buy a revolution. Still, singing the dream beats life in a whorehouse, doesn't it?[54] Shit. You can be "up to your boobies in white satin, with gardenias in your hair and no sugar cane for miles, but you can still be working on a plantation."[55] Singing the dream.

## CONTROL

She begins as a rags-to-riches tale, emerging "from a childhood of crushing abuse, armed only with a potent voice and a slender memory of an affectionate grandmother"[56] to create a starstruck career, *a life* of "undreamed-of-success."[57] She is proof that the dream is real.[58]

No matter how far she's come, though, she's notoriously unlucky in love.[59] Soon enough, she reverts to her less-than-desirable early life—she is unsophisticated, wild, promiscuous, prone to excess.[60] She just can't help herself. She eats too much, drinks too much, smokes too much, takes too many pills, and stays up much too late.[61] Though portraits of her excesses and transgressions are rarely connected to the burgeoning women's movement during her rise to fame in the 1920s and '30s (and beyond). Nor are they connected to the larger social, political, and cultural contexts in which she lives. Rather, her failure to capitalize on her talents and to live the American Dream is due to *personal* weaknesses and habits. "It would be a gigantic oversimplification to pretend that social conditions alone shaped her life, formed her vocal style, or led to her death."[62] Plenty of singers come from humble beginnings and remain untouched by scandal.[63] But for the torch singer it is "marijuana at fourteen, a jail term for prostitution at fifteen, and heroin addiction from her late twenties to her death."[64]

She is an incendiary exemplar: her abilities and achievements—while notable—are not enough to overcome a life always already spiraling out of control. In spite of her success, in spite of her stardom, she clings to the performances created in her material—unloved, a life unrequited.[65] Her life sounds like a line out of "My Man," the quintessential torch song: "I can't hold a man. . . . I'm nothing but a pair of lungs and a voice box."[66] Even her talents are beyond her control. The torch singer simply *sings*. And singing is "only wind and noise. I open my mouth and the sound comes out."[67] "I sing, I just sing."[68]

## HUNGER ARTIST

The singer is always hungry. She is starving, ravenous. She cooks pork chops and macaroni and cheese and fried chicken and potato salad and red beans, right in the can.[69] The cooking and the food satisfy her appetite, but these things don't fill the void of insults and misinterpretations.[70] She wolfs down turkey and dumplings, beets, fried bacon, ice cream cones and fries, pastrami sandwiches, sour green tomatoes, and rice pudding without the raisins, instant gratification.[71] She tears and digs and claws into her food.[72] To hell with delicacy and attractiveness.[73] She drinks Coca-Cola, beer, wine, and gin with a dash of water and a twist of lemon.[74] She overindulges—too much—a glutton. Her eating, like her music, is a style modeled after a star's life.[75] Her public makes what she puts in her mouth political, a matter of commerce.[76] People watch what she eats; they watch her weight.[77] They see she is starving—famished—and they greedily consume the artistry of her hunger. Franz Kafka was wrong. Interest in professional fasting has not diminished; the passion that streams from the throat of a caged animal is not hard to look at. Or listen to.[78]

## CONFESSION

No one knows the singer. Her story is a series of contradictory accounts, carefully constructed smokescreens, and outright lies.[79] She changes every detail—her name, her birth date, her father's identity, the story of her discovery, the tale of her influences and her style—to suit her fantasies about who she *really* is.[80] Once she becomes a performer—an actress, a player, a faker—she forgets. Embellishes. Obfuscates. You can't blame her, can you?

And yet, you can't stop yourself from looking at the photographs for what's behind the image, piercing you from the other side.[81] Can't stop reading the testimony—the noble attempts to set the record straight—trying to figure who's got it right. Does she? And you can't stop yourself from asking, "Did you really invite your lovers to beat you before your performances so you could sing with *authentic feeling*?"[82] You can't stop yourself from saying, "Come on, I need to know. I'm your biggest fan. *Confess*." Can you?

## TRUTH

Is the torch singer's story a confession—a testimony rooted in the truth-telling performances of spiritual and judicial testimony?[83] When narrating the events of her life, the torch singer and her biographers vow to tell the truth, the whole truth, and nothing but the truth, so help her—so help us. Within the realist, humanist tradition of such confessions, we assume that a singer can tell the truth about herself and her life, and further, that there is an essential and stable "Billie" or "Barbra" (an *I*, a *real self*) to be narrated and preserved in writing.[84] Don't we?

Torch songs also serve as confessional spaces in which to trace the facts and meanings of a life.[85] And because the torch singer is a star, her life story requires a complex logic of truth, coherence, and stability: the "life" story must correspond with the story told in the auto/biography and the story told in the music.[86] In this story, the torch singer becomes synonymous with her material—a living, breathing portrait of white, middle-class, heterosexual heartbreak—no matter that she might be poor; homosexual, bisexual, transsexual; a woman of color. No matter at all.

## STRANGE FRUIT

A torch singer is "structured by . . . [her] place in an economy of differences."[87] She lives amidst a "stream of signifiers and multiple identity constructions"; "turned again and again in stories that reflect and promote certain forms of selfhood identified with class, race, and nation as well as with sex."[88] Consider Holiday's decision to sing "Strange Fruit." *She* said "Strange Fruit" reminded her how her father died after being refused medical treatment at several hospitals because he was a black man.[89] *He* said, "Lady was non-political; when she first looked at 'Strange Fruit' she didn't know what to make of it. She never read anything but comic books."[90] To support this assessment, he offers the testimony of two of Holiday's friends, both of whom assert that, at least initially, she didn't understand the lyric.[91] As the story goes, Holiday had to be convinced to sing "Strange Fruit" by her mentor.[92] Though once she added the song to her repertoire, Holiday stumbled, fell. She descended from the pure speech of a natural singer giving her audiences untempered autobiography to the lowly rhetoric of a race woman. She became an actress who confused her self with her star persona, mistaking the artistic for the political.[93]

Yet no singer is completely natural—presenting her *real* self, voice, or story on stage or anywhere.[94] Like any ideology, star discourse exhibits an ironic self-awareness, a willingness to name itself[95] and to let the complex contradictions of me, not-me, you, not-you wrought in its performance go unspoken, but not to remain silent.[96] The torch singer's hazy, contradictory, fragmented performance and critique of untempered autobiography[97] becomes audible only in relief from the sound of her voice.[98] Here—on record, on stage, and in story—a torch singer is not the "utterly self-blinded, self-deluded straw target [her] theorists . . . make her out to be."[99] No, not at all.

### COMIC BOOKS

The singer makes music. She listens to records. She sings. She's not an intellectual. She doesn't read French philosophy or even the *New York Times.* She wouldn't understand the stuff. So when interviewers ask about her reading habits, she says she likes romance novels.[100] She says she just loves comic books.[101] She gets a big kick out of this. When the interviewers nod knowingly, smiling that just-as-I-suspected smile, the singer has to fight not to laugh. She knows what it means to be a girl singer in this world, and she gets her digs in where she can.

### REALLY

Okay, sure, yes, my torch singers are constructions and productions of my desire. I can—and do—experience and think through their performances and my pleasures in their sounds and voices and stories as a complex and potentially radical space of pleasure and critique. But I am wary of doing so at the expense of examining the ways such performances constrain, collapse, and do violence to their sounds, voices, and stories. Just as I am wary of the ways in which attention to the intersections of selves, star personae, and characters assumes that there is a stable, coherent, and volitional self to be experienced, known, and contrasted with other selves created and constituted in performance or anywhere. And yet torch singers as selves and voices and lives are told in such predictable, constraining, and violent ways. Their telling becomes as formulaic as a torch song, patterned after the heartbreak of white, middle-class, heterosexual desire. For what? For love, for a story to tell, for a voice, for a *life*. Their telling becomes a quest for the truth, for what's real:[102] Who are torch singers, *really*? How do I story them? Story myself? Story torch, really?

*Really*—an adverb, the double *l* a dividing line between the *real* and the *ly*, a dividing line within circumscribed, restricted, qualified, modified selves. Who are the real women who sing such songs? What do their voices and stories tell us about each other and ourselves? Do we find out who we really are? But what about *re-ally*—a transitive verb, beginning our alliance anew; always starting over? Re(-)ally, a series of linguistic performances demarcating erasures, misprints, and scars even while they refigure the constructions and constrictions of a life.

## MEDITATIONS ON LOVERS AND GHOSTS[103]

Asking the question of the torch singer—the question of really—requires not only reading and questioning and writing in, on, over star discourses, but also listening to her sing. Well, that's not quite right either, because listening requires reading and questioning and writing over. It requires that I speak to, of, and through her possibility, disappearance, and . . . pain.[104] This listening—my listening—isn't a how-to manual. It is not an explanation. It is, instead, a meditation; an inkling and linking of institution and individual, social structure and subject, history and biography, the living and the dead.[105]

Ear: Listening requires an "inter-subjective" attention that "does not aim at—or await certain determined, classified signs: not what is said or emitted, but who speaks, who emits," as well as who remains silent . . . though not unheard.[106] Such listening asks what a singer says as she whispers in our ears, as she speaks, softly, in "the interstices of the visible and the invisible."[107]

Voice: Listening requires a space in which "language encounters a voice."[108] This space is the *grain* of the voice, "a double posture, a double production: of language and of music."[109] In its slur and wail and sliding scale, a voice brings melody to bear on language.[110] When we listen to a torch singer, we listen to her silences, to how her voice speaks the unspoken.[111]

Body: Listening means moving beyond what can be said and understood about music "in the Academy, by Criticism, by Opinion."[112] If we listen to the grain of the singer's voice—to the body emerging from her throat—we can judge her performance on the body's enjoyment.[113] This body revels in the emotion of missing persons, the epistemology of haunting recognition.[114] It *sighs*; it reveals an "amorous absence."[115]

Loving: Listening requires an utterance, a "proffering, which has no scientific place: *I-love-you.*"[116] The occasion for *I-love-you*—"the point of departure for speaking it"—is music.[117] Listening to her sing, desire asks, how does her voice speak to *me*?[118]

Method: Listening requires a method, a practice, a style. It is the listening of an amateur (from the Latin *amator*, or lover) who gives her attention to "particularity, to specificity, to idiosyncrasy and detail."[119] This listening-as-method requires me to lean in, to press close so that the contact between my body and music's body is imbued with a ghostly, seething presence.[120]

Playing: Listening requires me to read and to write invisible things.[121] This listening does not "consist in receiving, in knowing, or in feeling [the] text, but in writing it anew, in crossing its writing with a fresh inscription . . . to operate [the] music, to draw it . . . into an unknown *praxis*."[122]

Acting: Listening requires me to reckon with how I enter into the story, with how the story changes me, with my own ghosts.[123] Otherwise, what "is the use of composing if it is to confine the product within the . . . solitude of listening to the radio? To compose, at least by propensity, is to give to do, not to give to hear *but to give to write*."[124]

Adverb: Listening requires that I link imagination and critique by conjuring the appearance of something that is absent; by calling attention to invisibility, marginality, and exclusion.[125] It asks what it would mean to "understand music not as the object of critique, but as its very practice."[126] It asks me to write about music as I listen: to modify the act—the verb, *critique*—with the additives and accumulations and alliances—the adverbs—of *listening*: critically, repetitively, persistently, patiently, attentively.

## LISTENING TO EDITH[127]

On the flight from Detroit to Paris, I read about the Edith Piaf Museum in the guidebook:

Paris. Open by appointment 1–6 p.m. Closed Friday, Saturday, Sunday, and bank holidays. Private museum in an apartment. Memorabilia of the singer. China collection. Free.

I circle the phone number. I turn the dog-eared page. I look up other addresses, places of Piaf memorabilia: 72 rue de Belleville, Piaf's birthplace, marked with a plaque dedicated by Maurice Chevalier, a fellow torch singer, which reads: "On the steps to this house there was born on December 19th, 1915, in utter destitution, Edith Piaf, whose voice was later to shatter the world."[128] The apartment at 115 rue de Belleville, where Piaf lived with her father, Louis Gassion. The corner of rue Troyon and avenue Macmahon, where Piaf was discovered by her first manager, Louis Leplee. Gerny's at rue Pierre Charron, where Piaf made her singing debut. 26 rue de Berri and 67 boulevard Lannes, two places Piaf called home.

I will make my pilgrimage to these addresses, tracing steps that she once walked, imagining myself coming home to apartments where she once lived, staring empty-voiced at street corners where she once sang. I will stand underneath the street lamp where she was born. I will pose and smile in the spaces of her beginnings while a Parisian shopkeeper takes my picture. And then I will feel wrong for making her ghost the object of my pursuit. I will refuse to visit the next destination—her grave at Le Pere Lachaise cemetery—deciding instead to listen for Piaf as she haunts Paris, a present history singing her (in)visibility.

Over the next few days, I will hear her voice radiating out of car radios and apartment windows. I will see her image in storefront displays and in books offered for sale at the Sunday morning market. I will feel her presence everywhere, in between. Walking down rue de la Gaîté, I will see a poster with the face of a woman—not Piaf but Evelyne Chancel—and I will think of a description I read of Piaf: "As she stood in the stark spotlight, she seemed all head and hands."[129] The photo of Chancel is startling; against the black background her face is ashen, with pencil-thin eyebrows drawn in a hyperbolic arch above black eyes. Her lips are painted hot pink, making her mouth float and blur on the chalky background. Her hands are fanned along her cheekbones, framing her face with red-tipped fingers. And the announcement, outlined and colored in pink:

UNIQUE A PARIS
*Evelyne Chancel*
Piaf mon am♥ur
Au
*Bistrot de la Gaîté*

The restaurant is closed for the afternoon, but the door is open. I push my way inside and pick up several of the postcard-size versions of the poster. I will return for the show tonight.

### PORTRAIT

I make a reservation for 7 p.m. at Piaf's Restaurant and Cabaret. I'm in San Francisco for a conference, and now seems like a good time to begin my fieldwork here, and Piaf's seems like the place—they present cabaret-style entertainment in the European tradition. Resident chanteuse Julie Hiryak sings chansons and accompanies herself on piano.

When my friends—Brenna and Dianne, women I've known for years—and I arrive, we are shown to a table in the back, near the piano. Along two sides of the narrow restaurant, the walls are crowded with photos and paintings of Edith Piaf. As we pass them on the way to our table, I feel as if I'm watching a strange film of her life: Here she leans into her lover Yves Montand and smiles in a film still for *Etoile sans Lumiére.* There she is posed in an early publicity photo, her hand at her brow, face pinched in trademark Piaf angst. Over here, she is a cartoon drawn on wobbly legs by a backstage onlooker. And there, she is singing, aged hands imploring the audience to regret nothing. Near our table, Piaf is frail but smiling in a hospital bed. And above where we sit, she wears her trademark black dress with the sweetheart neckline. She is clutching a glass of wine. She is here, everywhere, reduced to the outlines of her star persona—insatiable lover, overwrought actress, consummate performer, addict, drunk. Piaf is a mark, a smudge, a series of "instantaneous experiences which leave no trace, or rather whose trace is hated as irrational, superfluous, and 'overtaken.'"[130]

We order dinner—foie gras and salads and salmon and a nice bottle of red wine. Then Hiryak returns from a break and takes her place at the piano. She plays and sings, "Stuck between the Moon and New York City" and "It Had to Be You" and the theme song from the movie *Tootsie.* Dianne blinks. Brenna asks, "Is this torch singing?"

"I'm not sure." We watch Hiryak sing and she looks right through us.

Hiryak doesn't sing any Piaf numbers. The songs she does sing feel sugary, sticky sweet. I ask the waiter if we could request a few Piaf numbers at the break. I want to hear the *real* Piaf on the sound system. I look at the portrait hung above my table and see Edith staring, wild-eyed and pleading. I hear her asking to be released. *I am prisoner in these portraits and absent in the music. I am a missing person, a case of symptoms and screen memories, of spiraling affects . . . of violence and wounds.*[131] *Please.* I blink and look again. Edith's eyes have gone empty, dark. She is a case of disappearance.

After a while, I tune out the woman who appears here, a regular, three nights a week. I enjoy my foie gras and salad and salmon. I savor the wine and conversation. The music passes over me. And then Hiryak says she's had a request for some Piaf material. Oh, that's not what I meant! The restaurant is nearly empty now—only clusters of three and four at the tables near the piano remain. Hiryak begins to sing—"La Vie en Rose," "Je Ne Regrette Rien," "Bravo Pour le Clown," and something happens. The crowd of diners becomes an audience. We clap. We sing along. The music moves through us and we vibrate with Edith's uncanny presence. She is here, not quite real, an awareness, a compulsive repetition.[132] She is a memory spoken publicly, a vision and an allusion, leading us in song.

## SNAPSHOTS

I arrive at Bistrot de la Gaîté a few minutes early. The maître d' says he speaks very little English, but enough to help me order. I splurge on the foie gras and a bottle of red wine. The food arrives almost instantly and I enjoy myself immensely. While I eat, a tall, thin man seats himself behind the piano on a tiny stage at the front of the restaurant. He plays several Piaf songs, including "Milord," which has been running in my mind the entire trip. Walking in Montmartre or on the Metro, I'll just begin singing it—"da da da *daa* da da . . ."

The restaurant is filled with all manner of Piaf memorabilia—photographs and records and paintings. I am especially drawn to a painting of Piaf in the center of a rose. She is radiant and willful in the coil of petals. She rises from the stem, shoots out of it like an arrow, and pierces me.[133] I wonder if she would have enjoyed seeing her own image reflected on every surface in the room.

The lights dim and it's time for the show. A man on a ladder in the back of the restaurant works a makeshift spotlight. From his perch, he uses a microphone to announce Evelyne Chancel. As she takes the stage, he flutters a straw hat in front of the light. I watch him creating a fanfare for Chancel's entrance. He is perspiring and love struck. Chancel takes the stage and as with all of the performances I see in Paris—in French—I struggle to follow the dialogue. But something is different about this performance. She is not a Piaf impersonator; she is a fan. She is in love with Piaf.

Chancel wears a black dress with a heavy black cape. She looks at once like a nun and a governess, a socialite and a schoolgirl. Her hands peek through two long slits in the front of the cape. It is warm in the restaurant and in the spotlight she perspires. I wonder why she doesn't take off the cape, though I know it is necessary to her performance. It provides the stage and curtain for her hands—for Piaf's hands. She holds one hand at her chin and extends the other out toward the audience in a beckoning wave that curves back into her face and breasts. She shows us angry, trembling claws. These gestures are painted and photographed all around us and Chancel takes them into her body in an attempt to conjure Piaf.

She sings all the devotionals—"Mon Legionnaire," "Mon Dieu," and "La Vie en Rose." The audience sings along, almost drowning out Chancel. I sing along too, inserting what I imagine to be the words where my memory fails me. I raise my arms and shout, "Bravo! Bravo!" I look around the restaurant and see men and women—everyone—with their arms in the air, singing along and waving fine white dinner napkins like flags of surrender to the rush of nostalgia. And in this moment, napkin in the air, I feel Piaf's presence. Here, she is not mine alone; she is no longer my personal, recorded, domesticated possession.[134] Here, I share my desire for Piaf and the palpable longing to feel—even for a moment—the nervous flutter and stir of love. Chancel is the receiver, the medium for our haunted desires.

To close the show, the tall, perspiring man who has been fanning the flames of his love takes the stage to sing a number with Chancel. I don't recognize the tune, but it is surely a love song. The man is a poor singer. Chancel looks pained by his voice as he sings of his love for her. He is the stagehand, the star-struck fan permitted into her world for his instrumental effects. He asks Chancel's voice a question: Will you continue? Will you provide?[135] She does not respond. His song, of all songs, makes hot tears well in my eyes and a cry rise in my throat. I feel this pain not for the singer (or for the jilted lover in the song), but for the fan who does not penetrate the performance, the voice, or the woman. His voice sings *I-love-you.* His body sighs . . . an amorous absence.

When the number is over, Chancel ends the show with a flourish and many thanks to the audience. She leaves the stage, the spotlight is extinguished, and the lights come up. She moves toward her most vocal fans—two enthusiastic women close to the stage—and allows herself to be embraced and adored. I try to capture their reunion with my camera. I pop up behind the banquette like a celebrity photographer hiding in the bushes and snap the photo. All I am able to make out is the blurred image of one of the admirers, her hands extended in the air, palms out, fingers fanned to receive the voice and the woman. Though she is its subject, Piaf is absent from my stolen photo.[136] And then I look around the restaurant. She smiles out from the images hung here, pleased at what has taken place.

The maître d' comes by to collect the bill and I reluctantly leave the restaurant. I take a photo outside the Bistrot de la Gaîté, then walk down bustling and newly wet rue de la Gaîté to the Metro station. Paris hums with her presence. "Da da da *daa* da da . . ."

## COLLECTING

I arrive at the apartment museum at 1 p.m. My friend Melissa accompanies me as translator. We dial proprietor Bernard Marchois's number on the lobby phone. No answer. We check our watches. I check my notes. Yes, we said one. We wait. After a few minutes, a slight man accompanied by a small, white dog enters the vestibule.

"Are you?"

"Yes. So glad you've come."

We follow Marchois up a narrow staircase and into the apartment. He shows us into the museum while he gets the dog settled. Standing immediately in front of us is a black-and-white cardboard cutout of Piaf. I recognize the photo as one of later years. Marchois enters and tells us that the cutout was created as a lobby display for one of her last concerts at the Paris Olympia. He smiles. This is a life-size portrait, he says. He puts his arm around the cardboard statue. He is not a tall man, but Edith looks like a tiny bird under his arm—yes, a sparrow.

He shows us into the sitting room and Melissa and I look around. This place, like all of the others, is packed tight with Piaf memorabilia. Though these are *her* things—her records, her jewelry, her hastily scrawled letters, her black dress, her china. We sit on a couch (Is it hers? Did she sit here?). Marchois pulls up a chair. Melissa explains that we're interested in hearing about Piaf's performances, about Piaf the woman. He nods and smiles. He says, yes.

I ask him to tell us how they met. Melissa asks again, in French. He laughs. He explains that he met Piaf when he was a teenager.[137] An older couple—friends of the family—invited him to see Piaf at the Olympia. He went along willingly. Before the show, the couple took Marchois backstage to meet Piaf. He was disappointed. She was frail and plain. She looked like a cleaning lady.

> "Surprised?" Piaf asked. I nodded sheepishly.
> She laughed a round, full laugh. "You come back and see me after the show, eh?"
> I was sure I'd seen enough, but I nodded again.
> The show was electrifying. She opened her arms to us and pulled us in. She was a beacon. By the end of the show, I was smitten. I could barely contain my excitement as we made our way backstage. When we entered the dressing room, she turned that lightning smile on me.
> "So, what do you think of me *now*?"
> She saw everything in my eyes.
> She laughed. "Come," she said, and she pulled me into her embrace.[138]

Marchois's eyes glisten. He sighs. He says they were friends, never lovers, but his feelings about her never changed. He says she loved life, loved to laugh and play music, loved to sing. He says her songs were full of heartache, but that heartache was never hopeless. It was simply part of the equation of living. Her songs were signposts of the places she was in between—spaces of contradiction, tension, and immanent possibilities.[139] She loved sharing these places, these wounds of feeling. He says, again, she *loved* life.

I see the cardboard likeness of Piaf in the next room. I see the picture of Marchois with his arm around her—not the life-sized photo but what is pressing in from the other side of the image displayed within her tiny frame.[140] I see him sitting here, in an apartment filled with her teacups and earrings and stationery. I glance down at my notebook. My next question is, "Why do this? Why invite strangers into your home to talk about Edith Piaf?" I look up at him and I have my answer. He is an amateur, a careful collector of memories. He does this so that he might breathe life back in where only a vague memory or a bare trace was visible to those who bothered to look.[141] He lives among her things because looking at them and showing them to others is his lover's discourse. He is writing ghost stories in a language of commonplace things that take on an immense power.[142] And with each day, with each conversation, he proclaims his love and writes his memories anew.

We leave the museum and walk toward the Metro station. Melissa asks if I got what I wanted. I say, "Yes. No. I'm not sure, and maybe that's the point. I came to Paris looking for the real Edith Piaf, and I'm leaving with her ghost."

Melissa stops. "Why are you doing this? Why are you following a ghost around Paris?"

"Because following a ghost is about making contact, and that contact changes you. Because listening to the voice of a ghost means hearing and being and loving and writing the changes."[143]

## A GHOST

Dear Billie,

I'm listening to "They Can't Take That Away from Me," trying to decide when I fell for you, trying to decide when you began haunting me. Was it when I pressed your photographed lips to mine? When I read *Lady Sings the Blues* looking for clues about my own dreams, choices, and disappointments? When I began writing your initials—bh—next to fragments of texts on performances and philosophies that seem to speak something of your story and your music? When I began seeing and feeling you everywhere, in between? Like my falling for you, your haunting is pinned to a presence, rather than a moment. It happened when I looked at your many faces and understood not only your appearances, but also your disappearances. When I listened to your voice and understood the constructions and contradictions and immanent possibilities of your starry-eyed life. The way you haunt my dreams.[144]

This text, like all the others, haunts your presence. It loves and terrifies the very being it was intended to represent. You shatter the portrait of your self we see hanging in the textual frame of stardom.[145] What is useful in my desire to complicate and obfuscate the stories of your stardom—your excesses, your failures, your victimhood—and write over them with . . . what? Stories of your triumphs, your wit, your humility? Stories of my own?

Still, I remain a love-struck fan. Haunted, on fire. I hear you—and Edith and the others—watching over my shoulder as I write, always with me, the questioning, critical stars of my text.

Not quite memory or event, you leave marks of sound and rhythm on my language. You help me hear the voices of other torch singers, missing persons that never existed, *really* . . .[146]

## OTHER TRACES

*Acknowledgment.* The title of this chapter is a line from Billie Holiday, "They Can't Take That Away from Me," lyrics by George Gershwin and Ira Gershwin, *Billie Holiday—The Legacy* (1933–1958), Columbia/Legacy, 1991.

1. Richard Dyer, *Heavenly Bodies: Film Stars and Society* (New York: St. Martin's, 1986), 2.

2. Lauren Berlant, "Intimacy: A Special Issue," in *Intimacy*, ed. Lauren Berlant, 2 (Chicago: University of Chicago Press, 2000).

3. Avery Gordon, *Ghostly Matters: Haunting and the Sociological Imagination* (Minneapolis: University of Minnesota Press, 1997), 190.

4. Adapted from Howard Reich, "Her Way—Patricia Barber Continues to Evolve with Soft Sounds on Ravishing 'Nightclub,'" *Chicago Tribune*, September 24, 2000, www.patriciabarber.com/press/chicagotribune, par. 1 (accessed June 3, 2005), who writes, "The most consequential artists—the visionaries who either change the course of music or set standards to which others aspire—do not make compromises. Through sheer originality and force of will, they persuade the listening public to consider new ways of hearing jazz. Chicago these days seems to have an abundance of such loriously [*sic*] intrepid souls. . . . Among these visionaries, none has scoffed at commercial temptation more consistently than singer-pianist-songwriter Patricia Barber."

5. Leslie Gourse, *Sassy: The Life of Sarah Vaughan* (New York: Da Capo, 1994), 118. This is Gourse's characterization of accompanist Bob James's opinion of Sarah Vaughan's piano talent. Gourse writes, "He appreciated that Sassy was a superb piano player with a good understanding of arranging."

6. Rose Collis, *k.d. lang* (Somerset, England: Absolute Press, 1999), 101. This is Collis's description of k. d. lang's voice.

7. Gourse, *Sassy*, 3. This is Gourse's description of Sarah Vaughan's voice.

8. Elizabeth Hardwick, "Sleepless Nights," in *The Billie Holiday Companion: Seven Decades of Commentary*, ed. Leslie Gourse, 161 (New York: Schirmer, 1997). This is Hardwick's description of listening to jazz and listening to Billie Holiday.

9. Hardwick, "Sleepless Nights," 161, par. 5.

10. Adapted from Marcelle Clements, "Sighing, a French Sound Endures," *New York Times*, October 18, 1998, AR 33. The dialogue occurs between the interviewer, Clements, and an American woman who spoke of her "Francoise Hardy period." She notes, "That's all I could listen to. It was so sad and beautiful, just like me. I was drinking, needless to say. That's when I started drinking framboise, while I listened to chansons and I waited." When Clements asks, "For what?" she replies, "I don't know. . . . But there was something so sad, so tragic about my

life as I drank framboise . . . and I listened to her. I felt she understood the deep human sadness that characterized me, and that she, too, was waiting for something or other, yearning for whatever it was to come."

11. Wayne Koestenbaum, *The Queen's Throat: Opera, Homosexuality, and the Mystery of Desire* (New York: Poseidon, 1993), 81, writes, "Sexuality is inscrutable and we are made to feel the burden of unknowability: to feel responsible for finding, proving, remembering the source of this affliction, this benediction; for tracing it back to a scene or a fancy, to say, 'Here my desire began.'"

12. Robert O'Meally, *Lady Day: The Many Faces of Billie Holiday* (New York: Arcade, 1991).

13. Billie Holiday, *All or Nothing at All*, LP, Verve, n.d.; Edith Piaf, *La Vie en Rose*, LP, Columbia, n.d.; Lena Horne, *Stormy Weather*, LP, RCA/Victor, n.d.; Sarah Vaughan, *All Time Favorites*, LP, Mercury, n.d.; Barbra Streisand, *My Name Is Barbra*, LP, Columbia, n.d.; and k. d. lang, *Absolute Torch and Twang*, Sire, 1989.

14. Compiled from *Webster's New World Encyclopedia* (New York: Prentice Hall, 1992), 530; "Billie Holiday," n.d., www.music.excite.com/artist/biography/33213 (accessed April 15, 2001); and "Billie Holiday, Biography," n.d., *DownBeat*, www.downbeat.com/default.asp?sect=artists (accessed June 3, 2005).

15. Compiled from *Webster's*, 876; Monique Lange, *Piaf* (New York: Seaver, 1981), 90–91; and "Edith Piaf," n.d. , www.music.excite.com/artist/biography/18980 (accessed April 15, 2001).

16. Compiled from "Lena Horne," n.d., www.music.excite.com/artist/biography/11153 (accessed April 15, 2001), and "Lena Horne, Biography," *DownBeat*, n.d. www.downbeat.com/default.asp?sect=artists (accessed June 3, 2005).

17. Compiled from "Sarah Vaughan," n.d., www.music.excite.com/artist/biography/24353 (accessed April 15, 2001), and "Sarah Vaughan, Biography," *DownBeat*, n.d., www.downbeat.com/default.asp?sect=artists (accessed June 3, 2005).

18. Complied from *Webster's*, 1059; "Barbra Streisand," n.d., music.excite.com/artist/biography/22897 (accessed April 15, 2001); and "Barbra Streisand, Biography," Barbra Streisand website, n.d., www.barbrastreisand.com/bio_bio_pg2.html (accessed June 6, 2005).

19. "k.d. lang," n.d., www.music.excite.com/artist/biography/13521 (accessed April 15, 2001).

20. Complied from "k.d. lang," n.d., www.music.excite.com/artist/biography/13521 (accessed April 15, 2001); William Robertson, *k.d. lang: Carrying the Torch* (Toronto: ECW Press, 1992); and "k.d. lang, Biography," k. d. lang website, n.d., www.kdlang.com/biography2.htm (accessed June 15, 2005).

21. Koestenbaum, *Queen's Throat*, 19.

22. Koestenbaum, *Queen's Throat*, 28.

23. Dwight Conquergood, "Performing as a Moral Act: Ethical Dimensions of the Ethnography of Performance," *Text and Performance Quarterly* 5, no. 2 (April 1985): 6–7, describes such behavior as an "enthusiast's infatuation," marked by easy and superficial identification with the "other," refusing to become deeply engaged and thus trivializing the experience (and performance) of this other. For a more detailed discussion of Conquergood's "ethical pitfalls" ethnographers can encounter (and counter), see note 41 in chapter 8, "Circular Breathing."

24. I am referencing the distinction that J. L. Austin makes in *How to Do Things with Words* (Cambridge, MA: Harvard University Press, 1962), 6, between constative and performative utterances, where constative utterances *refer* to actions and performative utterances *are* actions. Austin gives a wedding vow as an example of a performative utterance—saying "I do" is the act (the doing) of marriage. A constative utterance, by contrast, represents or refers to an action—"I heard them say 'I do.'" This text constitutes a performative utterance of torch singers, of torch songs and torch singing, of music for torching.

25. Lena Horne, "Stormy Weather," lyrics by Ted Koehler and Harold Arlen, *Lena Horne: Stormy Weather*, BMG, 1990. My discussion is based on this recording.

26. My language is drawn from lang's recording of "Love's Great Ocean," lyrics by Ben Mink and k. d. lang, *Invincible Summer*, Warner Brothers, 2000.

27. My language is drawn from lang's recording of "What Better Said," lyrics by Abe Laboriel Jr. and k. d. lang, *Invincible Summer*, Warner Brothers, 2000.

28. R. Dyer, *Heavenly Bodies*, 5.

29. R. Dyer, *Heavenly Bodies*, 2.

30. In this section, I am dealing with the tripartite scheme Philip Auslander recommends for analyzing popular music performance in "Performance Analysis and Popular Music: A Manifesto," *Contemporary Theatre Review* 14, no. 1 (2004): 6–8. This scheme focuses on how performers enact three different identities or "strata" drawn from Simon Frith's *Performing Rites: On the Value of Popular Music* (Cambridge, MA: Harvard University Press, 1996), 186, 212: the "real" person, the performer's star image or persona, and the character in the (lyrical material of the) song. Of these three identities or strata, Auslander, "Performance Analysis," 7, writes, "The real person is the dimension of performance to which the audience has the least direct access, since the audience generally infers what the performer is like as a real person from his performance persona and the characters he [or she] portrays."

31. Auslander, "Performance Analysis," writes, "Frith proposes that we hear pop singers as 'personally expressive,' that is, as singing in their own persons, from their own experience. But two other layers are imposed on that one because popular musicians are 'involved in a process of double enactment: they enact both a star personality (their image) and a song personality,

the role that each lyric requires, and the pop star's art is to keep both acts in play at once.'" See also Frith, *Performing Rites*, 186, 212.

32. Auslander, "Performance Analysis," 7, writes, "Both the line between real person and performance persona and the line between persona and character may be blurry and indistinct, especially in the case of pop music performers whose work is heavily autobiographical." Elsewhere he writes, "The persona is of key importance because it is the signified to which the audience has the most direct and sustained access. . . . The persona is therefore the signified that mediates between the other two: the audience gains access to both the performer as a real person and the characters the performer portrays through the performer's elaboration of a persona" (12).

33. Auslander, "Performance Analysis," 9, draws on "Eugenio Barba's description of the actor's 'fictional body,'" noting, "It seems to me that the fictional body of a musical performer is the body of his [or her] performance persona, a body whose appearance is made to conform to the image of that persona."

34. Auslander, "Performance Analysis," 9, writes, "Part of the audience's pleasure in pop music comes from experiencing and consuming the personae of favorite artists in all their many forms and this experience is inseparable from the experience of the music itself and of the artists as musicians."

35. As an example, Auslander, "Performance Analysis," 10, writes, "The gender ambiguities of glam rockers' personae, for example, challenged the gender norms of American and European societies in the early 1970s. The performance of glam was a safe cultural space in which to experiment with versions of masculinity that clearly flouted those norms." However, Auslander tempers the resistive efficacy and culturally safe experimentation of glam, noting, "It was also entirely in line with the conventions of rock as a traditionally male-dominated cultural form. . . . Popular music is not entirely constrained by dominant ideologies, but neither is it entirely free of their influence."

36. Baz Kershaw, *The Radical in Performance: Between Brecht and Baudrillard* (London: Routledge, 1999), 7.

37. Auslander, "Performance Analysis," 6–7, relies on Richard Schechner's assertion that performers are simultaneously not being themselves and are also not not being themselves (see Schechner, "Performers and Spectators Transported and Transformed," *New Kenyon Review*, New Series 3, no. 4 [1981]: 88). Auslander uses David Bowie as an example: "This logic of the double negative is represented in one way by the professional names sometimes used by pop music performers. . . . David Jones renamed himself David Bowie; David Bowie is not David Jones, yet he also is not not David Jones."

38. As an example of this construction, see Angela Y. Davis, *Blues Legacies and Black Feminism: Gertrude "Ma" Rainey, Bessie Smith, and Billie Holiday* (New York: Pantheon, 1998), 179, who asserts that while Holiday's performances of love songs "offered other women the possibility of

understanding the social contradictions they embodied and enacted in their lives, [it was] an understanding she never achieved in her own life."

39. Michael Brooks, liner notes, *Billie Holiday—The Legacy (1933–58)*, Columbia/Legacy, 1991, 28, 31, voices this critique, contrasting Holiday's performance of "What a Little Moonlight Can Do," of which he writes, "Billie's [approach to singing the song was to] live the young girl caught up in the madness of first love" with her performance of "Strange Fruit," in which her "mistake was that she didn't let her natural instincts take charge and just sing, as she did with 'What a Little Moonlight Can Do.' Instead, she began to interpret."

40. One of the most shocking examples of such discourse is included in Leslie Gourse's "Preface" to *The Billie Holiday Companion: Seven Decades of Commentary* (New York: Schirmer, 1997), xiii, in which she notes, "All sources about Billie say that her men—husbands and managers—beat her up and took far more than their share of her money." She goes on to seemingly praise Holiday biographer Donald Clarke for being "the only one who has revealed that she invited these men to beat her up before her performances so she could sing with authentic feeling."

41. This is a point Judith Butler makes in "Performative Acts and Gender Constitution: An Essay in Phenomenology and Feminist Theory," in *Performing Feminisms: Feminist Critical Theory and Theatre*, ed. Sue-Ellen Case, 272–77, 278 (Baltimore: Johns Hopkins University Press, 1990), though with a slightly different emphasis and force. Butler is arguing that gender is not the expression of an essential, stable, volitional self, but rather that "the body becomes its gender through a series of acts," performed "by [an] actor who [is] always already on the stage, within the terms of the performance." Thus, gender is not a fact of being but rather a series of performative becomings. However, Butler is careful to point out that theatrical (performance) metaphors should not obscure very real "punitive and regulatory social conventions" (278). She writes, "In the theatre, one can say, 'this is just an act,' and de-realize the act, make acting into something quite distinct from what is real . . . the various conventions which announce that 'this is only a play' allow strict lines to be drawn between the performance and life. On the street or in the bus, the act becomes dangerous, if it does, precisely because there are not theatrical conventions to delimit the purely imaginary character of the act" (278). I am suggesting that while torch singing—as a performance—does not collapse the distinction between what happens in the theater and what happens on the bus, the "strict" lines between performance and life of which Butler speaks waver and break. The torch song, and thus the torch singer (real and performed) become more than "just" a performance and more than "just" a performer taking on a role.

42. R. Dyer, *Heavenly Bodies*, 147. This line was adapted from a comment Dyer includes in his analysis of the appeal of Judy Garland to gay male fans. A Garland fan writes, "I loved her because no matter how they put her down, she survived. When they said she couldn't sing; when they said she was drunk; when they said she was drugged; when they said she couldn't keep a man . . ."

43. From Amiri Baraka's "The Dark Lady of the Sonnets," reprinted in Gourse, *Billie Holiday Companion*, 182.

44. Baraka, "Dark Lady," 182.

45. This is another fan's comment about Garland in R. Dyer, *Heavenly Bodies*, 149.

46. Gene Lees, *Singers and the Song* (New York: Oxford University Press, 1987), 39, on Piaf.

47. Margaret Crosland, *Piaf* (New York: Fromm, 1987), 196.

48. Lees, *Singers*, 42, on Piaf.

49. Adapted from R. Dyer, *Heavenly Bodies*, 180.

50. James Haskins, *Lena: A Personal and Professional Biography of Lena Horne*, with Kathleen Benson (New York: Stein, 1984), 98, on Horne.

51. Comments made generally about the torch singers I've mentioned and Barber and Streisand in particular. See Alli Hirschman, "Q & Alli: A Modern Cool Companion," October 25, 1999, www.premonitionandmusic.com/artists/barber/interviews (accessed April 15, 2001), par. 3–4; and Edwards, *Streisand*, 519–20, respectively.

52. A list of the "extravagances" of Horne, lang, Piaf, Streisand, Vaughan, and Holiday. See Haskins, *Lena*, 149; Mim Udovitch, "k. d. lang: How Did a Lesbian, Feminist, Vegetarian Canadian Win a Grammy and the Hearts of America?" in *Rock She Wrote: Women Write about Rock, Pop, and Rap*, ed. Evelyn McDonnell and Ann Powers, 331 (New York: Delta, 1995); Crosland, *Piaf*, 141, 195–96; Edwards, *Streisand*, 24, 95–98; Gourse, *Sassy*, 224; and Donald Clarke, *Wishing on the Moon: The Life and Times of Billie Holiday* (New York: Viking, 1994), 290–92; respectively.

53. Comments made about Piaf, Streisand, and Holiday. See Lees, *Singers*, 42; Edwards, *Streisand*, 52; and Gourse, "Preface," ix-xvii, respectively.

54. Summarizing Piaf's life, Lees, *Singers*, 42, writes, "If the last years were hard, so they are for many people who have known nothing of the heights she attained. And singing your dreams to the air beats life in a Normandy whorehouse."

55. This line is from Billie Holiday, *Lady Sings the Blues*, with William Dufty (1956; New York: Penguin, 1992), 97. Citations are to the 1992 edition.

56. Leslie Gourse, "There Was No Middle Ground with Billie Holiday," in Gourse, *Billie Holiday Companion*, 140. The torch singer's story often begins with tales of poverty, racism, and physical and psychological abuse. See also Stuart Nicholson, *Billie Holiday* (Boston: Northeastern University Press, 1995), on Holiday; Crosland, *Piaf*, on Piaf; Haskins, *Lena*, on Horne; Gourse, *Sassy*, on Vaughan; and Edwards, *Streisand*, on Streisand.

57. Leonard Feather, "Lady Day," in Gourse, *Billie Holiday Companion*, 6. See also Crosland, *Piaf*, 193, on Piaf; Haskins, *Lena*, 33, on Horne; Gourse, *Sassy*, 14, on Vaughan; Edwards,

*Streisand*, 361, on Streisand; and Udovitch, "k. d. lang," 333, on lang. Such stories reinforce the individual success myth and the ideology of liberal individualism.

58. Dana L. Cloud, *Control and Consolation in American Culture and Politics: Rhetorics of Therapy* (Thousand Oaks, CA: Sage, 1998), 119, writes that popular biography likes to tell a "rags-to-riches" story as "'proof' that the dream of individual achievement against all odds is real," in turn "justif[ying] continuing inattention to structural factors, like race, gender, and class, that pose barriers to the dream for some Americans."

59. See Clarke, *Wishing on the Moon*, 290–92, on Holiday; Haskins, *Lena*, 85, on Horne; Lucy O'Brien, *She Bop: The Definitive History of Women in Rock, Pop, and Soul* (New York: Penguin, 1995), 53, on Piaf; Gourse, *Sassy*, 127, on Vaughan; and Edwards, *Streisand*, 360, on Streisand.

60. See Lees, *Singers*, 27, on Piaf, and Gourse, "Preface," xv, on Holiday.

61. See Feather, "Lady Day," 6, on Holiday; Gourse, *Sassy*, 30, on Vaughan; Lees, *Singers*, 27, on Piaf; and Edwards, *Streisand*, 261, on Streisand.

62. Feather's comments about Holiday—Feather, "Lady Day," 6. In addition to providing insight to how music critics and biographers viewed Holiday's life and choices, Feather's observations also speak more generally to how the story of a torch singer's life is typically interpreted and told.

63. For instance, Feather, "Lady Day," 6, contrasts Holiday's life story with that of Ella Fitzgerald's. I don't think it's a mistake to connect this distinction with how Holiday and Fitzgerald—both popular jazz singers—are categorized. While they are both labeled jazz singers, Holiday is also a *torch singer*. Fitzgerald is not.

64. Feather, "Lady Day," 6.

65. P. David Marshall, *Celebrity and Power: Fame in Contemporary Culture* (Minneapolis: University of Minnesota Press, 1997), 54, characterizes this relationship as semiotic: "A song, in essence, becomes a sign of the performer."

66. Garland quoted in Lees, *Singers*, 290.

67. Streisand quoted in Edwards, *Streisand*, 62.

68. Vaughan quoted in Gourse, *Sassy*, 48.

69. A collection of the foods Holiday, Vaughan, and Piaf liked to cook and eat. See Holiday, *Lady Sings the Blues*, 70, 194; Gourse, *Sassy*, 55–56; and Crosland, *Piaf*, 30.

70. I'm purposefully reinterpreting Gourse, *Sassy*, 56. Indirectly quoting Vaughan's road manager Johnnie Garry, Gourse writes, "Johnnie felt that her cooking helped make up for the insults of segregation that surrounded them in Miami."

71. Gourse, *Sassy*, 14, writes that Vaughan loved fried bacon. Edwards, *Streisand*, 263, 215–16, writes that Streisand ate turkey, dumplings, and beets in her performance of Dolly in *Hello,*

*Dolly!* Streisand also loves ice cream cones, French fries, hot pastrami sandwiches, and sour green tomatoes.

72. I'm drawing on Edwards's descriptions of Streisand's eating (Edwards, *Streisand*, 215–16). She writes, Streisand "sat in a chair and began to wolf down some fruit in a large basket near her," and she "sat down as she hungrily dug into the bag and pulled out a hot pastrami sandwich."

73. This is a contrary interpretation of Edwards, *Streisand*, 263. Edwards describes the scene in *Hello, Dolly!* in which Dolly wolfs down the turkey, dumplings, and beets. Streisand, while "eating heartily . . . had to maintain delicacy and attractiveness."

74. Favorite drinks of Streisand, Piaf, and Vaughan. See Edwards, *Streisand*, 215; Crosland, *Piaf*, 136–37; and Gourse, *Sassy*, 14.

75. Crosland, *Piaf*, 43, writes that Piaf's performance style was "no more than the mere possession of a voice. . . . Her style was her own life."

76. I'm referencing the public uproar surrounding lang's choice to appear in a commercial for the People for the Ethical Treatment of Animals (PETA) in which she says, "We all love animals, but why do we call some pets and some dinner? If you knew how meat was made, you'd lose your lunch. I know. I'm from cattle country and that's why I became a vegetarian" (quoted in Robertson, *Carrying the Torch*, 94). Following broadcast of the advertisement, lang (and her mother) received abusive phone calls, lang's records were banned from radio station play lists, and the "Home of k. d. lang" sign at the edge of Consort, Alberta (lang's hometown), was spray-painted with the words, "Eat beef dyke" (94).

77. This is especially true for Vaughan and Holiday. See Gourse, *Sassy*, 166, and Gourse, "Preface," ix, respectively. One of Holiday's first press notices, written by John Hammond for the April 1933 edition of *Melody Maker*, states, "This month, there has been a real find in the person of a singer called Billie Holiday . . . though only eighteen she weighs over 200 pounds, is incredibly beautiful and can sing as well as anybody I ever heard" (quoted in Farah Jasmine Griffin, *If You Can't Be Free, Be a Mystery: In Search of Billie Holiday* [New York: Free Press, 2001], 29).

78. These lines are drawn from Franz Kafka, "A Hunger Artist," in *Fiction 100: An Anthology of Short Stories*, 4th ed., ed. James H. Pickering, 642, 647 (New York: Macmillan, 1985).

79. Kathy Ferguson, *The Man Question: Visions of Subjectivity in Feminist Theory* (Berkeley: University of California Press, 1993), 11, writes, "We make up our claims to truth, Nietzsche argues, then we forget we made them up, then we forget that we forgot."

60. As an example, consider Holiday's autobiography, *Lady Sings the Blues*. The "source" of the material in the book has been the subject of much discussion. Some of Holiday's biographers attribute the account of her life, replete with its embellishments, distortions, and outright lies, to Holiday alone (see Gourse, "Preface," ix–x, and Henry Pleasants, "The Great American

Popular Singers," in Gourse, *Billie Holiday Companion*, 132). However, other critics assert that *Lady Sings the Blues* was constructed (fabricated even) almost entirely by journalist William Dufty and without Holiday's knowledge or permission. For this account, see Orin Keepnews, "Lady Sings the Blues," in Gourse, *Billie Holiday Companion*, 114, and Nat Hentoff, "The Real Lady Day," in Gourse, *Billie Holiday Companion*, 155. Griffin, *If You Can't Be Free*, 45–55, concurs with Keepnews and Hentoff; however, she recommends that rather than examine *Lady Sings the Blues* as an authentic or accurate portrait of Holiday's life, we read the autobiography as a performance of a stage persona. She notes, "The autobiography is not a song, but a series of them; it is a carefully constructed performance of a life" (48).

81. Adapted from Gordon, *Ghostly Matters*, 107, who writes, "The blind field is what the ghost's arrival signals. The blind field is never names as such in the photograph. How could it be? It is precisely what is pressing in from the other side of the fullness of the image displayed within the frame; the *punctum* only ever evokes it and the necessity of finding it."

82. Gourse, "Preface," xiii.

83. Leigh Gilmore, "Policing Truth: Confession, Gender, and Autobiographical Authority," in *Autobiography and Postmodernism*, ed. Kathleen Ashley, Leigh Gilmore, and Gerald Peters, 68 (Amherst: University of Massachusetts Press, 1994).

84. Leigh Gilmore, "The Mark of Autobiography: Postmodernism, Autobiography, and Genre," *Autobiography and Postmodernism*, ed. Kathleen Ashley, Leigh Gilmore, and Gerald Peters (Amherst: University of Massachusetts Press, 1994), 6–7. See also Norman Denzin, *Interpretive Biography*, Sage University Paper Series on Qualitative Research Methods, vol. 17 (Newbury Park: Sage, 1989), 19–23.

85. Michael A. Gonzales, "Torch Song Soliloquy: One Man's Poetic Tribute to Ladies Who Sing the Blues," *Mode*, February 1998, 55, on Piaf and Holiday.

86. Denzin, *Interpretive Biography*, 21. See also R. Dyer, *Heavenly Bodies*, 8–11.

87. Barbara Biesecker, "Coming to Terms with Recent Attempts to Write Women into the History of Rhetoric," *Philosophy and Rhetoric* 25, no. 2 (1992): 148.

88. Leigh Gilmore, *Autobiographics: A Feminist Theory of Women's Self-Representation* (Ithaca, NY: Cornell University Press, 1994), 148.

89. Holiday, *Lady Sings the Blues*, 84.

90. "He" is Holiday's biographer Clarke, *Wishing on the Moon*, 135.

91. Clarke, *Wishing on the Moon*, 164.

92. Barney Josephson.

93. Michael Denning, *The Cultural Front: The Laboring of American Culture in the Twentieth Century* (London: Verso, 1997), 338. See also Denzin, *Interpretive Biography*, 45, who writes

that biographies construct life stories as series of implicit and explicit hierarchies and oppositions (universal and particular, individual and society, self and other, emotional and rational, musician and actress, subject of the song and performer). The "essential" or "real" meanings of the subject are to be found in the resolution of these oppositions. Thus, Holiday is criticized for giving in to her dramatic, performative tendencies, rather than just singing. Performing "political" songs, including "Strange Fruit," transformed her natural talents into posturing performances (Brooks, liner notes, 28–31). Griffin, *If You Can't Be Free*, 30, provides an extended critique of this "naturalizing" discourse as it was applied to Holiday. Holiday the "natural" singer is out of history, out of context, and out of social convention. She notes, "Eventually the stories of her arrests and drug addiction joined with her stage persona of the torch singer to create a new image, that of the tragic, ever-suffering black woman singer who simply stands center stage and naturally sings of her woes. . . . As Robert O'Meally explains, this figure is a natural; she has no personal or artistic history, she has no musical skills. She feels but does not think. She has insatiable appetites for food, sex, alcohol, and drugs."

94. Stacy Wolf, *A Problem Like Maria: Gender and Sexuality in the American Musical* (Ann Arbor: University of Michigan Press, 2002), 35.

95. See Terry Eagleton, *Ideology: An Introduction* (London: Verso, 1991), 60–61, and James C. Scott, *Domination and the Arts of Resistance: Hidden Transcripts* (New Haven, CT: Yale University Press, 1990), 197.

96. Theresa Ebert, *Ludic Feminism and After: Postmodernism, Desire, and Labor in Late Capitalism* (Ann Arbor: University of Michigan Press, 1996), 7.

97. Denning, *Cultural Front*, 338.

98. Dana L. Cloud, "The Null Persona: Race and the Rhetoric of Silence in the Uprising of '34," *Rhetoric & Public Affairs* 2, no. 2 (1999): 176.

99. Eagleton, *Ideology*, 61.

100. Crosland, *Piaf*, 29.

101. Clarke, *Wishing on the Moon*, 164–65, on Holiday, and Gourse, *Sassy*, 46, on Vaughan.

102. In Piaf's preface to her autobiography—*My Life*, trans. and ed. Margaret Crosland (London: Owen, 1990), 10, which was dictated to Crosland near the end of Piaf's life—Piaf notes, "It's the more intimate secrets that weigh heavily upon me, the ones which have reached the public in distorted versions of the truth. I want to free myself from them once and for all by confessing them." Horne (Lena Horne and Richard Schickel, *Lena* [Garden City, NY: Doubleday, 1965]) says her autobiography marked a "decision to face my past" and the "self which existed in and was formed by it" (296). And the back cover of Holiday's *Lady Sings the Blues* proclaims, "In a memoir that is as poignant, lyrical, and dramatic as her legendary performances, Billie Holiday tells her own story." In the text, Holiday puts it with much less fanfare: "I've raked up my past so I can bury it" (183).

103. I am referring Roland Barthes's *A Lover's Discourse: Fragments*, trans. Richard Howard (New York: Hill & Wang, 1978), and Gordon's *Ghostly Matters.* Portions of this meditation and the following story about Piaf appear in revised form in Holman Jones, "Listening to the Bones: A Meditation on Torch Singers and Ghost Stories," in *The Green Window: Proceedings of the Giant City Conference on Performative Writing*, ed. Lynn C. Miller and Ronald J. Pelias, 8–18 (Carbondale: Southern Illinois University Press, 2001).

104. Della Pollock, "Performative Writing," in *The Ends of Performance*, ed. Peggy Phelan and Jill Lane, 79 (New York: New York University Press, 1998).

105. Gordon, *Ghostly Matters*, 19.

106. Roland Barthes, *The Responsibility of Forms: Critical Essays on Music, Art, and Representation*, trans. Richard Howard (Berkeley: University of California Press, 1985), 246.

107. Gordon, *Ghostly Matters*, 24.

108. Barthes, *Responsibility of Forms*, 269.

109. Barthes, *Responsibility of Forms*, 269.

110. Barthes, *Responsibility of Forms*, 271.

111. Gordon, *Ghostly Matters*, 150.

112. Barthes, *Responsibility of Forms*, 273.

113. Barthes, *Responsibility of Forms*, 277.

114. Gordon, *Ghostly Matters*, 63.

115. Barthes, *Lover's Discourse*, 15.

116. Barthes, *Lover's Discourse*, 149.

117. Barthes, *Lover's Discourse*, 149.

118. Adapted from Gordon, *Ghostly Matters*, 24, who asks, "How does the ghost speak to me?"

119. Barbara Engh, "Loving It: Music and Criticism in Roland Barthes," *Musicology and Difference: Gender and Sexuality in Music Scholarship*, ed. Ruth A. Solie, 75 (Berkeley: University of California Press, 1993).

120. Gordon, *Ghostly Matters*, 8.

121. Gordon, *Ghostly Matters*, 17.

122. Roland Barthes, *Image-Music-Text*, trans. Stephen Heath (New York: Hill, 1977), 153.

123. Gordon, *Ghostly Matters*, 22.

124. Barthes, *Image-Music-Text*, 153.

124. Gordon, *Ghostly Matters*, 24, 26.

126. Engh, "Loving It," 78.

127. Portions of this story about Piaf appear in revised form in Holman Jones, "Autoethnography: Making the Personal Political," in *The Sage Handbook of Qualitative Research*, 3rd ed., ed. Norman K. Denzin and Yvonna S. Lincoln, 774–76 (Thousand Oaks, CA: Sage, 2005).

128. Quoted in Crosland, *Piaf*, 18.

129. Lees, *Singers*, 25.

130. Max Horkheimer and Theodor Adorno, *Dialectic of Engagement* (1944; New York: Herder, 1972), 216. Citations are to the 1972 edition.

131. Gordon, *Ghostly Matters*, 25.

132. Neil Hertz, quoted in Gordon, *Ghostly Matters*, 56. Hertz is commenting on Sigmund Freud's theory of repetition. He notes, "Could we add that Freud was bound to perceive that relation as uncanny—not quite literary, but no longer quite real, either, the workings of a compulsion glimpsed 'through' an awareness of something-being-repeated."

133. Roland Barthes, *Camera Lucida: Reflections on Photography*, trans. Richard Howard (London: Fontana, 1986), 26.

134. Marshall, *Celebrity and Power*, 54.

135. Koestenbaum, *Queen's Throat*, 33.

136. Elaine Showalter, *The Female Malady: Women, Madness and English Culture 1830–1980* (New York: Pantheon, 1985), 152, notes that women "hysterics" were "not simply photographed once, but again and again, so that they became used to the camera and to the special status they received as photogenic subjects."

137. Bernard Marchois, personal interview, June 30, 2000.

138. Marchois, personal interview.

139. Scott, *Domination*, xii.

140. Gordon, *Ghostly Matters*, 107.

141. Gordon, *Ghostly Matters*, 22.

142. Raymond Carver, *Call If You Need Me: The Uncollected Fiction and Other Prose*, 1991 (New York: Vintage, 2000), 89. Carver writes, "It's possible, in a poem or short story, to write about commonplace things and objects using commonplace but precise language, and to endow those things—a chair, a window curtain, a fork, a stone, a woman's earring—with immense, even startling power."

143. Gordon, *Ghostly Matters*, 22.

144. Holiday, "They Can't Take That Away from Me."

145. Sidonie Smith, *A Poetics of Women's Autobiography: Marginality and the Fictions of Self-Representation* (Bloomington: Indiana University Press, 1987), 59.

146. Gordon, *Ghostly Matters*, 57, writes, "To allow the ghost to help you imagine what was lost that never even existed, really" (emphasis mine).

5

# Hearing Voices

In [her] performance of "My Man," an ironic edge in her voice warns against a facile, literal interpretation. And in case this is missed, the slow tempo with which she sings . . . emphasizes an ambivalent posture rather than an acquiescence to the violence described.

—*Angela Davis,* Blues Legacies and Black Feminism[1]

My search for "evidence" . . . became intimately linked with my desire—my desire for knowledge, answers, proof—and my desire to . . . hear [irony] in her voice. . . . Sometimes I couldn't tell which pieces of evidence were about the singer and which were about me.

—*adapted from Stacy Wolf, "Desire in Evidence"*[2]

Printing presses and copying machines may be seized, radio transmitters may be located, even typewriters and tape recorders may be taken, but short of killing its bearer, the human voice is irrepressible.

—*James Scott,* Domination and the Arts of Resistance[3]

---

## GOING HOME

I ask my mother to join me on a trip to hear torch singing in Chicago. I fly into Des Moines and rent a car, then drive to my parents' home. I will spend the night there and in the morning, my mother and I will drive to Chicago. But I get lost.

I'm trying to find my parents' house—not the house I grew up in, but the new house they bought on the outskirts of town. I've only been there once, but it's in my hometown, so I tell my mother I don't need directions. I drive around and around, looking for the entrance to the development. So many houses and they all look the same. I'm trying to go home, but I don't know the way.

On the third time by, I recognize my mother's car. Relieved, I pull into the driveway and quietly make my way into the house. It is late and my parents are asleep, but when I reach the top of the stairs, my father asks if my plane was delayed. I say yes, not wanting to admit my mistake.

The next morning, my mother and I drink coffee and look at the atlas. We load the car and stop for gas, and then we're on the highway to Chicago. I've never taken a trip alone with my mother. We've taken a few family vacations and she's visited me at this or that college town over the years, but we've never gone away together. I ask her if she's ever been to Chicago because I don't know the answer. She says, "*Sure*" and I take the bait.

"When?"

"Oh, a long time ago, before I met Dad."

"When you were married before? When you were married to . . ."

"Charlie?"

"Yeah."

"No. Before then even, right after high school, with a group of friends."

"What did you do?"

"Oh, you know. We went to the Field Museum and the Shedd Aquarium and the zoo. And we went to a few clubs at night, to hear music."

"I didn't know that."

My mother is silent for the next ten miles. Then she asks if I want to listen to the book on tape that she brought along. "Sure. What's it about?" I ask this question, though I know it's some sort of pulpy romance.

"Oh, you know. Some love story. But it's got a little mystery, too. I don't like the straight romance novels. There's got to be a murder or a stolen jewel or something to keep things interesting." She pushes the cassette into the player and we're transported to the Everglades, where we meet a tough-as-nails and strikingly handsome theme park owner who is the target of a murder plot (something about a large oil deposit directly under his property) and the beautiful and tougher-than-nails attorney who'll sort the whole thing out (but not before falling hopelessly in love with the strikingly handsome man). And we're off.

We arrive in Chicago just before the evening rush hour. We check into the hotel and decide to rest before going out for dinner and music. I've got several places I'd like to see—the Green Mill, Davenport's, Toulouse Jazz Cabaret—but we're only here for one night, and mom looks a little tired. I suggest we begin with dinner in the hotel restaurant and she agrees.

The restaurant is plush and decadent. I pick out a bottle of wine I think she will like. She decides she's going to have the salmon. I ask her if she wants to try the foie gras appetizer. She wrinkles her nose. "Have you tried it?" she asks.

"Sure. It's becoming sort of a fieldwork tradition. Let's get some."

The foie gras arrives and my mother tries a small bite. She smiles. She tries another bite and smiles again. She says that Dad will never believe that she's eating—how do you say it—fwar gwazzzzzz? She giggles. I'm not kidding. My mother is sitting across from me eating goose liver and giggling. I giggle, too.

And then a piano begins to play. We both turn around and search the room for the source of the sound. There, in the bar, a grand piano. So there's going to be music? As our dinners arrive, the Jennifer Graham Trio all the way from New York City takes the stage. Graham is tall and brunette and a bit younger than my mother, but only a bit. She sings "How Long Has This Been Going On?" and "You'll Never Know." My mother hums in tune with Jennifer. "So *this* is the kind of music you're writing about?"

"Yes. I love it."

"*Really?* I can't believe you're writing about these old songs! I bet I know every one of them."

"Did you use to sing these songs?"

"Sure."

"I guess I always think of you singing Johnny Mathis—'Chances Are' and 'Misty.'"

"Those, too."

"So what do you think about the Jennifer Graham Trio doing your material?"

"They're pretty good. She's got a good voice—not a great voice—but a good one."

"Maybe *you* should get up there."

"Ha! They wouldn't let me on stage. I'm too fat. I ruined my voice smoking all those cigarettes."

"You're not fat. And you still have your voice. You used to sing like this, in clubs, before you were married, right?"

"Never in clubs. Only weddings and things like that. Never in clubs."

"But you could have. Do you ever wonder about it? Do you wonder what it would've been like?"

My mother takes another bite of foie gras. She sips her wine. She smiles at me, but she doesn't reply.

## A TORCHED VOICE

Nothing touched the singer's voice. She could smoke two packs of cigarettes a day and still hit the high notes, at least when she was young.[4] And despite her youth, hers was a mature, womanly voice with a certain urgency, a throaty vulnerability.[5] She could take a note at the top of her range and bend it, *squeeze* it.[6] She could growl and rattle the low tones.[7] She could tease a song, cajole it. You could hear a sly but guileless humor peeking through her virtuoso technique.[8] Her art was her voice.

But smoking all the time, all the time, finally took its toll. Her voice grew heavier.[9] Her larking, daring quality diminished.[10] She began to use dramatic, dying notes.[11] Later, her voice took on a dismaying hue.[12] She sang with a painful rasp.[13] Her undertones and low notes began to sound almost *burnt*.[14] After that, her voice came and went. She refused to let on that anything had changed, and this bravery gave her a confusing majesty.[15]

And talking all the time, all the time, also took its toll. She talked about the miserable conditions on the road. She talked about the cheap hotels—when you could get one—the awful food, the thinly veiled racism and outright misogyny.[16] She talked about her material and her songwriting, along with her failure to make the *DownBeat* poll, to win this or that award, or simply to get credit for her work.[17] She talked about trying to break into other genres—television, opera, theater, Hollywood film—always too light or too dark or too androgynous or too butch or too ethnic or too something—to cross over.[18] And she talked about politics. She attended marches, sang protests, endorsed causes, and gave benefit concerts.[19]

With all the talking—with all the positioning and posturing—her music lost its optimism. Her singing lost its humor and spontaneity.[20] Not even her tremendous voice could make the commentary palatable. When the singer got on her soapbox, she became a bitch, a bore, a *diva*.[21] Her public wished she'd just shut up. They'd rather she remain silent. They'd rather that she be audible only in the sounds of her singing.

So the singer got back to the song, though she refused to quit smoking, or to quit talking. Her growls and bends and burnt-edged digressions became louder. Her mistakes were amplified in the playback. Nothing—not age, not abuse, not being hushed or dismissed or labeled—*nothing* touched the singer's voice.

## AN AUDIBLE SILENCE

The show is over, though Alice remains in her seat at the table left of center. She watches as the crowd rises and wraps itself against the weather and moves toward the door. She watches as a man rises from his seat, his hands pressed to the white tablecloth for balance. She sees him shake his head. She hears him say, "*Damn*, that was great. I've never seen the singer more in control, more in tune with the music, more connected with the audience. She was really *here*, present. . . . Damn."

Alice thinks about being here. She thinks about the man who is not her husband. She is glad he didn't come, glad she was alone with the music. Alice looks at the empty chair. She feels the singer and the music next to her still, breathless beside her and resonating in her body. The singer's voice rings in her ears. And as she looks at the faces of the people around her, readying themselves for the night, she sees the singer's words on their lips, hears the hum of her sound in their throats. She trembles with how the singer spoke to her and to everyone, together alone.[22]

Alice plays back the evening. She hears Vaughan run the scale, adding in more notes than even she thought possible, giving laughter to the lyric. She hears Streisand's slow build into an almost hysteric happiness at the moment of loss. She hears Piaf trade joy and loss, her song list a contrapuntal masterpiece. She hears Horne's sparse rendering of torrential lives. She hears lang playfully bending the notes, testing the limits of her material. And she hears Holiday's piercing disappointment inside a happy tune, cutting it to pieces. Alice hears all of these voices—personalities, positions—speaking at once. She hears irony. Speaking together, these voices move outside of individuality into a concerted, diva-esque reversal.[23] Alice is sure she hears a conversation—a debate rather than a monologue—on victimhood and a mythical American Dream. She hears something open, something *else* in the suppressed and missing notes, an audible silence.[24]

Alice wonders about her search for evidence in a voice and in a story. Which pieces of evidence are about the singer and which are about her? What does her wanting for knowledge, for answers, for *proof* say about her desire?[25] Alice wonders if she is dreaming. She blinks and looks around the darkened room. She touches the tablecloth in front of her, the seat beneath her. She thinks that in dreams—in her dreams at least—there is no sound. No, she can't be dreaming. She is hearing voices.

### HEARING VOICES

The sound of star discourse is the sound of metonymy; in clear, constant notes, quantities of women singers are reduced to a quality—victim, natural, addict, glutton.[26] The woman and the singer become a song. Listening to the sound of metonymy, quantities of listeners are also reduced to a quality; the list and the ending here, too, are the same. But when I listen to torch singing, I hear embellishment, excess, exuberance, coolness, camp. I hear irony. I pick up multiple meanings and hidden pleasures. I hear a third voice,[27] a thoroughly *diva discourse*—not the iconic talk of bitchiness or perfectionism or calculated control (a monolithic counterpoint to star discourses)—but an acquired dialect, a means of connecting with others in and through invisibility and oppression.[28] When I close my eyes and listen closely, I hear voices. Do you hear them, too?

I begin with "My Man," quintessential torch song—*the* standard form for unrequited love. The song requested and recorded and replayed by Brice, Holiday, Fitzgerald, Streisand, and countless others. The musical articulation of a feminist dilemma: How do you embrace romantic, heterosexual love within a systematically oppressive, violent patriarchy? Or do you? I've chosen Vaughan's version first,[29] and I transcribe the lyrics as I listen to her sing "My Man" over and over again. I see her, too, in black and white, caught singing another song in another performance. Still, this is the film that plays in my mind as I write: She is on a rooftop. It is late—well after midnight—and she is framed by city lights. Long earrings flash and brush her shoulders. She is still except for the clasp of her hands and a slight nod to Holiday's style in time with the music.[30] But her *voice*—her voice races in and around the scale, an acrobat. I push the play button, and she begins a cappella with "It cooost me a lot/but there's one thing that I've got/iiit's my . . . maaa-n," her voice winking on man, saying she's got a lot more than him. A wave of violins enters to laugh at the joke.

Her voice returns alone for "Cold or wet/tired you bet/but all that I'll soon for-get/with my maann," and this time the violins are melancholy in E and A minor. They offer a slow descent of quarter notes while she holds the lowdown man in her teasing vibrato. I breathe in sharply, my fingers poised above the keys, ready for the sadness. And then . . . I hear Vaughan *laughing* as she doubles high and low tones on "He's no-ot mu-uch fo-or looks/And no-oh her-ro ou-ut ah-of books." Her voice breaks—not with tears, but with a daring bravado—when she gets to "iii-it's my maann."

She raises her arms in front of her, an empty embrace, and smiles as a lone flute signals trouble. She begins slowly, "Two or three girls has he," then quickens the pace, "that he likes as well as meee," holding herself on the last note. She reaches low for "bu-hut-I-love-him." When the violins and flute offer no response, she goes it alone—"I don't know why I should"—then mirrors the question with an identical ascending scale answer, "he is-n't good." She pauses to fix the image. Her arms remain empty, an opening. The violins sigh slowly as she rushes down the scale with "He isn't true/he beats me too/What can I do," three perfect repetitions adding to her confession. My fingers too rush through these lines, wanting to leave their appearance on the page behind, to gain some distance from their awful admission.

I wait and the piano makes an easy entrance in bright tones. Vaughan comes in smiling, her voice full and lush on "Ooh, my ma-an/I lo-ove him sooo/he'll nev-er know." And then, underneath, "All my life is just despa-air, but I don't ca-are," I hear her giggling, mocking the lyric. She begins again, earnestly, "Whe-hen he takes me in his arms/the world is bright," but she can't resist playing with the ending, embellishing the words with repetition. The violins join her here, an echo of their earlier optimism, and together Vaughan's voice and the music deepen, "and it's bright/it's bright and it's a-all ri-ght." I hear Vaughan singing outside of the song, outside of the lyric, outside of the arms of the man.

She charges into "What's the diff-rence if I say/I'll go away," growling the "difference" and maintaining a single, steady tone for "if I say" and "I'll go away." She's sweet with "when I know I'll come back/on my knees/some-day," squeezing the last note so that the repentant words waver, uncertain. She does the last lines in a blur, slurring, "For-what-ever-my-man-is-I-am-his" before stopping to wonder on "for-ever, for-ever more." Her arms drop to her sides—her embrace withdrawn—but her smile remains. She's not finished.

The opulent orchestral mood of the song gives way to a bluesy drawl underneath her downward spiraling chorus, "Oh, oh, oh, oh, oh, ho, my-hi man-I-lo-ve-him-so. . . ." She digs down into distance, undermining and destabilizing[31] the centrality of her man, the image of a woman caught helpless in a story of romantic love. She swings and pushes through what he'll never know and all that despair, making room. She ends on "The world is bright, bright, bright, bright, and all right. . . . For whatever my man is/whatever my man is/I'm his forever/I'm his forever, for-ever mo-re/for-ever more." She is a double-talking, two-timing, sidestepping voice,[32] and listening to her makes me hear—and think—twice. Listening to Vaughan, I think I hear irony.

Irony requires detachment, a space that lets me get some distance on what I'm hearing.[33] Without that distance, I can't hear the "incongruity between literal and intended meanings—between what is said and what is meant, or between what is expected and what occurs."[34] Without that distance, I can't hear irony. Though irony doesn't exist until it has an audience—a listener—who actively identifies the incongruities.[35] *I* am necessary to make Vaughan's performance ironic. Together we transform literal meaning into irony in a four-step dance.[36] I want to try this out. *Step One:* Reject the literal meaning of the lyric.[37] Vaughan sings, "All my life is just despa-air, but I don't ca-are." Now, I can't just reject this line because I disagree with the idea that a man alone could make life hopeless or because I can pile on other meanings—maybe she's hungry or underpaid or terrifically depressed. Instead, I must reject the unspoken proposition on which the line depends: it doesn't make sense that a woman whose life is just *despair* wouldn't *care* (solely because a mean, abusive man takes her in his arms), even if the lyric rhymes. Things are not as they seem.

*Step Two:* Try out alternative interpretations or explanations.[38] But remember: these alternatives must be incongruous with what the literal statement seems to say—they must offer a retraction, a diminution, or an undercutting of some sort.[39] Perhaps her life isn't so despairing after all. Perhaps she doesn't care that her man has left her, while giving the appearance that she is devastated. Perhaps she's getting in her digs where she can.

So far, so good, but I'm not done yet. Simply deciding that *I* reject the literal meaning of a statement and that other, alternative explanations are possible and plausible doesn't get me irony. For that, I need *Step Three*: Determine whether the statements I reject are also rejected by the author.[40] Oh my. Which author? Albert Willemetz and Charles Jacques, authors of the French lyrics for "Mon Homme"? Maurice Yvain, who wrote the music? Channing Pollock, the English translator of "My Man"? Certainly not, not for this text. So, Vaughan. Which Vaughan? Vaughan the real person? Vaughan the star? Vaughan the character in song? Thankfully, Vaughan's voice—like nudges of an elbow and winks of an eye—gives me some clues.[41] Her *multiple* voices really—as woman, as singer, as character—invite me to hear multiple, unspoken meanings.[42] Hearing *laughter* in her voice is evidence that she, like me, hears and rejects what "all my life is just despair, but I don't care" implies.[43] Her laughter is also raucous accompaniment for a life that isn't as despairing as the lyric, for an attitude of thinly veiled nonchalance, for an opportunistic, underground critique.

And I can get more help here too—I can look for evidence in others' interpretations of Vaughan's voice. So I remind myself that Vaughan the woman, the "real" person, didn't much like torch songs. She considered them "corny" and amused and distanced herself by playing around with the lyrics.[44] I note how Vaughan the singer, the star, used her improvisatory skill to create a voice "gloating with joy about no longer being unhappy for any lost love."[45] And this helps me believe that Vaughan, as the woman in the song, is not only, not simply in despair, hopeless and helpless. Searching for clues, I listen for lyrics that conflict in some clear way with what I am sure Vaughan would say—*is saying*. Finding the proof I need, *Step Four* of the dance circles back: I have heard and seen—created—a performance in harmony with the unspoken beliefs I've attributed to Vaughan.[46] I *know* her performance is ironic.

And then the irony: irony is a fleeting recognition, an uncanny feeling rather than a moment of truth.[47] When encountering irony, I don't consciously ask if I have detected the clues, if I *get* it.[48] I *feel* it in my listening. And if I feel irony in my listening, is it important to explain how I hear irony in Vaughan's voice, and that you hear it, too? Is it important that I identify clues that show I *know* she is being ironic? Though I know that the consequences of a simply literal hearing of a misogynist recording are real.[49] I put another record on.

I listen to Streisand sing "My Man" live at the Winter Garden. With a piano playing quietly beneath her, Streisand says, "I would like, now, to do something that will let me pay my respects—my final respects—to the memory of the great lady who this play is about, and to the Winter Garden, and to *Funny*

*Girl*."[50] She doesn't do the first verse, which costs Vaughan and Holiday and the others a lot. Instead, she begins with the refrain, "Oh, my man," in a demure, tentative voice. I see Barbra at the end of the film,[51] on stage, saying goodbye to her man and to everything in weepy restraint. The applause drowns out "I love him so," then quiets for "he'll never know." She sings, "All my life is ju-st despair" with an abundant, round happiness. Did I hear her laugh on "just"? I'm not sure when I hear her tearful flutter on "but I-I-I-I don't care." The piano punctuates her clear, crisp enunciation on "When he takes me in his arms," and holds the note as she fades for "the world is bright." And then, with "ah-al ri-ight," guitar and snare drum add a blue tone.

In a hurry, she speaks, "What's-the diff-rence," then lifts off into song with "if I say/IIII'll go away/When I know I'll come back/on my knees"—she dots all the "I's" with pure, rich sound—before skidding into a spoken "some-day." She ends the chorus with a staccato "For what-ever my man is," then pauses to take a breath so she can rush the pause in the final two lines, slurring, "I am his" into "for-ever more."

Now she's ready for the first verse, which she speaks-sings in angry bursts, each word an accusation: "It. Cost. Me. A lot. But. There's. One. Thing. That. I've. Gooot," her voice sliding into a bawdy drawl. "III'ts. Myyyy. Man." And again, "Cold or wet. Tired—ah—you bet. But all that I soon forget. With myyyyy maaan." Here, the beat delivers the blows between Streisand's sung-spoken phrases. And again, "He's not much for looks. And no hero out of books," the embittered indictment giving way to a playful, winking, "He's my-hi man-an."

She giggles through "Two or three girls has he," then climbs the scale on "that he likes as well as me." I think I'm in on the joke, until she earnestly cries, "but I looooove himm," a full-scale reversal.[52] I listen to these lines again and again. I listen hard. And then I hear her giggle echoed in the piano and percussion, the laughter quickening under "I loooooove himm," and I think I know what she's up to. By the time she comes back in on the chorus, "Oh, my man/I love him so/he'll never know," she's turned again. Her voice is burlesque; too much. I hear her strip and tease, "All my life is just despair/but I don't care. . . . When he takes me in his arms/the world is bright/all right." The drum rolls and kicks as she tears into "What's the diff-rence if I say/I'll go away/When I know I'll come back/on my knees some-day." Then—boom, boom, boom, boom—the gate-crashing finale: "For whatever my man is/I am hi-is/for-ever mooooore." She shatters any poignant end to *Funny Girl*, any inevitable disposition, any harmonious resolution. As the applause thunders toward her, the transgressive victim takes a bow.

Streisand's "My Man" isn't Vaughan's "My Man." Where Vaughan coolly improvises and embellishes, Streisand belts and shouts. Are they both being ironic? Can they do that, singing so differently? Can they do that, singing a *standard*? Perhaps what I hear isn't stable, modern irony at all, but a postmodern sort of irony. Perhaps what I hear isn't an incongruity resolved in the harmony of interpretation (hearing how Vaughan's and Streisand's and my own reading of the performance are *alike*), but instead multiple, contingent, unstable, and discordant voices that abandon the quest for harmony altogether.[53]

The good news: postmodern irony has a unique ability to "*subvert* from within, to speak the language of the dominant order and at the same time suggest another meaning and another evaluation. This . . . mode of address deconstructs one discourse, even as it constructs another."[54] The not-so-good news: The "multiple, complex, and inconsistent messages postmodern, subversive irony advances can be confusing, thereby prompting an audience to dismiss the artifact as incoherent."[55] Hearing a subversive irony isn't an unconscious process, even if that's how it begins. Hearing a subversive, multivocal irony requires "actively *choosing* the . . . reading that subverts, rather than simply having it dawn on one."[56]

I remember that irony is a performance, a drama that contains many "voices, or personalities, or positions integrally affecting one another."[57] Streisand's "My Man" isn't a double-toned parody (though this sort of irony satisfies, too). Hers is a scale-running cacophony in which she plays—by turns—jilted lover, vindictive temptress, innocent bystander, and streetwise can-can dancer. Hearing all of these characters in her voice, a voluptuous abundance challenges any easy acceptance of the song's literal meaning. It's not Streisand's interpretation that catches my ear; it is her many, many voices. Perhaps I need some help here as well.

Though they were a staple of her early career, Streisand has publicly come out against "doormat" songs—songs that depict women "who can be strong only with and through their men."[58] She still sings torch songs, but does so at a distance, a self-conscious remove that allows audiences to "celebrat[e] her strength to overcome all the obstacles . . . she has overcome."[59] This is the kind of distance needed for an ironic reading. And—yes, *here it is*—what gets you about Streisand is her *voice* and not her interpretation.[60] Though maybe my search for proof of Vaughan's ironic interpretation or Streisand's ironic multitude of voices is simply my desire to hear evidence of a critical presence in torch singing. And maybe such desire is necessary to an active, transgressive reading.[61] Is that ironic, too? I keep listening.

I don't know whether Piaf sang "My Man." Her critics say she did; her curators say she didn't. I search, but I can't find a recording. What I find instead is a lilting "La Vie en Rose,"[62] one of the few recordings I discover of Piaf singing in English. Track 9 begins with a piano waterfall and rush of violins playing the versed melody. An oboe floats into range, followed by flute and tinkling piano, bringing Piaf's voice in on a wave. She sings, "Hoooold me close and hoooold me fast/the magic spell you caaaast/this is la vie en rose-ah," and her vibrato makes the words tremble.

The violins swell and she dives into "Whe-en you ki-ess me/heav-aen sighs/and though I close my eyeees, I see la vie en rose-ah." The violins tiptoe behind, echoing her purring, "Whe-en you press me to your heart/I'm in a world apart." They follow her up the scale, carrying her high into "a world where ro-ses bloom." Piaf—and I hear Vaughan here, too—and the violins spiral into "And when you spe-ak angels sing from above/everyday words seem to turn into love songs." And then the request, the demand: "Give your heart and soul to me/and life will always be/la vie en rose."

The music fades away and after a beat, Piaf speaks-sings the moment she fell: "I thought that love was just a word/they sang about in songs I heard/It took your kiss-es to re-veal/that I was wrong. . . ." She pauses a moment, a ringing dream, a breathy anticipation, and then her shimmering finish, "and love is real." When I hear Piaf sing, I see her in flash photography and film stills—hands and teeth and eyes in frozen detail—joy, anguish, laughter, fulsome loss. Always, always, I see her tiny frame disappear behind the rush of heavy velvet.[63]

Suddenly, her face reappears in the meeting of the curtains and her smile lights the dark auditorium. She begins another verse, with violins doing a foxtrot underneath her voice. She dances along through the first "la vie en rose," but when she sings, "When you press me to your heart," she languishes over the words. She drapes across each syllable, refusing to be hurried. Her voice takes on a burnished tone, tarnishing everyday "wo-rds" that seem to turn into "loo-ve songs," and coils into a sweet, single, "rooooosssee, ah dah dah dah . . ." And then—it takes me several listenings to hear this, too—she blows me a kiss, and says, "that's ah . . ." and I've lost her.

Piaf's unfinished sentence and her abrupt reappearance leave me waiting, wanting, with only questions at my fingertips: Is her performance ironic in interpretation—in the way she breaks into everyday words and questions whether they belong in love songs? Is it ironic in voice—in the many tempos and characters and shadings she tries on in a single-hued song? Or maybe it is ironic in its silence. I listen again to her soft-spoken bridge: "I thought that love was just a word/they sang about in songs I heard/It took your kiss-es to reveal/that I was wrong." She is silent for one, two, three beats punctuated by a faint ringing of a bell, saying wait, pay attention, don't miss this. . . . I hear her breathe in, and sing, "and love is real." Is Piaf calling attention to what can't be said[64]—about the illusion of love, about her own disappointments and struggles? Does the pause—an "act of saying"—reference Piaf's life outside the text?[65]

I look for the evidence: Piaf began her career singing songs of rejection for her supper and lunch and breakfast too, and the hunger never left her voice, even when she was a star and sang "La Vie en Rose."[66] She was a performer in and of 1930s and '40s France, a time marked by war, poverty, and a "pervasive sadness" that punctuated her material.[67] Did Piaf feel she couldn't sing directly about the conditions of her early life? The evidence doesn't point to any threat of violence or retaliation for doing so and thus for keeping quiet. Plus, she *did* sing overtly political songs, though she "would never have committed herself to any social or political movement."[68] It seems important also to say that, in contrast to Vaughan and Streisand, Piaf *preferred* to sing torchy ballads.[69] It seems important to say, too, that she worked to *close* the critical distance between herself and the song, as well as the distance between herself and the audience.[70]

Based on the evidence, do I abandon the idea that I can hear ironic silence—or any sort of irony—in Piaf's voice? Do I give up the possibility of a subversive performance, even when the pregnant pause in "La Vie en Rose" suggests how silence can be used to indirectly express the multiple and conflicting tensions of a life in pink and a life such as Piaf's? I want to say—because I am hopeful and because I've pinned a crush of analysis on a musical form that makes me sigh and cry and perhaps not much else—that at this point, the evidence is inconclusive. I search my record collection for another voice, another song.

I don't have Horne doing "My Man" either, so I decide to listen to her signature song, "Stormy Weather."[71] A bassoon begins a melody that conjures darkening skies and heavy clouds. The storm is quickened by a trumpet's siren and then Horne begins, "Don't know why/there's no sun up in the sky." I see her in white, almost transparent, a spectral image coming in and out of sight in time with her trilling vibrato.[72] Her voice sails up and over the threatening storm while the strings pluck a slow march. She sings, "stor-my wea-ther," her voice reaching sweet and low, and now the trumpet is a big, black bird, calling, "ah ha," to which Horne adds, "since my man and I ain't to-ge-ther." The strings echo this time, "ah ha," and Horne responds, "keeps rainin' aaaa-ll the ti-ime."

Horne sings, "Life is bare/glo-om and mis'ry ev'ry where/storm-y weather." The trumpets cackle, "ah ha" again. She brightly elaborates, "just ca-an't get my poor self ta-ge-ther," and the strings sigh, "ah ha." She ends the verse with a buoyant, "I'm wear-y aa-lllll the ti-me," and repeats the line in case we've missed it: "the ti-ime . . . so wear-y aa-llll the ti-ime."

At the bridge, the strings quicken the pace. Horne takes a deep breath and confesses, "When he went a-way/the blues walked in and met me. . . . If he stays a-way/ol' rock-in' chair will get me." She pushes out, "met me" and "get me," her voice turned brittle, no longer an echo of the strings' sighing "ah ha," and I think I hear her challenge her stormy circumstances. She rushes into, "All I do is pray/the lord a-bove will let me . . . wa-alk in the sun once more," hitting "pray" and "above" and "let me" with a shy force. I am with her. But she uses a feathery touch on "lord" and "walk in the sun," and now I'm not sure I hear a challenge. I'm not sure I hear her saying she can't stand the weather. Or whether she thinks the storm will pass.

She sings, "Can't go oooon/a-llll I have in life is gone . . . storm-y wea-ther," with the familiar, sunny optimism of the first verse. The trumpets and strings call, "ah ha" as she finishes the line, "Since my man and I ain't to-ge-ther/keeps rainin' a-llll the time." She pauses. She waits for an answer, then repeats, "keeps rainin' all the time."

At the bridge again, the strings wind up the scale. Horne continues her conversation with horns and strings, "I walk a-round heav-y hear-ted and sad" . . . "ah ha" . . . "night comes a-round and still feelin' bad" . . . "ah ha." And then her voice takes on a shrill, urgent tone, "Raain pourin' *down*, blindin' ev-ry *hope* I had." The strings and trumpets sound a gathering thunder, "bah, bah, bah bah!" Horne puts her hands over her ears and cries, "This pitterin' patterin' beatin' an' spatterin' *dri-ives* me mad!" Her voice shivers unaccompanied between speech and song and then the thunder claps again, "Ah!" She shouts, "Love! Love! Love! Love!" her voice softening with each blow. She relaxes into "This mis-ry's just toooo much for me." I hear her breathe in, deciding. . . . I hold my own breath in her silence.

She begins again, "Can't go on . . ." her smile forced, her voice barely contained by the lyric or the music's confidence. I wonder if she sounds hysterical here and I listen again. No, the song hasn't driven her mad, only down low, quaking, underground. She says she can't go on, but she does. The violins carry her out with the cool breeze, though not before the bassoon reappears, sounding notes of trouble in the happy ending.

Though Horne isn't singing "My Man," I hear echoes of Vaughan's laughter in her lively exchange with winds and strings. I hear strains of Streisand's bawdy tone when she spits out the pitterin' patterin' beatin' an' spatterin' sounds that drive her mad. I hear hints of Piaf's vibrato and lush pauses in her phrasing, although Horne doesn't languish over the lyrics as Piaf might. Instead, she rushes the words, pushing them into presence. The laughter and vibrato and phrasing and silence in Horne's voice sound . . . they sound irony.

For Horne, the evidence is more helpful and hopeful. Her silent pause between hesitantly anxious verses—between "this misery is just too much for me" and "can't go on"—signifies not only a decision to remain in a stormy relationship, but her own determination to keep singing despite the racism she encountered on the road and charges that she was a race traitor because she didn't always refuse to sing racially stereotypical songs.[73] Her silence on these things was, at least in part, prompted by fear of retaliation by promoters, critics, and audiences.[74] And although Horne chose to keep these slights and accusations to herself, they left marks on her phrasing and rhythm.[75] Her voice—especially her pauses and sighs—signals to audiences that Horne understands the emotional and social significance of what she is singing, even when her material is a simple love song.[76]

And then the evidence gets complicated, contradictory. Like Piaf, Horne preferred ballads; she thought they were better suited to her voice than "uppity" blues songs or jazz.[77] Early in her career, Horne—the woman, the singer, and certainly the actress—was criticized for remaining aloof and distant from the "characters" in her songs and cool to listeners.[78] As she matured as a performer, she learned to embody her material and open herself to an emotional exchange with her audience.[79] Horne's evolving performance style spans the difference between and among Vaughan and Streisand on one hand and Piaf on the other, leaving the question ringing in my ears: Is Horne being ironic while singing the torchy ballads she loves? *Can* she be ironic without creating critical distance among herself, her material, and her audience? And if the answers to these questions are yes, can I know that Horne *intends* to be ironic?

Intentions. I must decide that a singer means to reject the lyric; I must decide that she *intends* the irony I hear in her voice. I must remember, though, that I am not listening for what Horne the person intends, but rather, what Horne the star persona, the author implied in the performance, intends.[80] Looking at the lyrics and music, I can't say, "If the author did not intend irony, it would be odd, or outlandish, or inept, or stupid of [Horne] to do things in this way."[81] I *can* talk about the performance, a fleeting, ephemeral moment captured but not contained on disc or vinyl or film. The challenge for a *listener* is to pick up on those disparities and losses without fixing and classifying them—as irony or victim narrative or any other quality—so thoroughly that they become conclusions rather than possibilities.[82] The irony in Horne's "Stormy Weather"—in torch singing as performance—inheres in how her song is *voiced*, not in the lyrical content of the song. And I can hear irony in Vaughan and Streisand and Piaf and Horne's voices, even if their voices (and voicings) are contradictory, confounding, different.

Difference. Vaughan, Piaf, and Horne were, give or take a few years, contemporaries. They survived the depression and began their careers in the 1930s and '40s when music was one of the few ways women could make a move out of poverty and into stardom. They sang in between and underneath the racism, sexism, and silencing of the concert hall and city street. Their subversive readings voiced an explosive counterpoint to standard Tin Pan Alley lyrics.

Streisand was not a contemporary of Vaughan, Piaf, and Horne, though she was trained in the confrontational and performative idiom of cabaret. She made her professional debut in 1960 and rose to fame during feminism's second wave and the Vietnam War. She was (and is) openly political, devoting her name and her voice to social, cultural, and electoral causes, though she continues to sing the standards her audiences demand to hear.[83] So perhaps where

Vaughan, Piaf, and Horne's ironic readings of torch songs may have been forced underground by fears of professional and social repercussions, Streisand's voice gives an ironic spin to standards as a complement to her other, more overtly political acts. Counterpoint. Complement. And where do I put lang's voice in this story. . . . Chaos? Chagrin? Camp?

lang doesn't sing "My Man," and perhaps she doesn't need—or want—to. Perhaps she is not caught in the tension between heterosexual love and patriarchal oppression, though she still lives inside a system that constructs her as possession, as category, as difference itself.[84] And she loves the standards, the ballads, the torch songs.[85] In the absence of "My Man," I choose lang's "Save Me,"[86] the first track on her crossover from satiric country to torchy *Ingénue*. Drums and steel guitar introduce a soaring, expansive melody. I see lang squinting into sunlight, a golden carpet stretching out behind her.[87] Her voice enters with a sanguine, humble request, "Saaa-ve me/save me from you."

I have listened to this song hundreds of times, but listening now, I hear every beat, every blink, every slow intake of air. I listen carefully, trying again and again to record the lyrics, but I am distracted by the bare need of her voice. I press repeat and try again: "Save me . . ." The guitar and bass and snare and vibraphone set a luxuriously slow beat and lang's voice lingers over every syllable, leaving the lyric, leaving me, unfinished. Undone. "Save me . . ." The refrain gains depth and pulse in the hypnotic chorus of her voice. The steel guitar plays a simple melody once, twice, sounding a ghostly reply that slips into another verse. She sighs. Her sound falters and fades. I close my eyes. I stop writing. I savor the tranquil harmony of lang's plea. "Save me . . ."

I sit, waiting, fingers frozen. Track two, "The Mind of Love," and I see lang close her eyes and whisper into the microphone. Track three, "Miss Chatelaine," and I'm leaning in, watching her writhe on the stage floor, caught in the microphone cord. Track four, "Wash Me Clean," and I struggle to get my breath as she bounces and sways and traces delicate circles with bare feet.[88] I listen to each voice bleed into the next, enthralled. I see her in evening gowns, cowboy boots, three-piece suits, gauzy layers, a pompadour 'do, a flower behind her ear. She is the picture of mystery; of immanent, dissonant possibility.[89] She hums in doubled harmonies and fractured tones. My listening is pure artifice, an irrepressible passion. We are tender feeling, alive to a double sense.[90] She . . . I . . . *someone* . . . winks.

lang is often read as camp—extravagant, excessive—a woman walking around in western wear, taking herself "seriously, but not altogether seriously," and she agrees. She challenges convention and "plays around with stereotypes."[91] Cases in point and in print: her vegetarianism, her gender-bending identity politics. Just look at her "Meat Stinks" campaign for People for the Ethical Treatment of Animals (given by the girl who grew up in cattle country). Just look at her coming-out interview in the *Advocate* (given just as *Ingénue* was released). Just look at her cover photo for *Vanity Fair* (taken when lang was at the height of her popular success). There she is, head thrown back, face lathered up, ready for a close shave with Cindy Crawford. On stage and record, lang likes to play around with satire and parody, and she creates the requisite "distance" from her material to do so.[92] Though lang doesn't buy this analysis. Disputing the evidence, she says she isn't being distant or the least bit satirical in her singing.[93]

Hearing lang's (or anyone's) voice as camp—as a particular style of irony—is a listener's game. Hearing camp, a listener thrills at her own joy in having discovered a voice, in "having been *chosen*, solicited by it."[94] She savors her own power to fill degraded images "to the brim with meaning."[95] I don't think I hear *only* the playful voice of camp in her *Ingénue*. I hear a voice that creates, in beautiful harmonies, an irresolvable subject where only fragments were possible. And I *also* hear an open-ended ambiguity, an expansive *différence* that echoes in and across the divides of incongruity and purposeful delay. I hear a voice that, on the one hand, "indicates difference as distinction, inequality, or discernability" and on the other "expresses the interposition of delay, the interval of a spacing and temporalizing that puts off until 'later' what is presently denied, the possible that is presently impossible."[96]

I hear, too, the voices of Vaughan and Streisand and Piaf and Horne—lang's musical and vocal torchbearers. And where Vaughan and Piaf and Horne's voices are contrapuntal discourses hiding inside misogynist texts, and where Streisand's ballads complement an overt politics, lang creates ironic difference in her very voicing of song. I don't mean to say that lang doesn't exist outside the song, or that she doesn't recognize the push and pull of life and art or the material facts and consequences of her singing. Surely she does.[97] What I am suggesting is that hearing lang's voice closes the divide between text and interpretation, surface and depth. Hearing lang is a direct, sensuous encounter with many, many voices.

What I hear in my listening is multiple forms of irony: Irony as a felt presence, an "intuitive grasp of disparity" that I share with a voice.[98] Irony as a conscious means for coping with such disparity by creating subversive, transgressive readings.[99] Irony as a silence "audible only in relief from the sound of voices."[100] Irony as postponement and distinction—as difference[101] and contradiction. Each sort of irony is a creation of my own desire,[102] performed in acts of listening, hearing, and writing. I don't hear torch songs in one set of terms—individuality or victimhood or any singular characterization. I hear, instead, a performance of many positions and possibilities.[103] What I haven't heard yet is Holiday, and here I must choose.

There are many recorded versions of Holiday singing "My Man." I begin with one of the last, a live recording of Holiday's concert at Carnegie Hall in November 1956. Holiday's autobiography *Lady Sings the Blues* was published earlier that year, and *New York Times* writer Gilbert Millstein quotes Holiday extensively as a prelude to her Carnegie numbers.[104] He begins the concert by saying, "This is Billie Holiday's story. . . ."

> I've been told . . . nobody sings the word "hunger" like I do. Or the word "love." Maybe I [want to] remember what those words are all about. . . . All those towns from coast to coast where I got my lumps and my scars . . . every damn bit of it. . . . All I've learned in all those places from all those people is wrapped up in those two words. You've got to have something to eat and a little love in your life before you can hold still for any damn body's sermon on how to behave. Everything I am and everything I want out of life goes smack back to that. . . . Who can tell what detours are ahead? Another trial? Sure. Another jail? Maybe. But if you've beat the habit again . . . no jail on earth can worry you too much. Tired? You bet. But all that I'll soon forget with my man.[105]

The audience applauds Holiday's words while a solo clarinet plays the melody behind the line "I don't know why I should,"[106] then twists into a winding introduction. She clears her throat and waits. A piano follows the clarinet and ends the prelude with a pensive, soprano call: "da da-dah!" Holiday begins slow and low, blurring the lyric in some places and stopping on a dime in others. Her phrasing rolls off of my fingertips, so familiar I can close my eyes as I write: "I-hit-cost. Me-ah-lot. But-the-re's. One-thing. Th-at-I-I've. Got." Her speech-song rhythm is punctuated by a piano that plays sparse replies and staccato chords. Her voice rolls from low to high to low on "It-hits.

My-hi-ma-an. It-hits. My-hi-maa-an," and I hear her joking, playing around. I hear her smiling, winking, writing over these words with her sound.

Holiday punches the next line—the closing moments of her life story—"Cold-ah-wet. Ti-red-you-bet. Ah-ll-of-this-I'll-soon. For-get. With-my-maa-han." The piano echoes her on "cold," "wet," "tired," and "you bet," underlining her weary tone. She sails into "He-e's. Not-much-oh-n. Lo-oks. He-ee's-no-he-ero. Ah-out-of-bo-oks," then pauses, breathes, and admits, "But I-Iah-lo-ahve him. Yesss-I-hi-ah-lo-ah-ve hi-im." Her voice dips and rises with laughter, giving her away. She's confessing, but she's got her fingers crossed.

I hear her smile before "Two-or. Three-girls. Has-heeee. Thaat-he. Likes-as. Well-as. Meee." The piano races the scale and then waits for her "But-I-ah-lo-ove-him." She blinks slowly, turns her head, then ascends the scale on her own, "I-hi. Don't-know. Why. I-should," a question. And then the answer, a grave descent: "He-is-n't. Truee-ah. He-ah. Be-ats-me. Too-ah." And again Holiday waits, gathering her mocking voice into an accusation of its own: "Wh-ha-at-can-I-ah. Do-ho-oo?" I hear a troubled kinship with her enemy,[107] a surrender under protest.

The piano ascends the scale again, and Holiday lightens the mood, swinging into "Ooh-my. Man-I-ahn. I-love-him. So-oh. He'll-nee-ver-know-ah." Horns and winds make a tentative entrance and try to support her cheery reversal, but they sound confused, not sure of what they're rehearsing. She keeps going, singing, "All-my-life-is-just. Des-pair. But-I-ah-don't. Care-ah." I hear Holiday snap her fingers, marking the beat before, "When-he. Takes-me-in. His-arms. The-world-is. Bri-ght. A-ha-ll-ri-hi-ght." The band catches up to her, and then the piano stops the music for, "What's-the-diff-rence. If-I-say. I'll-go ah-way?" The hazy sound of the recording accentuates how she stretches and bends "*what's*" and "*diff-rence*." I see her standing stock-still, head thrown back, driving the words out—an exposé of difference—in rights, wages, independence. She keeps going, singing, "Wh-en-I-know. I'll-come-back-o-ahn. My-kne-es. So-ahme-da-hay." She stops, opening up a space of uncertainty, of delay. She sings, "Fooor-what-ever. My-man. Is-ss. I-ah-am-hi-iss. For-ev-ev-aher. Mo-oh-ore," and I know this isn't the end; I know there's more. Her lips stretch into a rueful smile and she nods with the applause.[108]

In rhythm, in phrasing, in the spaces between speech and song and indictment and confession, Holiday's voice speaks an ironic subversion. When she sings, "What's the difference if I say/I'll go away/When I know I'll come back/on my knees someday," her voice takes on such exaggerated highs and lows I feel sure we're rejecting the literal meaning of the lyric. I hear Vaughan's improvisation and embellishment in Holiday's voice. Or perhaps I hear Holiday's voice in Vaughan's.

I hear Streisand (or better, Streisand hears Holiday) when, together with her band,[109] she makes a playful cacophony of the chorus, "Oh my man I love him so/he'll never know/All my life is just despair/but I don't care." Holiday snaps and sets the beat before "When he takes me in his arms," in consummate control of an "out of control woman in love."[110] Though Holiday doesn't demand that the others sing along with her; she just keeps going, singing into the chaos of voices.

I hear Piaf and Horne—and Piaf and Horne hear Holiday—in the pregnant silence after "I know I'll come back on my knees"; a silence that voices the legacy of women on their knees, scrubbing floors and lowering their eyes. With her breath before "someday," I hear inevitability open into the promise of a someday that doesn't involve looking away or settling for an exquisite otherness, "whatever her man is," whatever the cost.

And I remember that Holiday is singing at Carnegie Hall because the police denied her the cabaret card required to sing in New York City clubs, even the "crummiest bars in town."[111] Singing "My Man" on the stage of success—in the space of *you've made it*—she sounds the impossible possibility of the torch song. Holiday is cool, composed; she lets her story speak for itself. I remember, too, how Vaughan and Horne refused to sing unless people of color were invited into the opulent and brilliantly lit theaters of their labor.[112] I remember how lang wrangled her way onto the resolutely heterosexual Grand Ole Opry stage and received a standing ovation from her detractors.[113]

Listening to Billie, I hear a diva discourse full of shadings and nuance—full of irony. Her voice is an instrument for "asserting power, preeminence, and invulnerability through language alone, of speaking strong."[114] And in the case of Holiday, the evidence of her vocal play and subversion is voluminous, almost overwhelming the singing itself.

Holiday's "multivoiced" style speaks competing perspectives on the meaning of her lyrics. She uses jazz tempo, vibrato, phrasing, slurred pronunciation, and melodic dissonance (among other things) to "key" listeners to her critique of the lyrics.[115] Her refusal to hit any note "straight" and her constantly changing tone disrupt the musical and lyrical narrative *as written*. Holiday performs the victim by maintaining the basic elements of a song (key, lyrics), while simultaneously casting doubt on/questioning this stable character-as-self through her vocal improvisation.[116]

Or perhaps Holiday's "My Man" uses an "ironic" edginess that "warns against a facile, literal interpretation" of the lyric.[117] And in case you miss it, her slow pace—"expressing uncertainty as to whether she should love him because 'he isn't true, he beats me too'—evidences an "ambivalent posture rather than an acquiescence to the violence described."[118]

In "My Man" and in other songs, Holiday's voice takes on a number of positions and characteristics: caution, playfulness, mockery, release, strength, restraint, nostalgia, frivolity, ambivalence.[119] Holiday's speech-song delivery and her behind-the-beat timing convey a tone of restraint and caution that undermines the literal meaning of her torchy lyrics.[120] Thus, rather than refusing to sing the Tin Pan Alley repertoire of her day (and denying herself a career), Holiday uses her voice to challenge racial, cultural, and gender oppression.[121]

And there's more: Holiday's vocal critique offers women "the possibility of understanding the social contradictions they embod[y] and enact . . . in their lives," even when Holiday couldn't achieve such an understanding in her own life.[122] What? Why qualify Holiday's voice, Holiday's performance, with a reminder of her victim's biography?[123] Holiday's life, like her voice, isn't a case of metonymy, a single quality. *Holiday* is an irony—a composition of multiple subjectivities (woman, star persona, character) that tries, by the interaction of terms upon one another, to produce a life and art that use *all* the terms.[124]

## EVIDENCE

The evidence shows how Holiday's many voices signify, and how listening to her is an act of aural signification—of hearing and encountering her multivocally disruptive and reconstructive talk. Reading and repeating this evidence, I feel, well, *relieved.* Others hear irony in Holiday's voice, too. And I feel right writing that I hear similar things in Vaughan and Piaf's vibrato, in Streisand and Piaf's speech-song delivery, in Holiday's delay and Horne's anticipation of the beat, in Vaughan and lang's luxurious phrasing, in Streisand and lang's unbridled exuberance. They are voices, personalities, positions, and subjectivities integrally influencing and affecting one another. And me. They create a "contentious conversation," arguing with and interrupting each other, yet finding "enough worth listening to so that they continue to talk."[125] I *get* that.

*Irony (Voice-Over Spoken by the Respected Male Musician):* You sound pretty satisfied with yourself.

*Me (Spoken by the Unidentified Woman):* I do?

*Irony:* I thought you said somewhere—way back in chapter 2 if I recall—that *true* irony isn't superior, it's *humble.*

*Me:* Yes, I remember writing that—well, actually, I remember writing that Burke wrote that.[126]

*Irony:* Of course. And didn't he mean that irony doesn't lord it over the other characters, ideas, or analyses? That irony isn't superior to what it rejects, but adopts an attitude of humility?

*Me:* I suppose so.

*Irony:* You're critical of Angela Davis's qualification about Holiday, lording her reservations about Holiday's ability to live the critique of her music over what she hears in her voice. Doesn't your "subversive postmodern argument, rife with multiple and contradictory messages" reek of superiority?[127]

*Me:* I don't think so. I'm saying that hearing voices means hearing multiple characters and interpretations, and not just the lyrical or musical content of the song. I'm saying that irony is about contradictions, about the "tension of holding incompatible things together because both or all are necessary and true."[128] It's a humble, sympathetic engagement with a performance and a story and a voice. And you're right. It doesn't point fingers.

*Irony:* Still sounds pretty elitist to me. And what about the danger of reifying the very discourses you seek to subvert?[129] Is that the story you want to tell?

*Me:* I want to tell a story about how hearing *signifies*: without a victim, no diva. Without the torch song, no debate. Without the torch singer, no critique.

*Irony:* So tell it.

*Me:*

*Irony:* Okay, I'll play. What does torch singing signify?

*Me:* That singing about men treating women badly can voice the abuses of racism and the terror of lynching.[130] That singing songs of unrequited love can question how middle-class consumerism and compulsory heterosexuality can ever buy happiness.[131] That singing doormat love songs can reference—even in silence—how difference has been systematically produced.[132] Torch singing signifies—through layered meaning and repetition and parody and pastiche—how human relationships are (con)substantial and not merely correlative or coincidental.

*Irony:* Not so fast. Tell me again, how do you *hear* these things?

*Me:* By listening for how they give voice to irony—to multiple subjectivities and meanings outside of the song—and looking for evidence and writing what I hear.

*Irony:* But isn't irony indeterminate? Isn't it an ineffable presence?

*Me:* Well, *yes.* I don't hear irony as a fixed or stable or singular sound that resonates across songs or performances. It's a fragmented discourse speaking out of silence and chaos.

*Irony:* Okay, so how do you *know* you're hearing irony?

*Me:* I don't, at least not certainly or conclusively. Torch singing is communication not by sound or words alone, but *by* voice, *in* performance.[133] And even if I might lack the means to create these voices in my own performance, I can't help but try to dream them into being.

*Irony:* A happy ending?

*Me:* I'm not finished. What I don't know is what torch singing gives to listeners—to listeners other than me. Do you think torch singing gives listeners something?

*Irony:* What?

*Me:* An invitation to critique? Tactics for resistance?

*Irony:*

*Me:* Okay, I'll play. Do you think torch singing has something to give?

*Irony:*

## RISING SUN

Mom and I don't make it to the Green Mill or Davenport's that night. Instead, after we finish dinner, we sit at the bar and listen to the Jennifer Graham Trio.

My notes on the evening are sparse:

*J. G. does most of the standards—"One for My Baby" and "Smoke Gets in Your Eyes" and "Darn That Dream."*

*She works to connect with the audience. She takes several requests.*

*Mom sings along quietly, gets applause at the bar.*

*Not a lot of "fieldwork," but we had a great time.*

We leave after the third set and take the elevator up to our room. We watch television for a while, then decide to go to bed. Before she goes to sleep, my mother places two inhalers on the nightstand, but she doesn't say anything. Okay, I'll play. "What are those?"

"They're for the asthma. I use them before bed and when I wake up."

"The *asthma? Two* inhalers?"

"Different medicines. I don't lose my breath like I used to." She takes three puffs from the first inhaler. "They really help."

"You used to lose your breath? You used to stop breathing?"

"Oh, no. I just felt like I wasn't getting enough *air*. But these help." She takes three puffs from the second inhaler. Then she lies back on the pillows and soon, she is fast asleep.

I lie awake in my own bed listening to her breathe in wet gasps. I think about her smoking, smoking all the time when I was a kid. I think about her singing, too, all through the house. I think about her trying to coax my sister and me into singing along and our giddy refusals. I remember something I read about singers and their mothers—something about how singers imitate and give voice to their mothers.[134] Eventually, though, that voice becomes a demanding child and the singer becomes a mother herself—a mother to the insistent flow of a voice.[135] But our voices—my sister's and my own—were no match for our mother's voice. I wonder if our voices—if *my* voice—is an empty space, a nowhere place unable to speak.

And then I remember the time, years ago, when my mother came to visit me in Dallas, where I'd moved right after college. The man I was dating and I took mom out to dinner. Afterward, we stopped at a place we knew had music on the weekends. That night the performer was a solo vocalist with a keyboard that turned him into a one-man band. He took nothing but requests and could play—and sing—anything the audience wanted to hear. Someone asked him to sing "House of the Rising Sun." He asked if someone in the audience would accompany him on stage. I nudged my mother. She said, "*No*." The man I was dating watched our exchange, then volunteered my mother to the singer. She gave him a withering look, but by then it was too late. The singer was calling her and the audience was applauding. She stood and walked grudgingly toward the stage.

After some whispered discussion about tempo and key, the singer played an introduction. My mother began singing, quietly at first, "There *is* a house," and then she let her voice come in full and strong on, "in New Orleans."[136] The small audience cheered. My mother smiled. She belted out the rest of the lyrics and ended with a grand sweep of her arms. The audience cheered, Again! Again!

So my mother sang "The House of the Rising Sun" again. And a third time. And when she came off the stage, she stopped to talk with her admirers down front. Then she walked toward the table where I was sitting. Her cheeks were flushed. Her breath came fast. I said that she sounded wonderful. She bent down to give me a hug. Then she stood and pointed and said, "Those folks over there want to buy me a drink. Okay if I talk with them for a while?" I nodded, and my mother returned to her fans.

I had forgotten about "The House of the Rising Sun." I had forgotten that on that night, at least, she was a singer. A diva. And now, as I lay in a hotel room in Chicago listening to my mother struggle for breath, I wonder if she is dreaming about being on stage, singing "The House of the Rising Sun" and "Chances Are" and "Smoke Gets in Your Eyes." I wonder if, in her dreams, my mother finds her voice.

### HEARING IT, TOO

Alice leaves the club—Home of Dolphina, the Girl in the Fish Bowl—and walks in the mist toward her hotel room. She stops and crosses the street. She takes the disposable camera from her coat pocket and snaps several pictures of the marquee announcing the singer's arrival. She pushes the camera back into her pocket and keeps walking.

She climbs the creaky stairs to the sparse rented room. She looks at her notes from the evening, blurry on the cocktail napkin. She turns the napkin over and writes,

I dream I am transparent, see-through.
I press up against words and rhythms
and they mark me with blue veins.
They pulse behind skin.

I read and talk and think and type,
making dime-store romances,
detective stories, great mysteries.

Pulp.

I am lost, unable to speak, to know.

I listen and watch and note,
trying to hear the hushed critique
trying to make language sing
trying to give music to voice.

Wondering if I do,
if you'll hear it too.

Alice folds the napkin and places it on the nightstand beside the bed. She shuts off the light and pushes her legs between the icy sheets. She listens to the rhythms of the city. She waits.

## MORE VOICES

1. Angela Y. Davis, *Blues Legacies and Black Feminism: Gertrude "Ma" Rainey, Bessie Smith, and Billie Holiday* (New York: Pantheon, 1998), 177, 178.

2. Stacy Wolf, "Desire in Evidence," *Text and Performance Quarterly* 17 (1997): 349, writes, "'Evidence is rhetorical,' Antoine Compagnon asserts. . . . But sometimes I couldn't tell which pieces of evidence were about [Mary] Martin and which were about me. . . . My search for 'evidence,' then, became intimately linked with my desire—my desire for knowledge, answers, proof—and my desire to see a lesbian presence in musicals, and to see 'lesbian' on Martin's body, to hear it in her voice, to read it in her self-presentations. . . ."

3. James C. Scott, *Domination and the Arts of Resistance: Hidden Transcripts* (New Haven, CT: Yale University Press, 1990), 142.

4. Leslie Gourse, *Sassy: The Life of Sarah Vaughan* (New York: Da Capo, 1994), 166, relates musician Walter Booker's observations on Vaughan's smoking and its lack of effect on her

voice. He notes, "When I stayed at her house, and I saw her smoking all the time, all the time, I didn't like to see that, because she was a great singer. It didn't seem to hurt her voice, though. . . . She could still get up to those high notes."

5. Anne Edwards, *Streisand: A Biography* (Boston: Little, Brown, 1997), 94. I am blurring the distinctions Edwards makes between Streisand's and Judy Garland's voices. Edwards writes, "Despite her youth, [Streisand's voice] was a mature woman's voice with a certain nasal urgency that was nothing like the youthful yearning, the throaty vulnerability that was so recognizably Judy Garland's at the same age."

6. Gourse, *Sassy*, 120, relates jazz critic Martin Williams's description of Vaughan's voice.

7. Gourse, *Sassy*, 120.

8. Gourse, *Sassy*, 120.

9. Leslie Gourse, "Preface." In *The Billie Holiday Companion: Seven Decades of Commentary*, ed. Leslie Gourse, xxii (New York: Schirmer, 1997).

10. Gourse, "Preface," xxii.

11. Gourse, "Preface," xxii.

12. Gourse, "Preface," xxii.

13. Gene Lees, *Singers and the Song* (New York: Oxford University Press, 1987), 40, describes Piaf's voice in her later years.

14. Gourse, "Preface," xxii.

15. Gourse, "Preface," xxii.

16. This is especially true for Holiday, Horne, and Vaughan. See Billie Holiday's *Lady Sings the Blues*, with William Dufty (1956; New York: Penguin, 1992), 70–82 (citations are to the 1992 edition); James Haskins, *Lena: A Personal and Professional Biography of Lena Horne*, with Kathleen Benson (New York: Stein, 1984), 153–58; and Gourse, *Sassy*, 14, respectively.

17. Holiday failed to win the *DownBeat* magazine poll for favorite singer (though she won many other awards); see Leslie Gourse, "There Was No Middle Ground with Billie Holiday," in *The Billie Holiday Companion: Seven Decades of Commentary*, ed. Leslie Gourse, 139–50 (New York: Schirmer, 1997), 147. Additionally, Holiday is credited (and claims credit) for writing the songs "Fine and Mellow" and "Billie's Blues," as well as collaborating with Arthur Herzog on "Don't Explain" and "God Bless the Child." In *Lady Sings the Blues*, Holiday takes credit (along with Sonny White and Abel Meerpool) for writing the music for Meerpool's lyrics for "Strange Fruit." Meerpool refutes this, saying he wrote both the music and the lyrics. For an account of this dispute see David Margolick, *Strange Fruit: Billie Holiday, Café Society, and an Early Cry for Civil Rights*, foreword by Hilton Als (Philadelphia: Running Press, 2000), 31–37. Piaf's biographers also dispute her songwriting activity. Lees claims Piaf wrote "almost nothing" (*Singers*, 26). Margaret

Crosland, *Piaf* (New York: Fromm, 1987), 83, 99, holds that Piaf wrote many songs of her own, including "La Vie en Rose," and often worked in collaboration with songwriters—Piaf would pen the lyrics and others, such as Marie Monnot, would compose the music.

18. After being signed by MGM, Horne was passed over for several film roles because she photographed "too white" next to African American actors. Haskins, *Lena*, 70–71, notes, "Eventually, cosmetics king Max Factor was called upon. He created a shade for Lena that he called 'Light Egyptian.' The unfortunate result of this development was that it could be applied to white actresses. . . . Lena . . . would eventually lose parts to white actresses because of this new make-up." Horne was also passed over for parts when she expressed concern about the racist portrayal of African Americans in the scripts (and on film) (Haskins, *Lena*, 102–3). Holiday also protests these portrayals in *Lady Sings the Blues*, 119. Commenting on her role in *New Orleans*, she notes, "I thought I was going to play myself in it. I thought I was going to be Billie Holiday doing a couple of songs in a nightclub setting and that would be it. I should have known better. . . . You just tell me one Negro girl who's made movies who didn't play a maid or a whore. I don't know any. I found out I was going to do a little singing, but I was still playing the part of a maid." This line also references lang's film debut in Percy Adlon's *Salmonberries*. Rose Collis, *k.d. lang* (Somerset, England: Absolute Press, 1999), 41, writes that lang plays Kotz, "an androgynous-looking, sullen, inarticulate loner, without a father figure and longing for love with another woman." Finally, this line invokes Edwards's assertion (*Streisand*, 424) that Streisand is "not beautiful by nonethnic standards."

19. Activities that Holiday, Horne, Streisand, and lang have undertaken. Holiday, of course, sang "Strange Fruit" and also performed at political rallies. Horne sang at political and civil rights rallies, marched on Washington, and recorded the protest song "Now"; Streisand has performed benefit concerts and donated millions to "liberal" causes, including the Democratic Party; and lang appeared in advertisements for the People for the Ethical Treatment of Animals. See Margolick, *Strange Fruit*, 44–52, and Michael Denning, *The Cultural Front: The Laboring of American Culture in the Twentieth Century* (London: Verso, 1997), 334, on Holiday; Haskins, *Lena*, 153–58, and Denning, *Cultural Front*, 335, on Horne; William Robertson, *k.d. lang: Carrying the Torch* (Toronto: ECW Press, 1992), 94–96, on lang; and Richard Zoglin, "The Way She Is," *Time*, May 16, 1994, 76–78, on Streisand, respectively.

20. I'm referencing Michael Brooks's critique (liner notes, *Billie Holiday—The Legacy [1933–58]*, Columbia/Legacy, 1991, 28) of Holiday's recording and continued performance of "Strange Fruit." He writes, "['Strange Fruit'] destroyed the joy and spontaneity that were an integral part of her artistry. The raw talent was shaped into something that was precious and unique, yet strangely lifeless."

21. Camille Paglia, "The Way She Was," in *Diva: Barbra Streisand and the Making of a Superstar*, ed. Ethlie Ann Vare, 224 (New York: Boulevard, 1996).

22. P. David Marshall, *Celebrity and Power: Fame in Contemporary Culture* (Minneapolis: University of Minnesota Press, 1997), 164, points out that music performance creates an

individual and personalized relationship between performer and audience, as well as communicates a sense of solidarity with (and among) an audience.

23. This description draws on Kenneth Burke's discussion (*A Grammar of Motives* [1945; Berkeley: University of California Press, 1969], 512, 517. Citations are to the 1969 edition.) of irony as dramatic and dialectic, rather than relativistic. He notes, "If you isolate any one agent in a drama, or any one advocate in a dialogue, and see the whole in terms of his position alone, you have the purely relativistic. . . . Irony arises when one tries, by the interaction of terms upon one another, to produce a development which uses all the terms. . . . They are all voices, or personalities, or positions integrally affecting one another. When the dialectic is properly formed, they are the number of characters needed to produce the total development" (512). It is dramatic and dialectic irony that allow for "'peripety,' the strategic moment of reversal" (517). I hope to imply such reversal in my move from "star" discourse to "diva" discourse in, about, and of the torch singer.

24. Writing about materialist feminist critique, Teresa Ebert, *Ludic Feminism and After: Postmodernism, Desire and Labor in Late Capitalism* (Ann Arbor: University of Michigan Press, 1996), 7, notes that it is a "mode of knowing that inquires into what is not said, into the silences and suppressed or missing, in order to uncover the concealed operations of power and the socio-economic relations connecting the myriad details and representations of our lives."

25. These sentences are adapted from Wolf, "Desire in Evidence," 349, who writes, "My search for 'evidence,' then, became intimately linked with my desire—my desire for knowledge, answers, proof."

26. Burke, *Grammar of Motives*, 503, 506, asserts that metonymy is a work of reduction, and further that reduction is a representation.

27. Hayden White, "Writing in the Middle Voice," *Stanford Literature Review* 9, no. 2 (1992): 180–81, 182, describes Derrida's (see Jacques Derrida, *Speech and Phenomena and Other Essays on Husserl's Theory of Signs*, trans. David B. Allison and Newton Garver [Evanston: Northwestern University Press, 1973], 137) *third, middle voice*, which works in a "metatransitive relationship between an agent, an act, and an effect." The middle voice is "at once productive of an affect and an object" and "constitutive of a particular kind of agent . . . by means of an action." This middle, third voice is descriptive of what I hear listening to torch singers who are at once agents, acts, and effects. They create a performative, diva discourse in which "torch" both "acts and is acted upon." Torch singing is, as Elin Diamond, "Introduction," *Performance and Cultural Politics* (London: Routledge, 1996), 1, puts it, a performance that is "always a doing and a thing done." See Diamond's essay and Judith Butler, *Gender Trouble: Feminism and the Subversion of Identity* (New York: Routledge, 1990), for a discussion of performativity and the relationship between and among performativity and performance.

28. Wayne Koestenbaum, *The Queen's Throat: Opera, Homosexuality, and the Mystery of Desire* (New York: Poseidon, 1993), 85.

29. Sarah Vaughan, "My Man," lyrics by Albert Willemetz and Jacques Charles, music by Maurice Yvain, trans. Channing Pollock, *Jazz 'Round Midnight,* rec. January 1967, Verve, 1992. My discussion is based on this recording.

30. *The Ladies Sing the Blues,* videocassette, V.I.E.W. Video, 1988. My description is drawn from footage of Vaughan singing "You're Mine."

31. Linda Hutcheon, "Introduction," in *Double Talking: Essays on Verbal and Visual Ironies in Canadian Contemporary Art and Literature,* ed. Linda Hutcheon, 30 (Toronto: ECW, 1991). Writing about postmodern irony, Hutcheon notes that it performs two functions, one destructive and one constructive. "The first kind is a kind of critical ironic stance that works to distance, undermine, unmask, relativize, destabilize. . . . This is primarily a form of critique which can at times border on the defensive, but which is always concerned with internally oppositional positions."

32. Hutcheon, "Introduction," 90. I'm playing with Hutcheon's comments on the constructive moments of irony, which work "to assert difference as positive . . . through double-talking doubled discourses."

33. Helene A. Shugart, "Postmodern Irony as Subversive Rhetorical Strategy," *Western Journal of Communication* 63, no. 4 (Fall 1999): 451–52.

34. Shugart, "Postmodern Irony," 434.

35. Shugart, "Postmodern Irony," 434–35.

36. This movement from literal interpretation to what Wayne C. Booth terms stable, modern irony is described in *A Rhetoric of Irony* (Chicago: University of Chicago Press, 1974).

37. Booth, *Rhetoric of Irony,* 10–11.

38. Booth, *Rhetoric of Irony,* 11.

39. Booth, *Rhetoric of Irony,* 11.

40. Booth, *Rhetoric of Irony,* 11.

41. Booth, *Rhetoric of Irony,* 53.

42. Booth, *Rhetoric of Irony,* 23.

43. Booth, *Rhetoric of Irony,* 11.

44. Gourse, *Sassy,* 33.

45. Gourse, *Sassy,* 121.

46. Booth, *Rhetoric of Irony,* 12.

47. Booth, *Rhetoric of Irony,* 23.

48. Booth, *Rhetoric of Irony*, 23.

49. Shugart, "Postmodern Irony," 434–35, notes that irony is a risky rhetorical strategy for subversion because the possibility that the audience won't "get it" means that a text "may well function hegemonically." The consequences of not hearing an ironic voice in torch singing are serious: If we hear (and read) a torch song literally, are we complicit with the violence, abuse, and victimization narrated in the lyrics? For an exploration of this question, see Susannah McCorkle, "'I Swear I Won't Call No Copper If I'm Beat Up by My Poppa,'" *New York Times Magazine*, January 9, 1994, 32–33.

50. Barbra Streisand, "My Man," lyrics by Albert Willemetz and Jacques Charles, music by Maurice Yvain, trans. Channing Pollock, *Barbra Streisand: Just for the Record*, Columbia, 1991. This line is drawn from Streisand's introduction to the number. My discussion is based on this recording.

51. *Funny Girl*, videocassette, dir. William Wyler, perf. Barbra Streisand, Omar Sharif, and Kay Medford, Columbia/Tristar, 1968.

52. Burke, *Grammar of Motives*, 517.

53. Shugart, "Postmodern Irony," 435. See also Burke, *Grammar of Motives*, 512, and Alan Wilde, *Horizons of Assent: Modernism, Postmodernism, and the Ironic Imagination* (Baltimore: Johns Hopkins University Press, 1981), 10.

54. Hutcheon, "Introduction," 16.

55. Shugart, "Postmodern Irony," 436.

56. Shugart, "Postmodern Irony," 436, emphasis mine.

57. Burke, *Grammar of Motives*, 521.

58. "Coming Star," in *Diva: Barbra Streisand and the Making of a Superstar*, ed. Ethlie Ann Vare, 18 (New York: Boulevard, 1996), and Edwards, *Streisand*, 361.

59. Edwards, *Streisand*, 500.

60. Quoted in Edwards, *Streisand*, 500, emphasis mine.

61. Adapted from Wolf, "Desire in Evidence," 350, who writes, "My desire encouraged and necessitated active, transgressive readings which always happen in historical work but which are denied, masked, or naturalized."

62. Edith Piaf, "La Vie en Rose," lyrics by Edith Piaf and Luis Guglielmi, trans. Mack David, *Sirens of Song: Classic Torch Singers*, Rhino, 1997. My discussion is based on this recording.

63. *Edith Piaf: La Vie en Rose*, videocassette, New River Media, 1985. My description is drawn from footage of Piaf singing "Milord."

64. Dana L. Cloud, "The Null Persona: Race and the Rhetoric of Silence in the Uprising of '34," *Rhetoric & Public Affairs* 2, no. 2 (1999): 193.

65. Adam Jaworski, *The Power of Silence: Social and Pragmatic Perspectives* (Newbury Park, CA: Sage, 1993), 44.

66. Monique Lange, *Piaf* (New York: Seaver, 1981), 24–28.

67. Crosland, *Piaf*, 193.

68. Crosland, *Piaf*, 189.

69. Crosland, *Piaf*, 189.

70. Edwards, *Streisand*, 500.

71. Lena Horne, "Stormy Weather," lyrics by Ted Koehler and Harold Arlen, *Lena Horne: Stormy Weather*, BMG, 1990. My discussion is based on this recording.

72. *The Ladies Sing the Blues*. My description is drawn from footage of Horne's film debut in which she sings "Boogie Woogie Dream" with the Duke Ellington Orchestra.

73. Haskins, *Lena*, 39, 56, and Gail Lumet Buckley, *The Hornes: An American Family* (New York: Knopf, 1986), 141.

74. Haskins, *Lena*, 154.

75. Haskins, *Lena*, 58–59.

76. Lumet Buckley, *The Hornes*, 141–43.

77. Lumet Buckley, *The Hornes*, 141.

78. Haskins, *Lena*, 84, 118.

79. Haskins, *Lena*, 198–199. Does this mean, then, that she learned to collapse woman into star persona into character in the song, and thus to welcome the violence of such text-into-life and life-into-text blurring I noted earlier?

80. Booth, *Rhetoric of Irony*, 11.

81. Booth, *Rhetoric of Irony*, 52–53.

82. Adapted from Peggy Phelan, "Introduction: The Ends of Performance," in *The Ends of Performance*, ed. Peggy Phelan and Jill Lane, 11 (New York: New York University Press, 1998), who, commenting on performance theory and writing, notes, "Our admiration for performance tempts us beyond our reason to make it ours, for better or worse. The challenge before us is to learn to love the thing we've lost without assimilating it so thoroughly that it becomes us rather than remaining itself."

83. Edwards, *Streisand*, 312–15, 326.

84. Colette Guillaumin, *Racism, Sexism, Power and Ideology* (London: Routledge, 1995), 186, 135, 223.

85. Robertson, *Carrying the Torch*, 101.

86. k. d. lang, "Save Me," lyrics by k. d. lang and Ben Mink, *Ingénue*, Sire, 1992. My discussion is based on this recording.

87. This description is based on the cover photo for lang's *Absolute Torch and Twang*, Sire, 1989.

88. My descriptions are drawn from lang's performance of "Pullin' Back the Reins" on *Saturday Night Live*, 1992, and her performance of "Summerfling" on *The Tonight Show*, June 2000.

89. Butler, *Gender Trouble*, 31, comments on how we perform (and denaturalize and mobilize) gender categories. She notes, "Even if heterosexist constructs circulate as the available sites of power/discourse from which to do gender at all, the question remains: What possibilities of recirculation exist? Which possibilities of doing gender repeat and displace through hyperbole, dissonance, internal confusion, and proliferation the very constructs by which they are mobilized?" lang's gender performance asks these questions and explores possible—contradictory and confounding—"answers."

90. Susan Sontag, *Against Interpretation* (New York: Dell, 1966), 281–293. These adjectives—alive to a double sense, artifice, irrepressible passion, and tender feeling—are all terms and/or phrases Sontag uses in her "Notes on Camp."

91. Mim Udovitch, "k.d. lang: How Did a Lesbian, Feminist, Vegetarian Canadian Win a Grammy and the Hearts of America?" in *Rock She Wrote: Women Write about Rock, Pop, and Rap*, ed. Evelyn McDonnell and Ann Powers, 331 (New York: Delta, 1995).

92. Sontag, *Against Interpretation*, 285, and Udovitch, "k.d. lang," 333.

93. Quoted in Udovitch, "k.d. lang," 333.

94. Koestenbaum, *Queen's Throat*, 117.

95. Koestenbaum, *Queen's Throat*, 117.

96. Derrida, *Speech and Phenomena*, 129.

97. See Udovitch, "k.d. lang"; Robertson, *Carrrying the Torch*; and Collis, *k.d. lang*.

98. Wilde, *Horizons of Assent*, 31.

99. Wilde, *Horizons of Assent*, 31.

100. Cloud, "Null Persona," 17.

101. Ernst Behler, *Irony and the Discourse of Modernity* (Seattle: University of Washington Press, 1990), 112.

102. Kathy E. Ferguson, *The Man Question: Visions of Subjectivity in Feminist Theory* (Berkeley: University of California Press, 1993), 157, writes, "Irony makes it possible for me to reside within the unstable theoretical space I have created."

103. Burke, *Grammar of Motives*, 512.

104. Gilbert Millstein, narrator, *The Essential Billie Holiday Carnegie Hall Concert*, rec. November 1956, Verve, 1989.

105. Holiday, *Lady Sings the Blues*, 168, 192.

106. Billie Holiday, "My Man," lyrics by Albert Willemetz and Jacques Charles, music by Maurice Yvain, trans. Channing Pollock, *The Essential Billie Holiday Carnegie Hall Concert*, rec. November 1956, Verve, 1989. My discussion is based on this recording.

107. Burke, *Grammar of Motives*, 514, notes, "True irony, humble irony, is based upon a sense of fundamental kinship with the enemy, as one *needs* him, is *indebted* to him, is not merely outside him as an observer but contains him from *within*, being consubstantial with him."

108. *Lady Day: The Many Faces of Billie Holiday*, videocassette, Kulture, 1990. My description is drawn from footage of Holiday performing "Fine and Mellow" and "Strange Fruit."

109. Buck Clayton, Tony Scott, Al Cohn, Carl Drinkard, Kenny Burrell, Carson Smith, and Chico Hamilton, as noted on the recording.

110. A. Davis, *Blues Legacies*, 175.

111. Holiday, *Lady Sings the Blues*, 148.

112. Gourse, *Sassy*, 56, and Haskins, *Lena*, 95.

113. Robertson, *Carrying the Torch*, 75, 78.

114. Koestenbaum, *Queen's Throat*, 132.

115. David Brackett, *Interpreting Popular Music* (New York: Cambridge University Press, 1995), 62–71. See also Denning, *Cultural Front*, 345–46.

116. Brackett, *Interpreting Popular Music*, 65.

117. A. Davis, *Blues Legacies*, 178.

118. A. Davis, *Blues Legacies*, 178.

119. A. Davis, *Blues Legacies*, 173–79.

120. A. Davis, *Blues Legacies*, 174, 177. Davis's characterization of Holiday's singing draws explicitly on notions of *signifying*, or indirect (hidden) expression, of which irony is a common

form. *Signifying* is a term developed by Henry Louis Gates Jr. (see *The Signifying Monkey: A Theory of African-American Literary Criticism* [New York: Oxford University Press, 1988]). Rooted in a black vernacular generated out of slavery and the need to create a "private yet communal" language, signifying is a collection of speech acts that function as a "double-voiced" metadiscourse—texts that talk to (and often critique) other texts (Gates, *Signifying Monkey*, xiv, xxv). Signifying constitutes a playful, doubled performative discursive practice that speaks with and comments on white culture, politics, and texts (xxxiv). Signifying is a performative practice available to anyone who wishes to speak and talk back to ideology, discourse, difference (A. Davis, *Blues Legacies*, 90). Holiday's "My Man" *signifies* because it enacts a textual and musical conversation that oscillates between latent and surface meaning, between that which can be said and that which can't be uttered. Her voice creates a "noisy disturbance in silence" that gestures toward the "*extradiscursive*, material relations of power which are perceived . . . to be unspeakable" outside of the song (Gates, *Signifying Monkeys*, 46; Cloud, "Null Persona," 179).

121. A. Davis, *Blues Legacies*, 176.

122. A. Davis, *Blues Legacies*, 179.

123. See also the exceptions A. Davis, *Blues Legacies*, makes on 173, 176, and 177.

124. Burke, *Grammar of Motives*, 512.

125. Ferguson, *Man Question*, 157.

126. Burke, *Grammar of Motives*, 512.

127. Shugart, "Postmodern Irony," 452.

128. Donna J. Haraway, *How Like a Leaf: An Interview with Thyrza Nichols Goodeve/Donna J. Haraway* (New York: Routledge, 2000), 171.

129. Haraway, *How Like a Leaf*, 454.

130. A. Davis, *Blues Legacies*, 170, and Denning, *Cultural Front*, 344.

131. William Howard Kenney, *Recorded Music in American Life: The Phonograph and Popular Memory, 1890–1945* (New York: Oxford University Press, 1999), 105–7.

132. Ebert, *Ludic Feminism*, 7.

133. Scott, *Domination*, 161, emphasis mine.

134. Koestenbaum, *Queen's Throat*, 96.

135. Koestenbaum, *Queen's Throat*, 96.

136. Nicholas Bacon, Libby Holmes, and Josh White, lyrics for "The House of the Rising Sun," DigitalDreamDoor.com, n.d., www.digitaldreamdoor.com/pages/lyrics/house_rising.html (accessed July 8, 2005).

# 6

# Love's Wounds

The speaking being is a wounded being, [her] speech wells up out of an aching for love.

*—Julia Kristeva, "Tales of Love"*[1]

Quarrelsome dreams sometimes rushed through her speech, and accounts of wounds she had inflicted.

*—Elizabeth Hardwick, "Sleepless Nights"*[2]

With her the song did all the work; all she had to do was bring out the bruised tenderness that is there in all old songs.

*—adapted from Geoff Dyer,* But Beautiful[3]

---

**SAMPLING**

A singer likes to sample. When she sits down to write, she begins by reciting the structures and phrasing and lyrics of others. She layers on ideas and quotations in expansive collages. She uses the music at hand—the melodies she finds at her fingertips—and puts them to use in ways they did not dream, not hesitating to change them or to try several of them at once.[4] She makes music's past—its theories and formations and structures—present, lived, immanent. She makes Music—a fixed and formal object—into a mutable, shimmering present. Music becomes visible, *felt* when she can trace the movements of the pieces that make up these assemblages.[5] Today's collage begins with a lyrical sampling on structures of feeling, to which she pins her own desires and puts to her own uses:

> A practical consciousness of a present kind
> thought as felt and feeling as thought.[6]
> What is actually being lived, and not only
> what is thought is being lived.[7]
> Social experiences in solution make
> music on the margins of language.[8]
> Evanescent constructions[9]
> never mere flux; built in
> the tangle of I and us.
> An exchange of seething absences,[10]
> a shared possession.
> This is the musicality of[11] listening,
> of hearing an ironic tone and fulsome silences,
> of seeing through the violence of a lyric,
> of feeling deep wounds in civilization,
> and longing for unforeseen pleasures,
> unspoken possibilities.[12]

She puts her fingers on the keys, eager to give her assembled fragments music. She rests them in the C position, on

CDEFG CDEFG

and then she pulls away. C is the paradigm key, signifier of musical literacy and formal education. She wonders if she should use G-flat, the key of jazz and blues, of orality and playing by ear.[13] She chooses these dark and lush notes to write an epilogue: A cultural, social, political, and performative hypothesis. This song sings love's wounds, its sounds clamor out of violence to be seen and heard.[14]

### WAITING

Alice is waiting for the man who is not her husband. Only this waiting doesn't happen in a theater before the music begins. This waiting happens outside the university library. As she waits, she searches the faces of the men and women who stream into the library—some reluctantly, some with fierce purpose—for the eyes of the man she loves. The man she loves? Alice realizes this waiting outside the university library. After a while, she sees his eyes and wide smile. She is careful to fix her gaze on his face, to not look away, to see no one but the man she has been waiting for.

Alice is waiting with the man who is not her husband in the music store checkout line. He is a lover of music, and because he loves Alice, he wants to share his music with her. He holds R.E.M. and The Specials—his choices. He holds The Beatles—their choice together. And Alice holds Billie Holiday, her choice. They buy their music and take it home. They can't agree on The Specials—Alice finds the music too rushed and angry; or on Holiday—he finds her too moody and regretful. But they agree on The Beatles, at least for now.

Alice is waiting for the man who is not her husband to finish scolding her. They are in a restaurant, and he is angry because Alice's eyes are not fixed on his. His says that when he talks, Alice's eyes scan the room. Alice blinks. She says she is sorry, then promises to see no one else.

Alice is waiting for the man who is not her husband to stop yelling. They are at home, arguing about who knows what. He is standing over her, his voice ringing in her ears. Alice puts up her hands, palms out, in surrender. And then she pushes him. She looks into his eyes and taunts him. Alice begins to shout, to move in close. He stands still, arms taut. She puts her hands on him again, and he raises his to her.

Alice is waiting for the bus. She has a suitcase full of clothes and records and notebooks filled with her handwriting—the things she managed to gather into her arms as she screamed and scratched her way out of the apartment. Alice stands on the street, crying. She tastes sweet, metallic blood in her mouth. She touches her face, but she doesn't see the bruises around her eyes.

Alice stays home—for now, her friend's tiny apartment—not wanting to attend her classes or go to work as a waitress; not wanting to explain. She is waiting for her blackened eyes to heal. When she does go out, she sees the man who is not her husband standing in the yard, waiting. Most days, she walks right by him, but today, she stops. She looks into his eyes and asks him what he wants. He says he is sorry. He says he doesn't know what happened. He says he wants her to come home.

Alice wishes she could say she didn't accept his apologies; she wishes she could say she didn't go back, even though that is exactly what she did. Of course, it was only a matter of time before the yelling and swinging of fists began again. Of course, Alice made threats and slammed doors and packed suitcases. Alice wishes she could say she finally realized she didn't provoke or deserve the bruises or the tears. That she didn't make her own jealous demands. That she didn't see the wounds of her rage on the man's face and hands and arms. Alice wishes she could say these things, but she cannot. What she can say is that she simply waited until the anger overwhelmed her love, and then she left.

Later, Alice writes a story about her affair with the man who is not her husband. She writes that their scornful, jealous love got her thinking. She writes that his efforts to control her voice and her vision gave her feminism. She writes that he gave her music, but she gave herself Billie Holiday.[15]

## RAISING MUSIC'S CONSCIOUSNESS

In *Feminine Endings: Music, Gender, and Sexuality*, Susan McClary writes, "To be sure, music's beauty is often overwhelming, its formal order magisterial. But the structures graphed by theorists and the beauty celebrated by aestheticians are often stained with such things as violence, misogyny, and racism. And perhaps more disturbing still to those who would present music as autonomous and invulnerable, it also frequently betrays fear—fear of women, fear of the body."[16]

This passage gets me thinking about the violence and fear in torch songs. It gets me thinking about the line in "My Man" that confesses, "He beats me too/what can I do?" It gets me thinking about how Holiday's voice stands up to that fear, confronts it subtly, ironically. I think about how the way Holiday sings "'My Man'—now playfully, now mournfully, now emphatically, and now frivolously—highlights the contradictions and ambiguities of women's location in love relationships and creates a space within which female subjectivity can move toward self-consciousness."[17] In Holiday's voice, words of violence invite recognition. Though unexamined identification and affirmation of experience—even the experience of oppression—isn't what feminists are after, right? "My Man" is a question of consciousness—of voices and selves and critiques—that is answered in how listeners hear a singer's voice and how they participate in the music.[18] "My Man" is also a question of fear and violence and music. And it gets me thinking.

I try to remember the moment I began thinking as a feminist, to pinpoint the moment my feminism began. Like all of the other moments of want and desire in this text, it began with a presence. A new graduate student, I read an essay by Anne Marie Hunter titled, "Numbering the Hairs of Our Heads: Male Social Control and the All-Seeing Male God," given to me by Mary, also a new graduate student. I liked Mary and so I read the article by Anne Marie Hunter. The piece was inspired by the author's experience working with battered women and Michel Foucault's writing about surveillance. I underlined Hunter's words about how women are watched—what they <u>wear</u>, what they <u>eat</u>, the <u>shapes their bodies</u> take. They are <u>visually vulnerable</u>, both in their own homes and in a social world that looks at, around, and right through them.[19] I underlined the passage that said a woman's visual vulnerability is connected to her <u>lover's possessiveness, jealousy, and intrusiveness</u>.[20] I underlined the words <u>"Women who work at home during the day report that their husbands or lovers call frequently (sometimes more than ten times each day) to make sure they are home and alone."</u>[21] I thought about my own homebound jealousies and questioning phone calls. And then I got to Hunter's explication of Foucault's Panopticon. I underlined one whole paragraph and part of a second:

> The Panopticon is a nineteenth-century model for a prison designed by Jeremy Bentham. The prison comprises a central guard tower surrounded by a circle of one-person cells. The cells have windows in both the outside and inside walls that allow light to pass through the cell from back to front. The guards in the central tower can thus see every action of each prisoner in silhouette at all times. The inmates do not know when they are being watched, but they know that they can be watched at any moment. The visibility of the inmates and the invisibility of the guards is key to the functioning of the system as a whole.
>
> In the Panopticon, Foucault found a model for his concept of disciplinary power, a way to illustrate how social control has been embodied and carried out in the modern era, a "mechanism of power reduced to an ideal form."[22]

I read the paragraphs again. The air in the room changed. I was cold with recognition. I hadn't thought about women's visibility in precisely this way before, though I knew I would never think about sight again without wondering how women are visions, surfaces, sites always already looked at.[23] The patriarchal social system is panoptic; it operates along a vast continuum that moves from the ways women's bodies are scrutinized to how they are valued—as employees, wives, and mothers—based on physical attractiveness and reproductive promise.[24] And like the prisoners in the Panopticon, women come to watch themselves, to police their own bodies and behavior.[25] Each picture of ideal bodies (and thus selves) in the media, each glance in the mirror, each physical and emotional intrusion in the workplace and at home becomes an act of "infinitesimal violence" that "forces a woman to shift focus, to see herself through the eyes of the Panopticon."[26]

And then I reread the article. In a footnote, Hunter writes that the visibility of women, on their own terms, is central to social liberation.[27] This liberation can be found in solidarity with other women who refuse to doubt and distrust themselves and their "internal knowledge and needs."[28] It can be found in women talking to women about redefining the panoptic gaze as a radical and pluralistic visibility.[29] Though Hunter recognizes the difficulties of overcoming women's own internalized and overt racism, sexism, homophobia, and misogyny, these are issues to be dealt with in *collective conversation.*

Reading and rereading this article, I became conscious of feminism—in this case, Hunter's radical-cultural-poststructural feminism, marked by critiques of patriarchy and discursive structures, along with the recommendation that women re-vision themselves in a collective "struggle for self-definition."[30] I became conscious of my self as a woman, as a social, cultural, political, and radical being. Hunter's writing and the work of other feminists made sense to me. Their texts spoke to me because they named something I didn't have a vocabulary for up until then: how raised fists and glances and words and structures can *all* embody acts of violence and how other structures and words and glances and raised fists can speak back to and against this violence.

Feminist texts also spoke to the other texts I loved, including torch songs. I listened to "My Man" and I heard something else, something new. I heard singers using a story about raised fists and glances and words and structures to make performances that spoke out, however subtly, against the circumstances of women's lives. Torch songs made violence visible on bodies while voices resonated with multiple meanings and visions. Quarrelsome dreams rushed through their speech. I heard their sound bend and bounce off the social arrangements, shadings, and gestures that shape what music can *mean*.[31]

Hearing women sing "My Man" and "Stormy Weather" and "Mean to Me," I became conscious of feminism and the resistive possibilities of torch singing. I heard and felt how torch songs story the "deeply social character of . . . personal experiences."[32] I understood the multiple and contradictory nature of torch songs, performers, and audiences meant that consciousness does not breathe life into an essential and stable and individual subject called Woman. Instead, torch singing insists that gender is performative, a musical becoming.[33] And rather than supercede sight with sound, torch singing enacts multiple visions and voices in conversation and contradiction.[34] *Here* my desire to hear a critique in torch singing began.

And along with my desire came questions: Is consciousness enough?[35] Does an emphasis on experience undercut concerted political action? What sort of resistance does torch singing constitute? And if torch singing does constitute a type of resistance, how are these performances read and interpreted by listeners? What kind of feminist am I—listening to these songs and stitching my desire to a patchwork feminist politics? These questions kept—and keep—me thinking and feeling and listening.

## BLINDNESS

I drive from Seattle to Portland on a Wednesday afternoon to see Rebecca Kilgore at the Benson Hotel. Kilgore lives in Portland, and playing the Lobby Court Bar is her regular gig. She has been singing with swing bands and jazz combos for twenty years, paying her dues. Tonight's performance will celebrate the release of her twenty-fourth appearance on CD, *Moments Like This*, and I am driving to Portland to mark the occasion.

In the car, I listen to the afternoon news on a Seattle radio station until I'm out of range. I switch to the only station I can find, one that's broadcasting an NBA playoff game. I listen as I cross the Columbia River and into Portland. I arrive in time to eat a quick dinner and make the 8 p.m. show. When I walk into the lobby of the Benson, the bar is crowded with people watching the game, which is now into overtime. I take the only available seat in the bar—the seat, I am convinced, farthest from the piano. I wonder out loud about whether they'll turn off the television so the music can start. The man sitting next to me looks over and says, "You're kidding, right?"

I look at my watch. 8:15. I tap my pencil on the bar. 8:30. The game goes into a second overtime. 8:45. I order a drink. 9:00. I start to worry that there won't be any music at all, that I've driven three hours to Portland on a Wednesday night and I won't hear a note of Rebecca Kilgore. 9:15. Mercifully, the game ends. I watch the musicians set up, relieved. I have no idea which team won the game. I am ready for the music. 9:30. Kilgore begins the set, but heated discussions about last-minute fouls and missed shots drown out her voice. 9:45. The basketball fans finally filter out of the bar, and the music demands the now small crowd's attention. I can hear her sing the standards with devotion—"Our Love Is Here to Stay," "My Heart Belongs to Daddy," "Lover Come Back to Me." Her voice is airy and lilting, interested in rhythms and cadence.

I'm most taken with Kilgore's rendition of "Lover." She does the song very up-tempo—almost staccato—which provides nice contrast with the lyrics, "Love had its day/that day is past/you've gone away/This aching heart of mine is singing/lover, come back to me."[36] I can hear Vaughan's relaxed, languorous rendition behind and beneath Kilgore's quick phrasing and I wonder if it's the contrast that's got me listening more attentively. And then it's time for a break.

I decide to buy a CD and I move toward where Kilgore is sitting. I want to ask her about torch singing, but I'm *nervous*. I don't know why. Maybe I'm a little starstruck, here in the Lobby Court Bar. I ask to buy a copy of the CD. She asks if I have correct change. Thankfully, I don't. I have to return to my table to look in my wallet. I scold myself. *Why are you here*? And then I return with my correct change and my question, "Do you ever sing 'My Man'?"

She thinks for a moment and speaks-sings, "Oh, my man I love him so? He'll never know"?

"Yes."

"It's got that line, 'He beats me too.' I don't do those kinds of songs."

"I ask because I'm writing a book about torch singing—about songs like 'My Man' and performers like Billie Holiday and Sarah Vaughan and Barbra Streisand."

"Oh?"

"Yes. I'm writing about how, when these women sing 'My Man,' their performances somehow say to audiences, 'Don't take these lyrics literally.'"

"Hmm."

"I believe there's more than a bit of irony in their interpretations of lyrics that are, on the surface, very negative in their portrayal of women."

"Have you seen Angela Davis's book on blues singers?"

"*Yes.* There's a chapter in that book about Holiday's love songs."

"It's a little too academic for me, and frankly I think she reads too much into Holiday's performances."

"How so?"

"I just don't know how she can be so sure that's what Holiday's doing—that she was really critiquing racism and sexism and what have you. Do you know Susannah McCorkle's article in the *New York Times Magazine* from a few years back?"

"Yes, I've seen it."

"Susannah is very smart about things like this—about lyrics and politics. You should read it again."

"I will. Thanks."

Now someone is behind me, speaking to Kilgore. She says, "Hello! I'm so glad you could come!" and I understand that my turn with her is over. I say, "Thank you," and move out of the way.

The second set begins with "Makin' Whoopie," then segues into "That's All," and "Ain't I Good to You?" after which Kilgore says, "That was a torch song for those of you interested in torch songs." I smile in acknowledgment, though I wonder if it *was* a torch song, if it was torch *singing.* Next, she does "They Can't Take That Away from Me." Even in her upbeat rendition, *this* seems more like torch singing, but I have to wonder again if that is because I can hear my Holiday sound track playing, "The way you haunt my dreams. . . . The way you changed my life."[37] I think that torch singing is a performance I've created to my own specifications. I'm searching for performances that fit *my* vision and *my* sound track—always disappointed, like a jilted lover. Is torch singing about blindness, about seeing what I want or not seeing at all? What kind of feminism is that?

## CASUALTIES

After the Portland trip, I dig through a bulging expandable file labeled "torch singing" for the McCorkle article. I find a blurry microfiche copy of the essay tucked in between the Oxford English Dictionary definition of "torch song," and a newspaper article on French cafe concerts. In the piece, McCorkle tells the story of how she fell in love with the popular songs of the 1930s and '40s and her new favorite singer, Billie Holiday.[38] Her love for torch songs and torch singers took McCorkle—a graduate of Berkeley, a liberated and politically committed woman—a bit off guard.[39] As she puts it, "I had a massive *crise de conscience* when I realized that what I most wanted to do in life was sing romantic standards."[40] Still, that's exactly what she did.

A year or two went by before McCorkle began to feel uncomfortable about singing songs of unrequited love. And after performing Holiday's "Don't Explain" one last time, she stopped singing "lyrics that romanticized cruelty and dependence."[41] She had "abandoned the barricades of political activism, but . . . [she] could still make a small contribution to a healthier society by not glamorizing masochism."[42] Also eliminated from her repertoire were "My Man," "Moanin' Low," and even Bessie Smith's "uppity" song, "Ain't Nobody's Business If I Do," because it contained the lines, "I swear I won't call no copper/if I'm beat up by my poppa."[43]

Soon after, McCorkle eliminated songs that portrayed gold-digging women, songs that did not translate from a female to male narrator, and songs that allowed women to adopt sexist attitudes toward men.[44] She was also bothered by how singing the word *gay* elicited laughter from audiences and wondered when gay and lesbian performers—including k. d. lang—would bring popular romantic ballads out of the closet by singing of same-sex lovers.[45]

This purging of material led McCorkle to wonder if, once she eliminated songs portraying sexism, material greed, racism, homophobia, or songs that sing the praises of smoking (a health hazard), there would be any songs left to sing.[46] She decided that songs of romance and heartache were still worth singing, adding the epilogue: it's not easy being a "politically correct chanteuse."[47]

I return the article to the file. McCorkle's tongue-in-cheek digs at political correctness aside, I wonder if she's saying that music—that performance itself—can't be political, so it's up to the performer to make choices about what lyrics to sing *before* she sings them. Though if that's true—if lyrics that portray women as dependent and men as cruel say to audiences, *this* is the way things are and perhaps, *should* be—music is doing its job rhetorically. And if that's true, it's possible for a singer to critique the lyrics she sings—to say this is the way things are and *shouldn't* be. It's possible for the audience to hear that critique. And if these things are true, is torch singing a critique sounded at the abandoned barricades of political activism?

Torch singing does not stand in for or shut down other forms of political protest and action. Torch singing is consciousness raising as a first step toward political change.[48] It does not say to audiences, *here* your activism begins. What torch singing does and says is, this is what is happening to women. Do you hear yourself in the song? Do you hear how it could be otherwise? Look around, and see the other women here, hearing and thinking and moving. Seeing yourself, recognizing yourself and identifying with the story told in the performance is a necessary part of any form of political resistance. Through parody and personal lives, irony and identity bending, consciousness and diva discourses, torch singing asks audiences to question their place in the stories of individual responsibility and victimhood. Lyrics are ideological discourses, and torch singing uses voice and music to work on those lyrics, those discourses.

Though this doesn't mean torch singing has to settle into or for a politics of the personal. In performance, singers and audience members might be moved out of passive subject positions—by the confrontational nature of the lyrics, by the participatory aspects of the form, by a voice that says, wait a minute; think again, feel again. And if audiences are listening to that voice, they can hear its hidden but ringing challenge: Do you hear an opening for another sort of conversation? Can you imagine how things might change?

Torch singing isn't a feminism shrouded in blindness, seeing and hearing what it wants or nothing at all. Singing songs about fear and violence *against* women *to* women, performers ask audiences to remember that visibility moves beneath surfaces, behind what can readily be seen in a "complex system of permission and prohibition, of presence and absence."[49] Torch singing tells an opportunistic and optimistic story about the "exclusions and invisibilities" spoken "behind the backs of the powerful"—opportunistic because it gets in its digs where it can, and optimistic because it hopes audiences can hear its critique in and outside the performance frame.[50] What kind of feminist writes about torch singing? One who says it's possible to hear torch singing as a performative practice that enacts and encourages critical engagement. A feminist who bears the trace and mark of her own violent musical consciousness and wonders how the others are tending their wounds.

Of course, my words about torch singing and feminism are formed in and around my hearing of the music and my desire to write what I hear. I wonder if that's what you hear, too. I wonder if that's what Susannah McCorkle might hear, if she could be persuaded by my words. I think that maybe, when this work is complete, I will send it to her. But I can't. I will finish these stories about torch singing, but not before McCorkle jumps to her death from a New York apartment window. She is fifty-five years old. She leaves a suicide note in which she surrenders her battle with depression.[51] I tell myself that singing romantic standards did not define Susannah McCorkle. Certainly torch singing did not cause her death, though it couldn't have saved her either. And it's not hard to remember that McCorkle isn't the first casualty. It's not hard to wonder whether we need these casualties, whether we need stories of women's struggles and losses so we can confront and examine our own despair without losing ourselves in it.[52]

## STANDARDS

I wanted to learn to play the piano, so I went to a piano dealer and rented a small upright for three months, a trial. I bought several beginners' books, and when the piano was delivered, I arranged them along the music stand above the keys. I was going to teach myself how to play. I had been writing about music for most of my life as a scholar, but it had been a long time since I had *played.*

I opened up the first book and read about clef and staff and whole-half-quarter notes and signatures. I paged ahead, to the practice songs: "The Big Parade" and "Copy Cats." But I wasn't sure which notes to play. I had forgotten how to read music. I had to turn back; I had to learn again. I read about ties and rests and repeat signs. I read about flats and sharps and naturals. Soon, though, I lost interest in the books. I sat at the piano and played what I already knew—by ear, by heart—"Silent Night" and "Chopsticks" and "Happy Birthday." I closed my self-instruction books and played these songs, over and over.

The same scene occurred at the piano each day for a week. I would begin with the books, attempting to teach myself, and would end up playing what I already knew or trying to play new songs by ear. I was having fun, but I wasn't sure I was learning to play the piano. I decided that I needed to take a lesson or two.

I called the number accompanying the newspaper advertisement for "adult beginners." A calm, male voice answered the phone. I told him about my rented piano and my desire to learn the basics over the summer. He said,

"Sure. Yes." We set an appointment for the following week. I continued my own instruction, adding a trial and error "Heart and Soul" to my repertoire.

The night of the lesson, I waited for the piano teacher on a plastic chair outside the closet-sized practice room. I looked at my hands, wondering if they were the hands of someone who could play the piano. I listened to the halted notes coming from inside the room, the efforts of another adult beginner. I chewed my fingernails.

The door swung open and the man with the calm voice reminded his student to practice what he had learned during the lesson for next week. And then it was my turn. The piano teacher asked me to sit at the piano. He asked me why I wanted to learn to play. I said I loved music. I said I'd always wanted to play the piano. He said, "Fine. Good. Do you know any songs?"

"Yes."

He nodded and I played "Heart and Soul" with all the heart and soul I had at that moment. He said, "Good. Fine."

"Do you read music?"

"Yes. Well, I could a long time ago."

"You'll remember. It's just like riding a bike."

He put the sheet music for "When the Saints Come Marching In" on the piano. He asked me to put my fingers in the C position. I raised my fingers above the keys, not sure where to set them down. He leaned over me and put my fingers on

CDEFG CDEFG

He said, "This is low and middle C."

"Okay."

"Go ahead, try the song."

I looked at the notes on the page. I looked at my fingers. I felt the piano teacher watching me. He leaned in and wrote,

C E F G C E F G C E F G E C E D

below the musical notes on the page. Still, I didn't know where to move my fingers. The piano teacher showed me which keys corresponded to which notes, moving my clumsy fingers along the keyboard. I began to sweat. I wanted to get up and run out of the tiny practice room, away from the expectant eyes of my teacher, but I stayed. I picked my way though "Saints" one note at a time. He said, "Fine. Good." He handed me the sheet music and said, "This is your homework. Practice it for your next lesson."

When I got home, I tried "Saints" several times, and soon my playing sounded like the song running in my head. Satisfied, I put my homework aside and ran through a few quick and immensely satisfying "Chopsticks" and "Heart and Souls." But the next day when I looked at the music for "Saints," I couldn't remember what to do. If I just listened and played, the song sounded right. But with the music I was lost. Soon, I gave up practicing "Saints" altogether and returned to my standards.

## PLAYING BY EAR

Lena Horne had no formal musical training. She learned by listening; she learned playing by ear. She began her career as a dancer, hired by white promoters to entertain white customers not because of her dancing abilities, but because of her exotic beauty. She had long legs, light skin, "good" hair, and she was young—a sweet sixteen.[53] She began singing ballads quite by accident, a replacement singer crooning "As Long as I Live" and "Cocktails for Two" with older, male partners.[54] This singing was a prop, a bit of stage business. Horne was one of nature's nearly flawless constructions, and her work was to be observed by as many people as possible.[55] At least that's what her critics said; at least that's what they saw when they looked at her.

Horne did not want or pretend to be a singer.[56] Still, she quit the club to become the sparrow, the thrush, the girl singer for a traveling orchestra. The road was hard for an African American orchestra playing to predominantly white audiences, and she spent many nights making entrances through service doors.[57] She returned to New York, hoping to establish herself as a headliner at the society clubs. She sang "Sleepy Time Down South" to audition for the owner who cared about talent and not about color.[58] At least she tried to sing the song, but after "Soft winds blowing through the pinewood trees/Folks down there live a life of ease,"[59] he stopped her. He asked, "Do you know what you're singing?"

"What do you mean?"

"Do you know what they do to Negroes in the South?"

Horne was startled by the question. She had never heard it before, had never asked it of herself. She did not understand the misery of Negroes in the

South. So she sang Holiday's song, "The Man I Love," and was allowed to proceed, but not before she was educated by the owner who cared about talent and not about color in the finer points of race and labor relations and blues idiom.[60]

She developed pride in herself and her background. She added protest songs to her repertoire. She began singing at political benefits. She was featured in left-wing newspapers and magazines. And when the witch-hunts began, she was blacklisted. Still, she kept on singing.[61]

Perhaps, during her time at Café Society, Horne was a political innocent in need of an education. Perhaps her consciousness was raised by radical white entrepreneurs like Barney Josephson and John Hammond. Perhaps she learned how race and gender and class and sexual preference are forms of double, triple—*multiple*—consciousness,[62] never reconciled, but held in mutual suspension and contradiction. Perhaps. What Horne learned at Café Society was that singing moved audiences to feel, to participate in a performance.[63] Singing was a reciprocal art. That she knew for sure.

Reciprocity is the idea that a performer will meet her audience halfway in creating the experience of the performance.[64] It refuses to construct the audience as passive and distant observers of an aesthetic event[65] or to hold the performer responsible for "engaging" the audience.[66] Reciprocity *implicates* the audience in the creation of the performance,[67] so that the performers "get something back from an audience that is reacting, that is involved with them."[68]

The same can be said of a torch singer's performance. Horne sings, "I'm numb again and I'm dumb again . . . bewitched, bothered and bewildered am I."[69] She sighs and impels her audience to "leap to its feet, stand and wildly applaud."[70] She "works on a crowd's insides, until the crowd is giving her as much as she gives the crowd. . . . She is not singing at them, and they realize they've got to give something back or it's no dice. She's crystallizing something for them that needs *their* help."[71] Her audience is not encouraged so much as *expected* to participate in the performance.[72]

Reciprocity is not achieved in an audience's *witnessing* of a performance. In a reciprocal relationship, a performer is designated the task of giving artistic expression to a community message or idea in *collaboration* with spectators.[73] This collaboration is a mutual effort to create an atmosphere of highly charged emotion appropriate to the unfolding drama.[74] Audience and performer display a "self-conscious willingness to engage more fully in the performance and a responsibility . . . to confirm what is happening."[75] When Horne sings "Summertime," her voice breaks and the audience is rapt. When she sings, a sensuous knowledge is created in the noisy silences and expectant absences of the music.[76] And when audiences hear Horne's voice, they meet her halfway.

## RED

The Lapin Agile cabaret in Montmartre, Paris, is situated halfway between a cemetery and a vineyard; halfway between decimation and exuberance, halfway between dissent and humor.[77] The cabaret began as a meeting place for avant-garde artists, writers, and poets.[78] Pablo Picasso, Guillaume Apollinaire, Maurice Utrillo, and Max Jacob[79] met there to drink wine, discuss cubism and pure poetry, and sing cabaret songs.[80] Jacob took the stage to sing clever puns, Maurice Utrillo would sketch for drink, and Picasso's blue period harlequin graced the far wall.[81] When my niece and I visit Paris, we walk past the cemetery and the vineyard and open the door to the salon of the avant-garde.

We are seated in a dark, square room with tables around the perimeter. The walls are adorned with posters and paintings, though Picasso's harlequin is missing. The entry to the room is closed with a red curtain on brass rings that shush along a metal rod. Sitting in the corner of the room, I imagine that the poet Gaston Coute is seated on the bench next to me, well into his second bottle of wine.[82]

The waiter comes to our table with cordial glasses filled with cherry liqueur. A piano player is positioned directly across from us. He plays several tunes I recognize, and a few I know by heart—"La Vie en Rose" and "Milord." I hum along, "da da da *da* da da . . ." After half an hour or so, a group of seven people—three women and four men—come into the room and sit at the center table. My eyes are drawn to the woman in red seated at the head of the table. She has glossy red lips that smile and talk and smoke and after a while, sing along with the piano player. The woman in red and the others sing quietly and sporadically at first, then gradually, with each song, their volume and performance are, somehow, *magnified.* Are the people at the center table projecting their voices? Or are they simply getting into the music? They sing to and for each other, though I see how they sense the watching eyes of others in the room.

After three or four songs, two of the men seated at the center table turn their chairs and bodies to face us. They continue singing to each other, but they also sing directly to us. And I understand that these men and the others are the *performers.*

Then the men and women seated at the center table begin taking turns singing solos. They turn their bodies toward us, though they remain seated. About halfway through these solos—which proceed around the table in turn—a large group is brought in and seated next to the piano. They, too, begin singing along. I wonder if they are also part of the show, but I'm not sure. At this point, I think *everyone* is a performer. And like the rest of the audience, I feel compelled to sing along, even in my fractured French.

A few songs later, a couple is seated next to us, and they begin smoking and singing along. I notice that the woman has a leather cigarette case much like the one my mother used to carry. She offers me a cigarette and I feel pleased—am I passing for French here in the dark? I decline without speaking so I don't give myself away.

As the solos progress, the performers get more and more effusive—the last three or four numbers are performed standing, with the singers encouraging the audience to sing along. And we do. After each member of the singing table does a solo, the group abruptly gets up and leaves the room. The waiter draws the red curtain behind them.

The piano player continues to play. A few more patrons are seated and then the woman in red—the woman with the crystalline, almost operatic voice and sleek, bobbed hair and laughing eyes—appears from behind the curtain. She stands, hands clasped in front of her, next to the piano. She smiles, showing us white teeth between red, red lips.

The piano player begins and the woman in red sings several traditional chansons. She sings with fervor and concentration, telling a story in each piece. I follow crimson fingernails as they speak the sweep of a valley or anticipate the arrival of a long-awaited lover. I see joy in the wrinkling of her nose and the light in her eyes. Her voice is full with longing for another time and place, and I meet her there.

For the twenty minutes she sings, I am alive with the tangible pressure of "somethingness"—a change in presence that does not wait for definition or interpretation.[83] I raise my glass to cherry-stained lips and call, "Bravo! Bravo!" with the crowd. And then the clink and hum of the brass curtain signals the end of the moment. She disappears into the lobby and in her place moves a rush of new patrons.

We wonder what will happen next. After the newcomers are seated and offered a cherry aperitif, a woman and man, also part of the center group, appear from behind the curtain. They sing a love ballad. The man stands behind the woman and the two of them sway and trill as if tropical breezes were in the air. The spell woven by the woman in red is broken. I look at my watch. 11:00. I lean toward my niece and say, "After they're through, do you want to go?" At the front counter, the woman in red raises her eyebrows when we request the check. I smile and say *merci beaucoup* once, twice, three times and each time she nods, her ruby smile widening.

The next day, we visit Sacré Cœur at Montmartre, then wander the brick streets around the cathedral. We spot a vineyard in the middle of a residential neighborhood. Its sparse vines line the hillside and we stop to take a photo. I wonder out loud if the Lapin Agile isn't near here, and then we turn around and see the cabaret directly in front of us.

I walk across the street and pose for a photo in front of the tiny house. I can hear the woman in red inside playing the piano and doing vocal exercises. I try the door, wondering how to ask if I might come inside and look around and maybe sit very quietly while you rehearse and ask what's your name and how long have you been singing and tell me about the chanson and do you think it's political or feminist and do you think audiences feel this and how and do you always wear red and your lips and your eyes and your hands and do you think I might . . .

I force my fingers into the bent latch and try the door, but it is locked. I watch small tears of blood form across my knuckles, and then I let go.

## USING HER VOICE

I have a tiny scar where my knuckles scraped against the latch. It is a small, white mark, barely noticeable between my index and middle fingers. The scar moves as I type field notes for the Paris trip, writing of my wound at the door of the Lapin Agile. I begin with a line I remember about torch singing: "In these emotionally charged environments, they warbled their elegies of retrospection and loss, with the result that the combination of sentiment, liquor, dim lights, and smoke-filled air was too much for many of the customers and tears rolled down their cheeks."[84] The Lapin Agile is an emotionally charged environment, a combination of sentiment, liquor, dim lights, and smoke-filled air; *too much.* I am reminded of Bertolt Brecht's criticism of empathic identification and catharsis in dramatic performance, which asserts that Western dramatic forms promote a purely empathic reaction with performers that in turn reinforces a dominant, oppressive ideology and evokes feelings of powerlessness in audiences. The empathic and resigned reactions of a dramatic spectator might include (with one significant revision), "Yes, I have felt like that too—Just like me—It's only natural—It'll never change—The sufferings of this woman appall me, because they are inescapable."[85]

This is the kind of emotional identification some feminists object to when critiquing the torch singer as a spokesperson for women's oppression—if the woman in the audience identifies with the "narrative's objectified, passive woman, she places herself in a masochistic position."[86] If she identifies with the "male hero, she becomes complicit with her own indirect objectification."[87] As dramatic spectacle, torch singing enacts a performance of emotional release; the torch singer and those in the audience who are carried away by her voice are casualties of their own despair.

But can't emotional, empathic identification lead to action? Isn't this what happened to Horne? Didn't she identify with the stories of blues and jazz?[88] Didn't she feel the power of music to inspire critical, political action, to set her own course?[89] Didn't she ask her audiences to meet her halfway, and didn't they respond?[90]

Brecht answers that he outlined an approach to epic theater that proposes an alternative to identification and demoralizing despair by encouraging spectators to critically engage dominant ideologies. The spectator of *epic* performance says, "I'd never have thought it—That's not the way—That's extraordinary, hardly believable—It's got to stop—The sufferings of this woman appall me because they are unnecessary."[91] Brecht's epic techniques are designed to outrage; to "isolate and manifest certain ideas and relationships that make ideology visible."[92]

Within the obscuring frame of a torch song, the singer uses the participatory and confrontational techniques of cabaret to move audiences out of passive, complacent spectatorship. Where Brecht's formulation seeks to publicly interrupt the covert but never all-encompassing workings of ideology, torch singing voices the invisible without getting caught. A torch singer mediates among public and hidden transcripts on gender, race, class, and sexual relations while giving a complex and ironic spin to the victim narrative. How? In an intimate and confrontational atmosphere, singers create a reciprocal relationship—a conversation—so that the palpable emotionality of a torch ballad might "jolt" audiences into critical awareness. Horne insists on reciprocity because it wagers against listening that stops at passive identification and immobilization. Reciprocity insists that it's not so much whether emotion or catharsis isn't necessary or productive, but what audiences *do* with their emotions and identifications that counts.

That's not to say, however, that Horne or anyone can be certain that audiences *hear* a resistant message or make critical interpretations. Realist assumptions about performance—assumptions that the performance will present a visually and aurally accurate (mimetic) representation of the world—can lead spectators to interpret antirealist (resistive) performance choices as *failed realist* choices.[93] And so a playful or ironic or dismissive reading of "He beats me too/what can I do" risks becoming a realist example of individual psychological failure, rather than a historically situated critique.[94]

What's more, audience activity "does not necessarily equal resistance, and that resistance is not necessarily progressive."[95] Even though the cabaret form and ironic vocalizations constitute antirealist—constructively resistive—performance choices, audience reception and reading practices are different for each spectator and the "meanings derived from any one performance . . . vary endlessly."[96]

The voice is one of the most viable and pliable instruments for sounding hidden resistance because the "communicator retains control over the manner of its dissemination."[97] What a singer needs is an audience attuned to the shadings and disguises and multiple messages of musically spoken irony. What she needs is an *aurally radical pedagogy* that gives listeners a "firm grasp of the codes of meaning being manipulated"—the "communicative force of . . . timing, tune, and nuance."[98] If your ear is trained to hear it, the critique of the torch song comes through loud and clear. This is playing by ear, a "practical consciousness of a present kind" that produces a "sensuous knowledge" in the moment of witnessing.[99]

Horne learned to sing by listening; playing by ear. She was conscious of the power of her voice as she sang "Now" and "Silent Spring" at Carnegie Hall. Radio stations and promoters banned her protests, but Horne wouldn't stop. Her performances make the audience part of something bigger than themselves. She demands that they be present, that they participate in the performance.

She does this so that they are moved out of their silence . . . and into dialogue and debate.[100]

**HOMEWORK**

I haven't practiced "When the Saints Come Marching In" once since my first lesson. And I've grown bored with "Heart and Soul," so for the past few days, I've been working on "My Man." So far, I've picked out the first two lines in G-flat, "It's cost me a lot/but there's one thing that I've got . . ." I hear Holiday's wary and weary tone in these notes, though I'm searching for Vaughan's giggling sound on "I-i-it's my ma-an."

I imagine the disappointment in the piano teacher's eyes when he sees I have not learned to play "Saints." I see his hands over mine, pressing my fingers to the keys, watching that I hit the right notes. I hear him tell me to take the music home again, to repeat my homework.

So when the day of my next lesson arrives, I call and cancel. I say something came up. And it's true. I have tickets to see Abbey Lincoln at Seattle's Jazz Showcase. I have been listening to Lincoln's voice all day—to her sparse style and luxurious sound. She sings in the simplest of terms, letting each note bend and twist on her tongue. I love the early recordings, the standards "Lonely House"[101] and "Come Sunday"[102] and "My Man."[103] Her "My Man" is a dare, a defiant stare. The piano plays a moody, thundering introduction and then Lincoln speaks-sings, "It's cos-t. *Me.* A lot. But there's one thing. That *I've.* Got"—punctuating me and I, along with the costs and losses. She adds, "It's myyyyy ma-an," in a tattling voice, signaling that her man's got some explaining to do. She announces that she's, "Cold or wet. Tiiirrred you bet," then climbs the scale on, "All of this. *I'll* soon for-get." She pauses to get her breath before her quiet admission, "With *myyyyyy* ma-an."

She moans and growls through "Ooooohhhhh. My man I. Love him so," the piano and cymbals coming into swing along with Lincoln and Holiday's sleepy phrasing. She uses a light, happy tone on "Heee'll nev-er knowww. *All my life* is just. Des-pair. But *I-I-I.* Don't care." She reaches lower for "When he takes mmeeee in his aa-rrrms," then grows sunny on "The world is. Bri-ight all-all-all-all-all ri-ight." She dips again on "What's the diff-rence. If I sa-ayyy," then opens up for "I-I-I'll go a-wayyy," before rushing into,"Whe-en I-I-I know. I'll-be-back. On-my-knees some-da-ay." Then she pauses, then bursts into "For what-ever my man ii-sss. I-I-ammm-hiii-iiiis. For-eeev-errr.

Mooooore." Her sound issues the challenge: What else do you hear? I answer: I can hear my own experience in the music's violence. I can hear the experiences of other women, different from me in every way, save one. I can move beyond passive acceptance of the victim's story and into critical attention: talking, writing, and acting in, on, and against the conditions that constrain my life and choices, women's lives and choices. I can begin by practicing, by doing my homework.

Lincoln has been singing in clubs and on record since the 1950s; she made her debut as a jazz singer on *Abbey Lincoln: That's Him!* On the cover, she is draped on a bed in a filmy white dress. She is the next "beautiful Black singer after Waters and Horne," noticeable not for her voice and musical talent (nurtured since childhood), but for her "lines, curves, arcs, and semi-circles, [all] in the tradition of the classic beauty."[104]

Like Horne, Holiday, Vaughan, Piaf, and Streisand, Lincoln began her career singing standards. Her simple phrasing and blues shadings are reminiscent of Holiday's style.[105] Though Lincoln's voice isn't full of despair. It is, instead, resoundingly disobedient. Like Horne and Holiday, she tried to cross over into film, but she didn't want to fill the role or the wardrobe of a "Black Marilyn Monroe."[106] When she began to wear her hair *natural*, everything changed.[107] She became political, insisting on civil rights[108] and "bristling" with feminine independence."[109] She fell out of favor. The critics whispered that she had become a *race woman* and a *feminist*.

Relegated to the fringes of jazz and politics, Lincoln became a composer. She wrote her own stories—stories in which women survive instead of faltering.[110] Her voice matured, its brilliant trill taking on a plaintive color and sanguine tone. She kept singing, her voice a "strong black wind blowing, gently on and on."[111]

And now, more than forty years after her debut, she steps onto small stages in supper clubs and jazz houses and sings what she has learned. She teaches her audiences how music is part devotion, part vigilant critique—against the assaults of stardom, against the wounds of a torch song.[112] Tonight, those lessons include "Blues for Momma."[113] Alongside a ringing guitar melody, Lincoln's voice pulses, a quiet siren sounding. She sings, "Hey lor-dy Ma-ma.[114] Heard you wasn't feel-in' good." There's a laughing, knowing tone in her voice when she sings, "They spread-in' dir-ty rumors. A-round the neigh-borhood." On the lines that reference "My Man," Lincoln is both incredulous and earnest, "They say you're, you're mean and evil. Heh. And don't know what to do. That's the rea-son that he's gone. . . . And left you black-and-blue." And on the refrain, her voice is doubled and lowdown; fractured and blue, asking, "Hey lordy Mama, what you gonna do? Hey lordy Mama, what you gon-na do-oo? *What* you gon-na do?" Her guitarist sings backup on this refrain, following Lincoln's lead and reflecting her questions, "What you gonna do? What you gonna do?"

She references familiar stories about stormy weather, a cheating man, and gossiping indictments of a woman who loves to fuss and fight, a woman who brings her good man down, a woman acting like a man. She asks, "Hey lordy Mama, what you gon-na do-oo? What you gon-na do?" She tries out one possible ending: "Well, a man can hate a wo-man/a man can hate his life/and learn to live with sor-row/and struggle with the strife. . . ." She pauses, considering . . . "huh." She wonders if "a man can hate a wo-man. A woman-hate-a man. And live without re-demp-tion. Any-way they can." And then the ringing question, "Hey lordy Mama/what you gon-na do-oo? What you gon-na do?"

In the last verse, Lincoln offers another possibility. She begins, "Well the wheels of life keep turnin'" and the guitarist says, "Yes." Lincoln goes on, "and they bring about a change." The guitar player agrees, singing, "bring about a change." Then Lincoln references another Holiday tune, "Strange Fruit." She sings, "Sometimes the fruit is bit-ter." The guitarist replies, "Yes, it is." Lincoln continues, "Sometimes life is strange," not waiting for a reply before she sings, "Wheels of life keep turnin'." Lincoln ascends the scale as she sings, "Beginnings bring an end" before settling on hope: "There's al-ways a to-mor-row. And one day he'll need a frie-end. Hey lordy Mama, what you gon-na do-oo. What you gon-na do?" Lincoln leaves the story open, with an expansive play of repetition: "Hey lordy Mama. Hey lordy Mama. What, you gonna do? What, what you gon-na do-oooo? What you gonna do-oooo?" The conversation reflects the displacements and condensations of power relationships[115] while leaving room for glimpses of possibility.

She is Lincoln, and she is also Holiday and Vaughan and Piaf, looking into my eyes[116] and speaking to me.[117] She laughs, "Shake your shoul-ders. Do a *dance.* Ne-ver mind a sad romance"[118] and we hear each other's stories. She calls, "A time has come. A cor-ner turned. It's clear-er now. The les-sons learned. And time will tell. And fires burn," and I answer in my attentiveness, in willingness to meet her halfway, in my resolve to tell on, in, and through our differences.

**Seeing and Hearing**

Before I sit down to write about seeing and hearing Lincoln, I return to "Numbering the Hairs of Our Heads." I reread the underlined passage that says, "white women are not outside the channels through which surveillance, and the power that attends it, circulate."[119] I reread Toni Morrison's assertion that "it is a source of amusement . . . to black women to listen to feminist talk of liberation while somebody's nice black grandmother shoulders the daily responsibility of child rearing and floor mopping and the liberated one comes home to examine the housekeeping. . . ."[120] Hunter's and Morrison's comments underline a critique of feminism's white, middle-class, heterosexual second wave raised by women of color, women of the working class, women whose desires don't dance to the pulse of a compulsory heterosexuality. Their comments raise the question of difference, along with the question of standpoints.

Standpoints are ways of seeing and hearing the world. They are not static, nor are they bestowed on individuals by virtue of their race, class, gender, or sexual preference.[121] They are *constructed*; rooted in the facts and acts that compose women's lives. Standpoints "name where we are and are not"—they are partial and particular, mobile and "situated knowledges" learned in the body, in how and what we learn to see and hear.[122] Feminist tactics that depend on complexity and contradiction, standpoints work to transform "individuals into resistant, oppositional, and collective subjects."[123]

Creating and deploying standpoints is a process—a performance—that relies on the sounds and sights our bodies make, together and alone, in the shift and movement among identification and counteridentification. In torch singing performances, audiences are presented with varying and conflicting identities and images of women's experience and are asked to identify with some images and to reject (counteridentify with) others.[124] Standpoints also make room for exploring and exploding—through identification and disidentification—differences that bring together and hold women apart, not only *between* and *among* social/cultural/political categories, but also *within* subject positions.[125]

Standpoints, or "identities-in-difference,"[126] suggest that the opposition of empathy and outrage (dramatic and epic performance) might also be read as a nesting of contradictory, though not separate, positions—for example, empathy-in-difference and outrage-in-marginalization. Here, the emotional response of audiences isn't symptomatic of a willingness to relinquish complexity, critical perspective, or the ability to act. Instead, complexity, perspective, and action are incited by an emotional experience and empathy is a necessary and productive means for identifying with others within and across difference.[127] Audiences are asked to read between and across the lines of a torch song; to imagine how we have felt like that, too—"Just like me, just like you" *as well as* "That's not the way I am, you are, we are . . . these false representations have got to stop . . . these sufferings appall us because they are unnecessary." Such readings don't require textual or musical literacy—knowledge that comes with formal training in paradigm keys. They ask that we learn by listening, that we play it by ear.

This is what I felt as I listened to Lincoln's voice, what I imagined when her eyes met mine. Our experiences are not synonymous, unified; Lincoln started singing when the world was looking for an African American Marilyn Monroe. She became a jazz musician instead, playing around with rhythm and sound so she wouldn't become a casualty of the music.[128] She sings to honor her teachers—Billie Holiday among them—and her performances are an inspiration to the students of her sound.[129] I was born in 1966, not long after Lincoln was "blacklisted" by Hollywood and popular music.[130] I haven't been asked to represent white women or to pose for an identity I did not choose. I haven't been denied access to do the work I wanted. I am not a musician; I can't compose music or even carry a tune. I am humbled by the knowledge that Lincoln's protests and struggles made my own feminism possible. And yet, sitting in the audience and listening to Lincoln's voice and looking into her eyes, I recognized how our stories speak together—not in spite of our differences, but in and because of them. I felt how we created contingent, contested understandings in between and across the divide of our lives, all in time with the music.

After seeing and hearing Lincoln, I don't return to the piano lessons or to work on "When the Saints Come Marching In." Instead, I keep listening and playing, adding new songs to my repertoire—first "My Man," then "Stormy Weather" and "Save Me," then "Not to Worry." I place my fingers on the keys and let them find their way into the music, into new positions, into spaces full of possibility.

## OPENING

Years later, Alice rewrites the ending to the story about her musical consciousness raising. In the new ending, the man who is not her husband and violence and Billie Holiday and feminism help her learn how torch singing acts on the violence written into a torch song—how it tends love's wounds.

And then she writes over this statement, too, deciding that torch singing creates an opening—that it doesn't so much tend the wounds as make space for an emergent resistance, "*something to be done.*"[131]

## OTHER VISIONS, OTHER SOUNDS

1. Julia Kristeva, "Tales of Love," in *The Portable Kristeva*, ed. Kelly Oliver, 171 (New York: Columbia University Press, 1997).

2. Elizabeth Hardwick, "Billie Holiday: Sleepless Nights," in *The Billie Holiday Companion: Seven Decades of Commentary*, ed. Leslie Gourse, 166 (New York: Schirmer, 1997).

3. Adapted from Geoff Dyer, *But Beautiful: A Book about Jazz* (New York: North Point, 1996), 133, who, writing about Chet Baker, notes, "With Chet the song did all the work; all Chet had to do was bring out the bruised tenderness that is there in all old songs."

4. Jacques Derrida, *Writing and Difference*, trans. Alan Bass (Chicago: University of Chicago Press, 1978), 285. I am "sampling" Derrida's writing about Claude Lévi-Strauss's notion of the bricoleur. Derrida writes, "The *bricoleur*, says Lévi-Strauss, is someone who uses 'the means at hand,' that is, the instruments he finds at his disposition around him, those which are already there, which had not been especially conceived with an eye to the operation for which they are to be used and to which one tries by trial and error to adapt them, not hesitating to change them whenever it appears necessary, or to try several of them at once, even if their form and their origin are heterogeneous—and so forth."

5. Krim Benterrak, Stephen Muecke, and Paddy Roe, *Reading the Country: Introduction to Nomadology* (Fremantle, Australia: Fremantle Arts, 1984), 148, emphasis mine. The authors write, "*Bricolage* becomes visible when we can *trace* the origins of the different pieces making up the whole."

6. Of "structures of feeling," Raymond Williams, *Marxism and Literature* (New York: Oxford University Press, 1977), 132, writes, "We are talking about characteristic elements of impulse, restraint, and tone; specifically affective elements of consciousness and relationships: not feeling against thought, but thought as felt and feeling as thought: practical consciousness of a present kind, in a living and interrelating continuity."

7. Williams, *Marxism and Literature*, 131. Williams writes, "Practical consciousness is almost always different from official consciousness, and this is not only a matter of relative freedom or control. For practical consciousness is what is actually being lived, and not only what it is thought is being lived."

8. Williams, *Marxism and Literature*, 133–34. Williams notes, "For structures of feeling can be defined as social experiences in solution, as distinct from other social semantic formations

which have been precipitated and are more evidently and more immediately available. . . .Yet this specific solution is never mere flux. It is a structured formation . . . [that] is at the very edge of semantic availability."

9. Terry Eagleton, *Walter Benjamin; or, Towards a Revolutionary Criticism* (London: Verso, 1981), 48, writes, "Structures of feeling are "those elusive, impalpable forms of social consciousness which are at once as evanescent as 'feelings' suggests, but nevertheless display a significant configuration captured in the term 'structure.'"

10. Sampling Williams, *Marxism and Literature*, Avery F. Gordon, *Ghostly Matters: Haunting and the Sociological Imagination* (Minneapolis: University of Minnesota Press, 1997), 200, writes, "A structure of feeling is precisely that conception, or sensuous knowledge, of a historical materialism characterized constitutively by the tangle of the subjective and the objective, experience and belief, feeling and thought, the immediate and the general, the personal and the social. A structure of feeling 'articulates presence' as the tangled exchange of noisy silences and seething absences."

11. Gordon, *Ghostly Matters*, 201. Gordon writes, "I have offered a cultural hypothesis: haunting is a shared structure of feeling, a shared possession, a specific type of sociality. . . . Haunting is the sociality of living with ghosts, a sociality both tangible and tactile as well as ephemeral and imaginary."

12. Gordon, *Ghostly Matters*, 207. Gordon notes, "When I am a spooky phantom you want to avoid, when there is nothing but the shadow of a public civic life, when bedrooms and boardrooms are clamorous ghost chambers, deep 'wounds in civilization' are in haunting evidence. . . . The ghost always registers the actual 'degraded present' in which we are inextricably and historically entangled and the longing for the arrival of a future, entangled certainly, but ripe in the plentitude of nonsacrificial freedoms and exuberant unforeseen pleasures."

13. These lines are drawn from Farah Jasmine Griffin's extended analysis (*If You Can't Be Free, Be a Mystery: In Search of Billie Holiday* [New York: Free Press, 2001], 88–89) of a recorded rehearsal of Billie Holiday, pianist Jimmy Rowles, and bassist Artie Shapiro. Griffin asserts that this recording evidences Holiday's musical expertise and rhythmic sophistication. The discussion among Holiday, Rowles, and Shapiro centers on Holiday's preference for singing in G-flat. Griffin writes,

> G-flat is one of the hardest keys in which to play, especially for those who are used to playing in the key of C or the C-major scale. However, the key has a long history with blues and jazz musicians. [Salim] Washington says G-flat is an especially difficult key for those who learned to play by reading music as opposed to those who learned to play by ear. "This opposition between literacy and orality is significant in this case because those who learn to play by reading music invariably learn from a paradigm which contains no sharps or flats: the key of C. Those who learn to play by ear, depending on their instrument, do not necessarily . . . learn from a paradigm key."

For an extended discussion of Holiday's musicianship—particularly her way with instrumental techniques—see Kate Daubney, "Songbird or Subversive? Instrumental Vocalisation Technique in the Songs of Billie Holiday," *Journal of Gender Studies* 11, no. 1 (2002): 17–28.

14. I am sampling Gordon, *Ghostly Matters*, 201.

15. See Stacy Holman Jones, "The Way We Were, Are, and Might Be: Torch Singing as Autoethnography," in *Ethnographically Speaking: Autoethnography, Literature, and Aesthetics*, ed. Arthur P. Bochner and Carolyn Ellis, 47–48 (Walnut Creek, CA: AltaMira, 2001).

16. Susan McClary, *Feminine Endings: Music, Gender, and Sexuality* (Minneapolis: University of Minnesota Press, 1991), 4.

17. Angela Y. Davis, *Blues Legacies and Black Feminism: Gertrude "Ma" Rainey, Bessie Smith, and Billie Holiday* (New York: Pantheon, 1998), 178–79.

18. A. Davis, *Blue Legacies*, 179–80.

19. Anne Marie Hunter, "Numbering the Hairs of Our Heads: Male Social Control and the All-Seeing Male God," *Journal of Feminist Studies in Religion* 8, no. 2 (1992): 8.

20. Lenore Walker, quoted in Hunter, "Numbering the Hairs," 9.

21. Hunter, "Numbering the Hairs," 8.

22. Hunter, "Numbering the Hairs," 14.

23. Hunter, "Numbering the Hairs," 22. For an extended discussion of the ways in which women's bodies are sites and sights of what Foucault terms the "micro–physics of power" as well as how women's bodies are a particular feminine manifestation and performance of such power dynamics, see Sandra Lee Bartky, "Foucault, Femininity, and the Modernization of Patriarchal Power," in *Femininity and Domination: Studies in the Phenomenology of Oppression*, 63–82 (New York: Routledge, 1991).

24. Hunter, "Numbering the Hairs," 17.

25. Hunter, "Numbering the Hairs," 15.

26. Hunter, "Numbering the Hairs," 22.

27. Hunter, "Numbering the Hairs," 8.

28. Audre Lorde quoted in Hunter, "Numbering the Hairs," 22.

29. Hunter, "Numbering the Hairs," 22–23.

30. Hunter, "Numbering the Hairs," 26.

31. Jill Dolan, *Presence and Desire: Essays on Gender, Sexuality, Performance* (Ann Arbor: University of Michigan Press, 1933), 47–48. This line borrows from Dolan, who in describing the materialist feminist perspective on theater criticism writes, "The theater apparatus, then, includes the stage, lights, sets, casting, blocking, gestures, the location of the auditorium and the cost of the tickets, the advertising, the length of the run—all the material and ideological forces that shape what a theater event means."

32. A. Davis, *Blues Legacies*, 56.

33. I am referencing Judith Butler, *Gender Trouble: Feminism and the Subversion of Identity* (New York: Routledge, 1990), 140–41, 145, when she writes, "Gender ought not to be construed as a stable identity or locus of agency from which various acts follow; rather gender is an identity tenuously constituted in time, instituted in an exterior space through a *stylized repetition of acts*. . . . If gender attributes, however, are not expressive but performative, then these attributes effectively constitute the identity they are said to express or reveal. . . . The injunction *to be* a given gender produces necessary failures, a variety of incoherent configurations that in their multiplicity exceed and defy the injunction by which they are generated."

34. I make this comment in terms of how I hear torch singing, as well as in response to "shifts in emphasis from space to time, from sight and vision to sound and voice, from text to performance, from authority to vulnerability" in ethnography, as noted by Dwight Conquergood in "Rethinking Ethnography: Towards a Critical Cultural Politics," *Communication Monographs* 58 (June 1991): 183. Conquergood is encouraging ethnography's shift from the "visualist bias of positivism" and the "detachment and distance" of "sight and surveillance" in favor of the aural privileging of "temporal process, proximity, and incorporation" meant to return the researcher's (and researched's) bodies, hearts, and minds to the doing and writing of ethnography. In my research on torch singing, I found the complex interactions between vision and voice to be at the heart of torch singing's critique, though I, too, want to privilege hearing and the sounds of voices in this text.

35. Dana L. Cloud, *Control and Consolation in American Culture and Politics: Rhetorics of Therapy* (Thousand Oaks, CA: Sage, 1998), 111.

36. Sarah Vaughan, "Lover, Come Back to Me," lyrics by Oscar Hammerstein II and Sigmund Romberg, *Embraceable You*, Laserlight, 1996. My discussion is based on this recording.

37. George Gershwin and Ira Gershwin, lyrics for "They Can't Take That Away from Me," LyricsFreak, n.d., www.lyricsfreak.com/b/billie-holiday/18026.html (accessed June 3, 2005).

38. Susannah McCorkle, "'I Swear I Won't Call No Copper If I'm Beat Up by My Poppa,'" *New York Times Magazine*, January 9, 1994, 33.

39. McCorkle, "'I Swear I Won't Call No Copper,'" 33.

40. McCorkle, "'I Swear I Won't Call No Copper,'" 33.

41. McCorkle, "'I Swear I Won't Call No Copper,'" 33.

42. McCorkle, "'I Swear I Won't Call No Copper,'" 33.

43. McCorkle, "'I Swear I Won't Call No Copper,'" 33. See Percival Granger, Robert Prince, and Clarence Williams, lyrics for "Ain't Nobody's Business If I Do," Running Horse Lyrics Page, n.d., www.therunninghorse.ukpub.net/lyrics.html (accessed July 8, 2005).

44. McCorkle, "'I Swear I Won't Call No Copper,'" 33.

45. McCorkle, "'I Swear I Won't Call No Copper,'" 33.

46. McCorkle, "'I Swear I Won't Call No Copper,'" 33.

47. McCorkle, "'I Swear I Won't Call No Copper,'" 33.

48. I am borrowing this phrase from Cloud, *Control and Consolation*, 128, who writes, "Feminism's second wave attempted to raise consciousness of women who shared their oppression in common as a first step toward political change."

49. Laura Kipnis, "Feminism: The Political Consequence of Postmodernism?" in *Universal Abandon? The Politics of Postmodernism*, ed. Andrew Ross, 158 (Minneapolis: University of Minnesota Press, 1988).

50. Gordon, *Ghostly Matters*, 16, and James C. Scott, *Domination and the Arts of Resistance: Hidden Transcripts* (New Haven, CT: Yale University Press, 1990), xiii.

51. See "Susannah McCorkle, 55; Jazz-Pop Singer and Writer," *Washington Post*, May 19, 2001, www.washingtonpost.com/wp-dyn/acticles/A50453-2001May19.html (accessed May 19, 2001), and Gwenda Blair, "Jazz Bird," *New York* magazine, June 3, 2002, www.newyorkmetro.com/nymetro/arts/music/jazz/reviews/6064 (accessed June 16, 2005).

52. Griffin, *If You Can't Be Free*, 28, discusses the popular conception of Billie Holiday as a tragic figure. She writes, "Holiday's performances allow her listeners to experience the cathartic release of their own personal sense of sorrow and tragedy. We think of her in tragic terms because there are elements of her life that reinforce our own sense of tragedy and that allow us to confront and explore our own despair without losing ourselves in it."

53. James Haskins, *Lena: A Personal and Professional Biography of Lena Horne*, with Kathleen Benson (New York: Stein, 1984), 23, 26, describes Horne as "tall, slim, light-skinned, [with] 'good' hair, and . . . young." According to Haskins, this light-skinned, straight-haired, beautiful, young "look" was *the* look of the Cotton Club chorus girls.

54. Gail Lumet Buckley, *The Hornes: An American Family* (New York: Knopf, 1986), 120–21.

55. Music critic Nat Hentoff quoted in Haskins, *Lena*, 180.

56. Lumet Buckley, *The Hornes*, 120.

57. Haskins, *Lena*, 39–40.

58. Lumet Buckley, *The Hornes*, 140–41, describes Horne's audition for Café Society owner Barney Josephson.

59. Leon René, Otis René Jr., and Clarence Muse, lyrics for "Sleepytime Down South," n.d., http://users.bart.nlo/ecduzit/billy/song/song261.html (accessed April 20, 2001).

60. Lumet Buckley, *The Hornes*, 141, and Lena Horne and Richard Schickel, *Lena* (Garden City, NY: Doubleday, 1965), 113–15. This conversation is constructed from accounts given by Lumet Buckley and Horne of her audition for Barney Josephson.

61. Horne and Schickel, *Lena*, 117–119. See also Michael Denning, *The Cultural Front: The Laboring of American Culture in the Twentieth Century* (London: Verso, 1997), 339, 347.

62. I'm referencing W. E. B. Du Bois's concept of "double consciousness" outlined in *The Souls of Black Folk: Essays and Sketches* (New York: Fawcett, 1961), 17. Du Bois writes that double consciousness is a doubled existence experienced by African Americans, a sense of "always looking at one's self through the eyes of others."

63. Denning, *Cultural Front*, 339.

64. bell hooks, "Performance Practice as a Site of Opposition," in *Let's Get It On: The Politics of Black Performance*, ed. Catherine Ugwu, 221 (Seattle: Bay, 1995).

65. Henry J. Elam Jr., *Taking It to the Streets: The Social Protest Theater of Luis Valdez and Amiri Baraka* (Ann Arbor: University of Michigan Press, 1997), 78.

66. hooks, "Performance Practice," 221.

67. Oyin Ogunba, "Traditional African Festival Drama," in *Theatre in Africa*, ed. Oyin Ogunba and Abiola Irele, 22 (Ibadan, Nigeria: Ibadan University Press, 1978), emphasis mine. Reciprocity is a key feature of African American performance.

68. Jon Panish, *The Color of Jazz: Race and Representation in Postwar American Culture* (Jackson: University of Mississippi Press, 1997), 80.

69. Lena Horne, "Bewitched, Bothered, and Bewildered," lyrics by Lorenz Hart and Richard Rodgers, *Lena Horne—The Lady and Her Music: Live on Broadway*, Warner Brothers, 1995. My discussion is based on this recording.

70. Robert E. Johnson, "Lena Horne Burns Broadway with Hot Songs and Biting Rap," *Jet* (July 23, 1981): 55.

71. Ralph Harris, Horne's road manager, quoted in Haskins, *Lena*, 136.

72. Elam, *Taking It to the Streets*, 112.

73. Ogunba, "Traditional African Festival Drama," 18.

74. Ogunba, "Traditional African Festival Drama," 22–23.

75. Elam, *Taking It to the Streets*, 112.

76. Gordon, *Ghostly Matters*, 200.

77. These lines are drawn from Lisa Appignanesi, *The Cabaret*, 2nd ed. (New York: Grove, 1984), 64, who notes that the inception of the Lapin Agile corresponded with the "years whose

imaginative exuberance was to give direction to art for the next half-century," and asserts that "the cabaret became increasingly a salon for the avant-garde. . . . Its artistic dissent paralleled the cabaret's parody of entrenched values, both social and artistic. Humour—ranging in kind from a comic childlikeness to biting satire—marked both; and seriously exploited the popular elements in art."

78. Appignanesi, *Cabaret*, 64.

79. Picasso, Apollinaire, and Utrillo were painters; Jacob was a writer.

80. Appignanesi, *Cabaret*, 65–67.

81. Appignanesi, *Cabaret*, 69–70.

82. Appignanesi, *Cabaret*, 70–71. She notes, "The poet, Gaston Coute, author of *Chansons d'un gars qu'a mal tourné*, could often be seen lying dead drunk on a bench."

83. Writing about structures of feeling, Williams, *Marxism and Literature*, 132, notes that they are social rather than personal experience in two ways: "First, in that they are changes in presence (while they are being lived this is obvious; when they have been lived it is still their substantial characteristic); second, in that although they are emergent or pre-emergent, they do not have to await definition, classification, or rationalization before they exert palpable pressures and set effective limits on experience and on action."

84. John Moore, "'The Hieroglyphics of Love': The Torch Singers and Interpretation," *Popular Music* 8, no. 1 (1989): 42. The highly charged and emotional atmosphere evoked in Moore's description is referenced in biographies and criticism. See Will Friedwald, *Jazz Singing: America's Great Voices from Bessie Smith to Bebop and Beyond* (New York: Da Capo, 1996), on Holiday; Johnson, "Lena Horne Burns Broadway," on Horne; Leslie Gourse: *Sassy: The Life of Sarah Vaughan* (New York: Da Capo, 1994), on Vaughan; Margaret Crosland, *Piaf* (New York: Fromm, 1987), on Piaf; and William Robertson, *k. d. lang: Carrying the Torch* (Toronto: ECW Press, 1992) on lang, respectively.

85. Bertolt Brecht, *Brecht on Theatre*, ed. John Willett (New York: Hill, 1991), 71.

86. Jill Dolan, "The Discourse of Feminisms: The Spectator and Representation," in *The Routledge Reader in Gender and Performance*, ed. Lizbeth Goodman, with Jane de Gay, 291 (London: Routledge, 1998). See also hooks, "Performance Practice," 211.

87. Dolan, "Discourse of Feminisms," 291.

88. Horne and Schickel, *Lena*, 114.

89. Horne and Schickel, *Lena*, 117–19.

90. Horne and Schickel, *Lena*, 290.

91. Brecht, *Brecht on Theatre*, 71.

92. Janelle Reinelt, "Beyond Brecht: Britain's New Feminist Drama," in *Performing Feminisms: Feminist Critical Theory and Theatre,* ed. Sue-Ellen Case, 150 (Baltimore: Johns Hopkins University Press, 1990).

93. Stacy Wolf, "Talking about Pornography, Talking about Theatre: Ethnography, Critical Pedagogy, and the Production of 'Educated' Audiences of 'Etta Jenks' in Madison," *Theatre Research International* 19, no. 1 (1994): 29–37, par. 36, www.infotrac.com (accessed June 4, 2005).

94. Wolf, "Talking about Pornography," par. 39.

95. David Sholle quoted in Wolf, "Talking about Pornography," par. 36.

96. Dolan, *Presence and Desire,* 293.

97. Scott, *Domination,* 161.

98. Scott, *Domination,* 139, 155, 137.

99. Williams, *Marxism and Literature,* 132, and Gordon, *Ghostly Matters,* 200.

100. Horne and Schickel, *Lena,* 288–91, writes that "Silent Spring" is a song dedicated to the memory of the four children who died in the bombing of the Sixteenth Street Baptist Church in Birmingham, Alabama, in September 1963, with lyrics by E. Y. Harburg and Harold Arlen. "Now" is a civil rights protest song set to the tune of "Hava Nagillah," with lyrics by Adolph Green and Betty Comden. Horne sang both of these numbers at a Student Nonviolent Coordinating Committee fundraiser held at Carnegie Hall, which she headlined along with Frank Sinatra (who was raising money for the International Orphan's Fund). Of the evening's performance, Horne writes, "Everybody in the audience felt that he [sic] was a part of something big and good. I was so thrilled that I had to say something. 'I don't make speeches,' I said, 'but tonight I have this overwhelming pride that I am a New Yorker.' Everybody yelled and clapped and clapped—for themselves, I thought, because they were all participating in something bigger than himself." See also Haskins, *Lena,* 154–58, and Lumet Buckley, *The Hornes,* 247–48.

101. Abbey Lincoln, "Lonely House," lyrics by Langston Hughes and Kurt Weill, *Abbey Is Blue,* rec. 1959, Riverside, 1987.

102. Abbey Lincoln, "Come Sunday," lyrics by Duke Ellington, *Abbey Is Blue,* rec. 1959, Fantasy, 1987.

103. Abbey Lincoln, "My Man," lyrics by Albert Willemetz and Jacques Charles, music by Maurice Yvain, trans. Channing Pollock, *Abbey Lincoln: That's Him,* rec. 1958, Fantasy, 1988. My discussion is based on this recording.

104. Lyricist, producer, and manager Bob Russell, quoted in Gary Giddens, *Visions of Jazz: The First Century* (New York: Oxford University Press, 1998), 576.

105. Giddens, *Visions of Jazz*, 578.

106. J. Nelson, "Abbey Lincoln," *Essence* 22, no. 12 (April 1991): 72, notes, "Abbey Lincoln has come a long way since her early days as a 'colored' sex kitten, a 'Black Marilyn Monroe . . . in the Marilyn Monroe Dress,' a skintight number that hugs her voluptuous body" (and that Monroe wore in *Gentlemen Prefer Blondes*). Lincoln made her film debut in *The Girl Can't Help It* and later appeared in the civil rights-inspired film *Nothing but a Man* and starred opposite Sidney Poitier in *For the Love of Ivy*. See "Abbey Lincoln, Biography," n.d., www.bsoinc.com/AbbeyLincoln.html, par. 5 (accessed April 20, 2001).

107. Giddens, *Visions of Jazz*, 576–77.

108. Lincoln collaborated with Max Roach, Coleman Hawkins, and Olatunji on *We Insist! Freedom Now Suite* (Candid Records, 1958).

109. Giddens, *Visions of Jazz*, 577.

110. Giddens, *Visions of Jazz*, 581, notes that like Holiday and Piaf, Lincoln is "urgently personal in singing standard songs. With this difference: They sang of survival while faltering; Lincoln presents an image of revitalization and strength."

111. Nikki Giovanni quoted in Giddens, *Visions of Jazz*, 576.

112. This line is drawn from Griffin, *If You Can't Be Free*, 189–90, who writes that Lincoln's work (essays, poems, song lyrics, music, performances, and interviews) contributes to "the black woman intellectual's responsibility to Holiday: to maintain a vigilant critique against efforts that assault her personhood and her intellect. In defending her, we defend ourselves." Griffin also writes that Lincoln's music is a meditative, creative act, a "form of devotion." While Griffin's work focuses specifically on Holiday (and here, the comparisons made between Holiday and Lincoln and the work of black woman intellectuals), I'd like to suggest that Lincoln's singing *also* contributes to a critique against efforts to assault a torch singer's personhood and intellect, as well as how torch singing might constitute a form of devotion.

113. Abbey Lincoln, "Blues for Momma," lyrics by Abbey Lincoln and Nina Simone, *A Turtle's Dream*, Verve, 1995. My discussion is based on this recording.

114. In Lincoln's liner notes, "Momma" is always capitalized. I have followed Lincoln's convention in this text.

115. This line is drawn from Eric Lott, *Love and Theft: Blackface Minstrelsy and the American Working Class* (New York: Oxford University Press, 1993), 8, who writes that blackface performances (which I cite in chapter 3, "Sing Me a Torch Song," as instances of performing hidden transcripts), *signify* (rather than repeat) power relations in a "distorted mirror, reflecting displacements and condensations and discontinuities between which [power relationships] and the social field there exist lags, unevennesses, multiple determinations."

116. Crosland, *Piaf*, 194, on Piaf; Alice Adams, *Listening to Billie* (New York: Knopf, 1978), 7, on Holiday; and Haskins, *Lena*, 134, on Horne.

117. Giddens, *Visions of Jazz*, 580, asserts that Lincoln gave "an audience the delusion that [she] was speaking individually to each member. . . . That kind of bond between performer and onlooker exemplifies a collaborative subversion of reality and common sense." Unlike Giddens, my experience of Lincoln's performance did not give me the "delusion" she was speaking to me. And where we might have engaged in a "collaborative subversion," it was not of reality and common sense, but rather of the normative discourses surrounding race, class, gender, and sexual preference.

118. Abbey Lincoln, "Not to Worry," *A Turtle's Dream*, Verve, 1995. My discussion is based on this recording.

119. Hunter, "Numbering the Hairs," 12.

120. Toni Morrison quoted in Hunter, "Numbering the Hairs," 12.

121. Nancy C. M. Hartsock, "Comment on Hekman's 'Truth and Method: Feminist Standpoint Theory Revisited': Truth or Justice," *Signs: Journal of Women in Culture and Society* 22, no. 2 (Winter 1997): 367–375, http://sbweb2.med.icanet.com/infotrac, par. 16 (accessed June 4, 2005).

122. Donna J. Haraway, "Situated Knowledges: The Science Question in Feminism and the Privilege of Partial Perspective," *Feminist Studies* 14, no. 3 (1988): 582, 583.

123. Hartsock, "Comment," par. 17.

124. Dolan, *Presence and Desire*, 48.

125. José Esteban Muñoz, *Disidentifications: Queers of Color and the Performance of Politics* (Minneapolis: University of Minnesota Press, 1999), 19, writes, "Disidentification negotiates strategies of resistance within the flux of discourse and power. It understands that counterdiscourses, like discourse, can always fluctuate for different ideological ends and a politicized agent must have the ability to adapt and shift as quickly as power does within discourse." See also Chandra Talpade Mohanty, *Feminism without Borders: Decolonizing Theory, Practicing Solidarity* (Durham, NC: Duke University Press, 2003), 226.

126. "Identities-in-difference" is Muñoz's (*Disidentifications*, 6, 7) term, which he borrows from the ideas of Third World Feminists and radical women of color (including Chela Sandoval's differential consciousness, discussed in chapter 7, "Hopeful Openness"). Such identities-in-difference are processual becoming, performative "sites of emergence."

127. Josephine Lee, "Pity and Terror as Public Acts: Reading Feminist Politics in the Plays of Maria Irene Fornes," in *Staging Resistance: Essays on Political Theater*, ed. Jeanne Colleran and Jenny S. Spencer, 184 (Ann Arbor: University of Michigan Press, 1998).

128. Lincoln quoted in Griffin, *If You Can't Be Free*, 182, says, "I discovered that you become what you sing. You can't repeat lyrics night after night as though they were prayer without having them come true in your own life."

129. Griffin, *If You Can't Be Free*, 188, 191, asserts that Lincoln's "Billie Holiday tributes are an offering to an honored ancestor" and believes that "Abbey Lincoln stands at the crossroads as an important link between the tradition initiated and embodied by Billie Holiday and that which points to our future. Her work and interpretation of her life through that work can serve not as a model, but an inspiration to all young people, especially young black women, regardless of their chosen paths." Griffin, *If You Can't Be Free*, 180, also argues based on her reading of Abbey Lincoln's 1966 essay "Who Will Revere the Black Woman" (reprinted in *Black Woman*, ed. Toni Cade, 82–87 [New York: New American Library, 1970]), that Lincoln did not believe "black and white women can join in a movement for women's liberation." Griffin's analysis of Lincoln's recent work does not suggest whether she believes Lincoln still holds this opinion. Like Griffin, I speak from my particular, situated location, and like Griffin, I find Lincoln's music to be an inspiration and an important voice in the feminist conversation that seeks to bridge (while still acknowledging) racial distances.

130. Griffin, *If You Can't Be Free*, 182, 169, writes, "By the end of the sixties, Lincoln found herself blacklisted in the U.S." She uses the term *blacklisted* to describe the industry's reaction to Lincoln's decision to become a "serious" jazz musician committed to "black culture and the black freedom struggle."

131. Gordon, *Ghostly Matters*, 202, writes that Williams's structure of feeling proposes an "emergent solution," "something to be done."

# 7

# Hopeful Openness

Picture how in the expansive scan of narrative space connections between things are always partial . . . there is always something more to say, always an uncaptured excess that provokes further questions, new associations that just come, and fresh gaps in understanding.

—*Kathleen Stewart,* A Space on the Side of the Road[1]

Space is not merely a container in which human action transpires but instead simultaneously a product and producer of action.

—*Kirk W. Fuoss, "Performance as Contestation"*[2]

We must not deny the way aesthetics serves as the foundation for emerging visions. It is, for some of us, critical space that inspires and encourages artistic endeavor. The ways we interpret that space and inhabit it differ.

—*bell hooks,* Yearning[3]

---

**WAITING, POSSIBLE**

The first time I see Janet Rayor, she is a big, beautiful bird. She is a long-legged gazelle prancing daintily among the cocktail tables and scattered chairs in Seattle's Blue Window Bar. Like the other patrons, I crane my neck to see her towering above me. Her lips are pursed and her eyes dart wildly around the room. Audience members giggle and blush when she moves over them, pecking mischievously. Her head bobs and sways. Pink and purple down catches the air and hovers above our heads. Rayor is a dancer, an actress, a cabaret performer. She teeters deftly on stilts, transforming herself into a floating curiosity, and we eagerly follow her every move.

After a while, the happy hour crowd loses interest and returns to their drinks and after-work conversations. I continue to watch her move through the bar, marveling at her grace. Rayor takes one last turn through the audience and then ducks into the dressing room.

I get up and follow her on the pretense of looking for the restroom. The dressing room door is ajar, and I see Rayor remove feathers and beads. I see her exposed legs strapped into what seem to me—a woman afraid of heights—heart-stoppingly high stilts. I see her head bowed, her neck curved to the line of the ceiling. I know I am trespassing here, watching Rayor's backstage rituals, looking through the space between yours and mine into a scene that doesn't include me. I look away, ashamed at my intrusion. I keep moving down the hall, into the dead end. I turn and walk back toward the bar. When I pass the dressing room a second time, I can't resist looking, but the door is closed.

Rayor returns as the singer in Rouge, an ensemble that plays French cabaret music—Piaf, Jacques Brel, and Josephine Baker.[4] She sings many of the Piaf numbers I've come to love—"La Vie en Rose" and "Bravo Pour le Clown" and "La Foule." "La Foule" is one of Rayor's favorites. She loves the language and the beauty of the lyric, the dreamlike quality of the story. She loves how the man and the woman find each other in a crowd, how they become "one body."[5] She loves, too, the moment of separation, when the lovers are pulled away from each other and become, once again, alone.

She has always wanted to sing this song. It fits her mood, her zest for living, her voice. Only I don't know these things, at least not yet. I haven't worked up the courage to introduce myself to Rayor, to ask if she wouldn't mind talking about cabaret and Piaf and torch singing. I haven't accepted an invitation to drive to her house on a cloudy Thursday for an interview. I haven't been invited into her kitchen for tea and conversation while she washes and dries the dishes. I haven't watched Rayor pull up a chair to sit and talk, only to push and dance around it instead.

## AN EMPTY SPACE

I wait for you, an empty space inside an empty auditorium. Minutes stretch into hours and then suddenly the house is flooded with light. I wait for you to rush into the room, deciding. I wait for you to choose your place and settle in with elbows on tables and belongings scattered all around us. It's not quite like being at home, among your own things and people, though I can imagine you there, talking and laughing and sipping wine and waiting for something to happen. You bring your private habits and sorrows here—twisting and tearing at paper napkins, waiting for the music to start. I can't seem to give or bend to quiet your worries. I can't seem to tell you that this moment isn't alone, separate, homebound. I can't seem to say that this space—not owing to being public but perhaps because of it—is uncertain, a provocation to desire.[6] I can't ask you to imagine how you'll find yourself both inside and outside the music, both seduced and watchful.[7] Though I can imagine what you'll say within remembered scenes and unfolding events.[8] I can't do or ask or say these things, but I can wait. I can wait until you look into the emptiness around you and see an opening to things unheard and places unknown.

I wait for you, an empty space inside an empty auditorium. I am at right angles, constrained, fixed. I am a bit embarrassed at how formulaic I've become—a variation on a theme, a standard. Still, I derive pleasure and possibility in placement, in repetition, in constant reiteration. I am a form that demands a certain twist, a change in perspective, an ironic poetic that only you can give me.[9] I don't see myself as vacant, vacuous, empty. Only waiting, possible.

**PLAYBACK**

Alice dreams she is in the red theater, only now the crowd is gone and the stage is empty. She plays back the music, this time at a slower speed, endless revolutions per minute. She savors each note, each twist and bend and growl and running scale. In the spaces between notes, between bars, and between words, Alice hears an opening, a gathering presence. She hears it in the haunting reminders of Holiday's and Streisand's and Piaf's voices,[10] and yes, in Vaughan's trilling bravado.[11] Vaughan's style—her range, her improvisation, her constant variation of pitch and color and weight—calls attention to what previously had been covered over by music and lyrical form.[12] A voice hovers over the music, narrating what Alice hears: Vaughan uses her voice to savor an emotional pulse in the music[13] and create a thrilling connection of singer, song, and audience. Her voice has wings; it is luscious and tensile, disciplined and nuanced.[14] She creates a new way to sing and to think about singing.[15] She swings in and around so many terms, positions, structures: jazz musician and pop star, recording artist and concert diva, commercial success and creativity, self-indulgence and a desire to keep the music interesting.[16]

But Alice dreams in the gaps and pauses and spaces *between* voice and sound. Moments tick by in the silences surrounded by each note—silences that are taut, brimming with anticipation.[17] Alice blinks. She waits for the sound to return. She shifts in her chair; she teeters on the edge of her seat. She twists and tears the napkin bleeding with her words.[18] She cranes her neck, trying to get a better picture of the stage. She fixes her gaze on the singer. She looks around her and watches the lips of the others, silently mouthing the words.

Vaughan releases another note and her voice bends, dips low and breaks into an opening that reflects every surface in the room. Alice's eyes fill with tears. She is called to the stage.[19] Lyrics drag behind rhythm and emotion, so by the time Alice hears the words, they are filled with her own reverberations.[20] The song remains the same; its sounding is what induces excess, seepage, a permeation of boundaries, an emotional space.[21] Alice touches the table in front of her, the seat beneath her. She closes her eyes and wavers in and out of Vaughan's voice, in and out of subject positions, in and out of recognition and rejection, agitation and celebration, difference.[22] She is here, hearing and breathless with anticipation. She opens her mouth to speak, but no sound comes out.

Alice's eyes fly open. She sits up, unsure of where she is. She turns on the light. She looks at her legs outlined by the thin sheets, at her words waiting in the folds of the napkin on the bedside table. She gets out of bed and pulls a small composition book out of her bag. She writes fast, trying to record the frantic release of her dream.

> *Emotional space, the distance between the notes of a song or two lines of dialogue or two bars of music. . . . The silences are taut, full of anticipation. It impels us to participate in the performance and to connect with one another in the sounds of alienation, ecstasy, cultural divisions, and commonalties. . . .*[23] *Emotional space brings women's private lives into public view, questioning any easy distinction between the two. Emotional space complicates the opposition of subject positions, spectators and performers, emotion and intellect, literal meanings and critical interpretations, performance and reality, art and politics.*[24] *Torch singers sing good-woman-got-down songs—personal and cultural and political low points—in the space and pause, fits and starts of desire. Audience and performer hear themselves in the music, but not in irreducible tones or characteristics or personalities. They listen as much for the spaces between the notes as they do for the choice of sound, of tone. Their voices wait to see what happens.*[25]

Alice returns the composition book to her bag. She checks the clock. She shuts off the light and curls down into the sheets. She closes her eyes and waits for sleep.

## DRAWING IN

I buy the CD. I get on the mailing list. I follow Rayor and Rouge through new arrangements and CD release parties and late-night sing-alongs and still I can't seem to manage to ask my questions, to make my requests. Instead, I send Rayor an e-mail explaining myself. She invites me to phone and talk, and I leave several messages. And then, expecting to speak into the machine again, I call Rayor one morning and am surprised by her breathy, "Hello?"

"Janet Rayor?"

"Yes?"

"This is Stacy Holman Jones. I sent you an e-mail? I called last week. . . ."

"Oh, yes. You wanted to do an interview."

"Right. I was hoping we could find a time in the next few weeks to—"

"I'm doing some gardening now, but I could do it in an hour or so."

"Oh, well, I have a class to teach today. Maybe some time . . ."

"Tomorrow?"

"Sure. What time?"

"Why don't you come over at eleven?"

I set the time and get directions to Rayor's house. And at eleven the next morning, I knock on her screen door. After several minutes, she answers, looking, well, *surprised.* I tell her I'm here for our interview.

"Oh, *yes,*" she says, "come in. I'm just helping someone with some stilts." I wait in the doorway as Rayor shows a woman how to fasten the stilts to her legs. After the woman has her directions and her stilts, she leaves. Rayor clears a chair and a place at her kitchen table and invites me to sit.

"Do you mind if I clean up the kitchen a bit while we talk?"

I say, "Sure, no, not at all."

She smiles and says, "Tell me again what you want to talk about?"

I tell her, "Torch singing, Edith Piaf," and we're off, talking about Piaf, about French cabaret and café concerts, about chansons and American torch songs. I ask her about the connections among these forms, and she pulls her hands out of the dish soap and dries them on a towel as she talks.

> I love, *love* the torch songs, but . . . I'm not into those victim messages that are so heavy in English torch songs. . . . My life does not revolve around men. It may feel like it at times, but I highly resent that. In my own relationship if that's happening, then I'm not really happy with it. So I got into the French music . . . the lyrics and the stories are highly engaging, they're poetic, they're very interesting, they're about very full people. . . . "If you love me, I can laugh at all of it." That's a richer message . . . than, "I really loved you and in the end, if you die, I'm going to die too."[26]

She offers me tea—licorice or orange. Absently, I ask for orange. I am playing Rayor's words over in my head and thinking about the poetics of torch singing, about how a performance can create beauty and complexity even when the lyrics *aren't* rich or evocative or interesting. How the beauty and complexity of torch singing is a *call*, a sounding that directs our attention toward what is absent.[27] I ask her to tell me about how she connects with audiences, singing French songs to English speakers. She says,

> Piaf would pick a very few gestures that became the song. . . . Some of that came actually from her own nerves about performing and that she had to do something with her hands. But it was also to pick one thing that was very evocative in the song that people come deeply inside with. I'm singing in French where most people do not understand what I'm saying. . . . I want images that people can understand what the words are, that they can get some idea of what I'm saying in a very spare way. . . . And there's a lot of times where I'm very still so that they have to just get it from my voice. But partly my gestures are about how to get to that deep place, something that's very essential.[28]

I ask about the deep place, the something essential and inside. She stops. She thinks. I stop. I think about how music can make a livable space for critical voices. Rayor sighs. She brushes crumbs from the countertop and into the sink and says,

> There's a certain amount of what you'd expect in a more populist cabaret, café type of situation. . . . I want people to want to sing and dance and to love more deeply. . . . I want people to be vitalized. . . . What I would like people to feel is more *alive*. There's no question that I go for that. I have people who say, "Oh, it just opened up this whole side of me . . . and it was just this incredible flash." . . . I feel like I've done something if people are crying or laughing or anything like that. . . . So there is this . . . *response* that I'm going for that way. And that people get that, there's no question.[29]

I smile. I nod. I say, "I understand." Rayor excuses herself and disappears into the back of the house. I check the tape in the recorder. I make a few notes on the unused pad I brought to the interview: *Opening up, creating a dialogue, engaging and disrupting efforts to make a closed and stable discourse.*[30] *A sounding, a call for charged participation within the push and pull of location and movement, identification and difference.*[31] *Claiming rights and access to music and to language and action—alive to possibility.*[32] *A hopeful openness to the diverse possibilities of . . .*

"Now," Rayor says, "what were we saying?"

"Responses. The responses you're going for. How do you make them possible, make them happen?"

She smiles. She pulls out a chair, but she does not sit down. Instead, she leans over the back and stretches and bends, warming up. She says,

> There isn't the fourth wall of musical theater. There isn't the fourth wall of the opera. You're much more [saying,] "I'm telling you a story, I realize you are out there in the audience." And that's a very different thing than . . . other art forms. I have a certain formula, even though I change my program constantly. You have to have a ballad at a certain point, you have to have an English song at a certain point before you lose an audience, where they're just going, "My mind's bursting, I've had too much French." . . . It's usually fourth or fifth . . . there's always an English song then. And always a ballad the third song in. . . . Actually, I am not all that fond of "La Vie en Rose," but it's a necessary [song] to sing well. It's also the one I wait [to do]. . . . People stay because they want . . . to hear "La Vie en Rose." So you wait a little bit. So there's a theatricality of waiting.[33]

I think about form and formulas. The torch song is a formula, a standard structure designed for mass production and consistently popular appeal. But torch singing isn't formulaic. It takes a voice—noisy, multiple, competing voices[34]—to give the text of a torch song liveness and liveliness. Torch singing is a storytelling marked by palpitating vulnerability; a witnessing made by someone who has been there and back.[35] Torch singing is the theatricality of waiting to see what happens when audiences engage with a text, a performance, and a story.

Rayor asks if I have any more questions. I say, "No, yes, I have just one. Which songs are your favorites?"

"I've always loved 'T'es Beau.' There's humor in it, there's deep passion, it's one of the more sweet songs, there's something so kind and loving. . . . I love, 'my hand trembles, touching you.'"[36]

She touches my hand as she says this. I say, "Yes. It draws you into a space of desire . . . and possibility."

"It does."

I stand and thank her. She gives me a card announcing Rouge's next engagement, set for next Friday. I say that I'll come. I thank her again. She smiles and holds the screen door for me as I move through the doorway and down the stairs. When I reach the sidewalk, I look back, wanting to thank her again, but the door is closed.

## SPACES OF ENGAGEMENT

When I enter the café, I see Rayor in the corner of the room, listening to the musicians play the sound check. She crosses the floor and moves in behind the microphone. She covers one ear and sings a few bars. She turns to look at the violinist and the guitar player and all three nod. She turns around again and looks right at me. She smiles and walks toward my table. She bends down and whispers in my ear, "Glad you could come. I lost my voice a few days ago and it's barely back, so I'm saving it."

I nod. I smile. I open my mouth to speak, but no sound emerges.

She smiles and whispers, "Enjoy the show." She returns to the stage.

The first set includes Piaf's "Les Amants," which Rayor introduces by telling a story about lovers in Paris walking, eating at cafés, shopping for clothes at secondhand stores. She points to the red and strappy and very high heels on her feet. She raises up on her toes and pirouettes and laughs into the microphone. She says, "Paris." She sings Josephine Baker's "So Easy to Love" in English, the fourth song in the set, as promised. During the tango-inspired instrumental, "T'es Beau," she comes off the stage and invites an audience member to dance. She laces her fingers into his and they spin around the tables closest to the stage while the onlookers clap and cheer.

At the set break, I leave the table and look for the restroom. It is a small space, no bigger than a closet, and I run my hand along the wall looking for the light switch. I find the light and flip the switch. I close the door and slide the bolt into the hinge. On the back of the door, a filmy black dress hangs regally on a papered hanger. It is short-sleeved, crepe, with a sweetheart neckline and tiny rhinestone buttons down the front. I look at the yellowed French boutique label and know that this is one of Rayor's secondhand Parisian treasures.

I run my hand along the fabric. I take the hanger from the nail and press the dress to my waist. I turn and look at myself in the mirror, trying on the dress and an afternoon of searching through vintage fabrics for just the right thing to take home and on stage. I turn and watch my reflection. The dress lifts and floats around my legs as I spin. I imagine dust dancing in the sunlight streaming through storefront windows. I see myself peeking around dressing room curtains, looking for my lover and saying, "What do you think? Do you like this one? Does it look right? What do you think?" I see myself in the dress, sitting at a tiny table in a candlelit restaurant sipping champagne and waving a fine white dinner napkin in the air while I sing along and shout, "Bravo! Bravo!"

I return the hanger to the nail on the restroom door. I look again at myself in the mirror, at my plain T-shirt and jeans. I can see the dress behind me, waiting for Rayor to put it on before the next set. It is a costume—hers and mine—and also the dress of a woman neither of us know. I think, too, about how music—Rayor's and mine and a woman neither of us know—is a costume, a space of engagement. An engagement is an act, a state, an appointment, an arrangement, an ancient promise, a condition of employment, an interlocking conflict, an encounter. An engagement asks that we try something on, that we tie the knot, that we make contact, that we examine the connections, that we don't look away.[37]

I splash water on my face and watch my eyes in the mirror. I see the dress behind me, waiting for a body. It is a flimsy imitation of haute couture, a hand-me-down, a scavenged identity. I think about how music can be a put on, a passing pleasure, a moment of separation and transcendence.[38]

I turn away from the mirror and look at the dress again, waiting for a purpose, an occasion. It waits on the back of the door, as it waited in the vintage clothing store and in the closets of its other owners, to be chosen. It waits while its wearer undresses or emerges fresh from the shower, sticky with talc. It waits to be worn. It is a standard form waiting to be filled—with flesh, with heartbeat, with admiring glances, with movement and meaning and music. Its wearer might feel superior or supreme; she might try to transcend the universe, time, experience, barriers, and oppressions. She might want to hear separation and the collapse of difference in her music. She might want to take solace in a song, a narrative for Woman's suffering. She might want to lose herself in lyrics that figure critique as an act for other places and another dress.[39] Its wearer might also feel humble, obligated to make good on the promise of encounter and conflict. She might want to hear irony and double entendre and counter melodies in her music. She might want to use a song as an invitation to demand another sort of relationship, another set of meanings, a new kind of form—one deeply inside history[40] and alive with unforeseen pleasures.[41]

I touch the dress again, embarrassed at the designs I have on it. It is a garment, a case of appearance. I cannot read or speak or interpret "on" such a dress. I can only speak "in it, in its fashion."[42] I check the lock and slip the dress off the hanger. I kick off my shoes and pull my T-shirt over my head. I hear a knock at the door. I hear Rayor saying, "Hello? Are you almost finished in there? I need to change."

I pull the T-shirt back over my head. I scramble into my shoes and shove the dress onto the hanger. I open the door, breathless and pink cheeked. "Hi, *sorry*."

She smiles. "No problem. The ladies room is doubling as my dressing room. Did you see it? The black dress on the back of the door?"

"Yes. It's beautiful."

"I got it in Paris years ago. Very Piaf, don't you think?"

"Very." I squeeze out the door and past her.

She smiles again. She steps into the tiny space and closes the door behind her.

## MAKING ROOM

I return to my table and turn over the napkin I've been using to record song titles and introductions and audience responses and write about engagement and transcendence in performance.

> *A politics of transcendence proposes separation and collapses difference in the name of women's—and feminist—community. It assumes women are unified by a common experience of oppression without asking how they might be located in history; it announces women's collective vision and recommends we transcend engagement, agency, struggle.*[43]
>
> *A politics of engagement, on the other hand, recognizes the fragmented, discontinuous nature of experience as it happens in time and space and history; it claims a particular, peculiar, territorial notion of coalition; it works for collective vision and strives to change relationships and structures in a temporality of struggle.*[44]
>
> *Performance can be an occasion to transcend differences in search of common understanding. Performance can be a space of dialogue where different voices, experiences, and positions can question, debate, and challenge each other.*[45] *Performance might also be a means for creating an oppositional consciousness that is*

*voiced outside of the concert hall or living room—in the voting booth, at the company picnic, on the assembly floor, in the supermarket checkout line. Because it is a performance, music is at once a representation of an ideology and the dissection and exposition of that ideology.*[46]

*The radical possibilities in music are immanently practical, not black and white, easy to interpret as apolitical or resistive. The challenge is to stay open, to avoid assigning superiority or certain meaning to either the transcendent or the engaged and to listen instead for transcendence and engagement as they mark and cross borders and connections.*[47] *Torch singing makes room for something to be done and does something to make room—a space, a gap, an opening for the power of stories.*[48]

The musicians begin warming up. I put down the pen and look toward the stage. Rayor is there, behind the microphone in the black dress. She welcomes us back for the last set and thanks us for being such a wonderful audience, so alive and vibrant. She begins with "La Vie en Rose" because we have been waiting to hear it. I lean in, ready for this familiar reward.

**Choosing**

I close my eyes and listen, though I don't imagine myself in Piaf's dress or in Paris or a life in pink. Instead, I see Katie rushing to cross a busy New York street.[49] She is late for her shift to collect signatures and distribute leaflets urging her government to Ban the Bomb. She is in charge, informed, and loud. She is Jewish, political, and proud.

Katie looks up from her work—her cause, her passion—and sees Hubbell (once her work, her cause, and her passion) emerge from a car across the street. He is beautiful, intractable, all-American.

Hubbell waves. Katie rushes to cross the busy New York street. They kiss, then embrace. A beautiful, perhaps intractable, and certainly all-American woman moves into the scene. She is Hubbell's fiancée. Katie, Hubbell, and the fiancée make small talk and empty promises to meet for drinks, then say goodbye. Katie returns to her work to Ban the Bomb.

But this isn't the end. Now Hubbell crosses the busy New York street. He tells Katie that she never gives up. She says that she only gives up when she is absolutely forced to. They kiss, embrace, and say goodbye.

Hubbell returns to his fiancée. Katie returns, once again, to her work. Streisand sings, "Memories . . ."[50]

I cry each time I see the final scene between Katie and Hubbell in *The Way We Were.* I have to see only that last scene, hear only those last sounds. "Memories . . ." I cry for Katie and Hubbell, for the way they tried, but just couldn't make their relationship work. I cry for Katie's refusal to give up on her causes or her heart. I cry for how she feels forced to choose between her passion and her love.

I have long loved *The Way We Were,*[51] in spite of its swooning melodrama—or perhaps because of it. I feel the harsh choices and tensions and disappointments of the movie, even though it is missing a crucial scene—the one in which Hubbell comes home from his work as a Hollywood screenwriter and tells Katie the studio is going to fire him because he has a subversive wife.[52] He means that Katie is too involved in protesting the blacklisting of Hollywood actors and screenwriters in the era of McCarthyism. They are sitting down to dinner and wine in their Malibu beach house. Waves crash in the background. Katie is pregnant and glamorous, with red, red lipstick and a cause.

Katie says, "So if I close my eyes and let those fascists get away with destroying people's lives all in the name of patriotism, you won't have a subversive wife?"

"Katie, nothing is going to change."

"If I sit by and shut up and play the good girl, you won't have a subversive wife?"

Hubbell raises his eyebrows, but says nothing.

"If we get a divorce, you won't have a subversive wife?"[53]

Hubbell looks away.

"If I let them cut this scene and simply say, 'Isn't it funny how decisions are forced on you, willy-nilly,' the audience won't have to watch another boring political debate at the end of the movie?"[54]

Hubbell gets up from the couch. He turns his back on Katie and looks out the French doors at the ocean.

"If I ask only that you stay with me until the baby is born, the audience will remain alert and engaged with the story, even though it doesn't make *sense*?"

Hubbell nods, but he does not look at Katie.

"And when I see you in front of the Plaza hotel and say that I was forced to give up on you, the audience will think it's because I talked too much or because you didn't like my perfume, my family, my pot roast . . . and not because I couldn't betray my friends or my beliefs, even for you?"

Hubbell opens the door and steps onto the sand.

"And the audience will think that when I sing 'Memories' it means that I'd rather have you than my politics?"

Hubbell walks toward the water. The sound of the ocean rushes into the room, almost drowning out Katie's speech. She has to yell to be heard over the waves.

"So the audience will think that you didn't have a subversive wife after all?"

The audience never missed the scene where politics and love collide and choices are made.[55] But I miss this scene when I watch *The Way We Were.* I miss it because this scene asks whether politics and emotion are an either/or proposition. It asks what spaces of critique are opened up when people are articulate in their criticism and agitated to act, as Katie was. It asks what happens when people are silenced, when crucial scenes are cut out of the film—right there on the positive print with a razor blade—and they are left to speak, instead, inside a sentimental song while the credits roll.[56] I wonder why, when people are moved to act out politically—for example, during the labor protests of the 1930s or the civil rights movement and feminism's second wave in the 1960s and 1970s—music is a powerful form for overt protest.[57] I wonder why, when people are silenced or even complacent or content, music is space for marking time, of enduring, rather than resisting.[58] I wonder if it isn't so clear, if it *depends.*

I hear Streisand sing, "What's too painful to remember/we simply choose to forget," and I think that's what happened to the razored scene too political for the audience to sit through. She sings, "But it's the laughter/we will remember," and I think about how I choose to remember the laughter in a torch singer's voice, along with the disappointment. I think of Katie, shouting at Hubbell that "*People are their principles!*" In the very next scene, she stands by her car, a sporty convertible. She is talking to her radical friend, Paula, who says, "What's more important?" She means love or politics.

Katie says, "*He* is." She means Hubbell.

"That's your *choice*, Katie."

Katie gets in the car and starts the engine. She speeds away, determined to stand by her man instead of her principles. But of course that's not what happens. It's not clear who leaves whom or whether love wins out over politics or politics over love. It depends on which movie you see, on which scenes you remember or rewrite, on which story you hear, on how you shift the gears of that sporty convertible.

## SHIFTING

I don't know how to drive a manual transmission car. I am self-conscious about this. I sometimes joke that I am the only adult woman in America who does not know how to drive a stick shift, though I have tried to learn several times. I will climb into the car of a friend and she will be calm and encouraging and helpful as I grind the gears and move us along in jolts and hesitations. I will kill the engine, several times. I will sigh and try again. I will squeal the tires and get frustrated, *mad.* I will whine, "There are *too many things to do at once.*" I will shout, "I've got enough to learn without learning this!" I will beg to quit, to go home. My friend will be firm, but soon she will give in to my demands.

When I get into my own automatic transmission car, I am thankful for each smooth transition. I worry when the engine hesitates, when it seems to be racing ahead without shifting gears. I worry that my transmission will fail and I will be stuck, unable to move. I turn up the radio so I don't have to listen to these pauses and delays.

Gear shifting is a metaphor for movement within and among critical consciousnesses and politics—including, but not limited to, feminism. The gears represent points of contact among forms of oppositional ideologies and the usefulness of being able to move in and out of subject positions depending on our goals and abilities to speak and act.[59] Gear shifting represents how subjectivity and representation move and change, as well as how four shifting modes of resistance are used by subordinated classes in their efforts to resist domination and oppression.[60]

We can inhabit an "equal rights" mode, charging that differences in status are only matters of appearance and demanding legitimization within existing social structures.[61]

We can engage a "revolutionary" mode, proudly proclaiming our differences from those in power (in both form and content) and calling for a reordering and restructuring of dominant culture.[62]

We can claim a "supremacist" mode, asserting a superiority that allows us to provide society with a "higher ethical and moral vision" and leadership.[63]

We can employ a "separatist" mode, choosing to "protect and nurture [our] differences" through "complete separation from the dominant social order."[64]

These modes of consciousness-in-opposition are not mutually exclusive—no one ideology is the final answer.[65] They are not easily engaged, but instead require concerted effort—a commitment to self-consciously taking a position as a tactical response in the moment, a technology of power.[66] They are a source of mobility, allowing movement between and through oppositional ideologies, even when you grind the gears. Gear shifting animates the call for a politics of engagement and tactical subjectivity based on time, place, and history in its capacity to reinvent subjectivity depending on the "kinds of oppression to be confronted."[67] Those who learn to shift—to move in varying speeds and forces—create a fifth position, a mobile "differential consciousness" that works as a clutch, a medium and mechanism that "permits the driver to select, engage, and disengage gears in a system for the transmission of power."[68]

Even though I never learned to shift the gears of a car, I have learned how to listen. I can hear when the motor is ready—when it is revving—for change. I can also hear how gear shifting operates in torch singing. Differential oppositional consciousness functions in and through social, cultural, and political hierarchies, locations, and systems of value. The mode of consciousness chosen at any given moment is a tactical move. Torch singing also functions within these differentials, enacting the "recovery, revenge, and reparation" of a failed romance, a recording industry, a star's discourse, a dominant ideology.[69] I hear the gears engage when Vaughan and Horne demand racial equality in ticket sales and admissions to their live performances and their own compensation.[70] I hear Vaughan and Horne saying that differences in status are arbitrary and demanding that their work and their fans be treated equitably within the existing structures of recording contracts and concert venues, not to mention their struggles to gain legitimacy within the larger social structures of American politics, race relations, and human relationships. I hear them engage a fight for equality. I hear Horne say, "I don't run away from controversy."[71]

I hear the gears shift in how Piaf sings songs of the resistance, in how Horne sings civil rights anthems, in how Holiday pauses to sing "Strange Fruit" at the end of every set.[72] Their critics and biographers are not convinced or sure that these women sing to break with the existing social order.[73] Their voices call attention to difference and provide a backbeat for other efforts to create social change.[74] When singing these songs becomes uncomfortable and inconvenient and bad for business, Piaf and Horne and Holiday keep them in the lineup because the oppressions that inspired the music haven't changed or disappeared.[75]

I hear a shift in how Piaf and Vaughan and Streisand demand total musical and artistic control over their performances because they know what's best.[76] Their superior attitude is denigrated as tyrannical, nihilistic, pathological.[77] Still their vision is unwavering; their voices take audiences to unimagined places while living up to their own high expectations.[78]

I hear another shift in how lang sees her coming out as a moment for creating a separate space of intimacy with the women in her audience.[79] She believes women have "to realize that we're different, and we have to find some way of making that difference known inside ourselves."[80] A stage is a location of power and empowerment, and lang holds out hope that her art can engage and transcend her sexuality—that her voice can be located in time and space and history and still retain a desirous charge.[81]

I also hear how a singer's voice emerges out of "correlations, intensities, junctures, and crises" *inside* a torch song.[82] I hear Streisand's talent for even, sustained notes. I hear Vaughan demolish and rewrite the text with her improvisations. I hear Holiday and Horne's cool wisdom and Piaf's supreme zest for living. I hear lang's playful tease make a lyric all her own. I hear the laughter and silence and bawdy cacophony of their voices.

Listening to these women, I shift in and through modes of consciousness, and what I hear at any given moment is a tactical move. In some positions, a political critique is clear and deliberate and direct—music is a *form* of opposition and political action.[83] In others, I hear strains of community building and boundary marking. Music is a site, an opening, a *space* for deliberation and connection and contention.[84] And sometimes—between and among notes and lines and fixed positions—I hear everything at once. Fits and starts and stalls and reversals are part of a narrative worked self-consciously, part of the effort of resistive writing. I am writing to make room, to create a space for what happens in between note and line, emotion and intellect, thought and action.

## DEEPLY INSIDE

I open my eyes as Rayor sings the last lines of "La Vie en Rose." I scold myself for not paying attention, for hearing Streisand's voice and picturing Katie and the scenes from *The Way We Were* instead. I remember that Katie wanted to move to France and study French cookery while Hubbell finished his novel. Maybe that's why I let myself get carried away from here—from the fieldwork and the black dress and the songs of Piaf—and into a story about cut scenes and convertibles.

I look at my hands on the table in front of me, at the empty chair next to me. I consider the space there, a simple form that is open, possible, waiting to be filled. The chair, the dress, the convertible, the torch song are not simply containers, but also products and producers of action.[85] They are invitations into a place of interpretation, into a lyrical space that gives *pause.*[86] Pause for what? Pause for whom? Pause for trying on a text and a performance. Pause for emotional space, for filling in my own meanings and ironic understandings. Pause for reciprocal conversations that create shared knowledges, momentary identifications, and new visions out of found objects and received forms. Pause to shift gears, to disengage and reengage standpoints, positions, and purposes. Pause to consider the "density and force" of musical politics.[87]

Torch singing is "not an end, a blueprint for thinking and acting, but a constant beginning again—a search, an argument, an unfinished longing. The very effort to imagine it, then, is itself a continuous effort to reopen stories and spaces of cultural critique that are just as continuously being slammed shut with every new 'solution'" to the problem of music and performance and resistance.[88]

The door to the café opens and night air rushes in around my legs. I look up and listen to Rouge's finale, a rousing and frenetic "Bravo Pour le Clown." In Rayor's version, the clown goes a little wild, a little crazy, a little drunk with the applause and each successive "Bravo! Bravo!" from the crowd. I shout and cheer and clap with the rest of the audience. I follow along, getting a little wild, a little crazy, a little drunk with the music, deeply inside.

## OPENING

Alice sits up in bed. She's heard a sound, a knock, a presence. She searches the room, squinting while her eyes adjust to the sunlight streaming through the window. She can't see what's changed, though she knows something is different. She gets out of bed. She looks across the room and sees that the door is ajar. So that's what woke her. She moves to push it shut and feels a cool breeze wash over her legs. She decides to leave the door open and climbs back into bed.

## SPACES OF ENTRY

*Acknowledgments.* The title of this chapter is inspired and borrowed from Jill Dolan, "Rehearsing Democracy: Advocacy, Public Intellectuals, and Civic Engagement in Theatre and Performance Studies," *Theatre Topics* 11, no. 1 (2001): 2. She writes of performances that "model a hopeful openness to the diverse possibilities of democracy." Additionally, portions of this chapter appear in revised form in Stacy Holman Jones, "Emotional Space: Performing the Resistive Possibilities of Torch Singing," *Qualitative Inquiry* 8, no. 6 (2002): 738–59.

1. Kathleen Stewart, *A Space on the Side of the Road: Cultural Poetics in an "Other" America* (Princeton, NJ: Princeton University Press, 1996), 32.

2. Kirk W. Fuoss, "Performance as Contestation: An Agonistic Perspective on the Insurgent Assembly," in *Exceptional Spaces: Essays in Performance and History*, ed. Della Pollock, 109 (Chapel Hill: University of North Carolina Press, 1998).

3. bell hooks, *Yearning: Race, Gender, and Cultural Politics* (Boston: South End, 1990), 112.

4. Rayor founded Rouge in 1995 on finding a personal connection to the poetry, melodic range, and drama in the music of Edith Piaf and Jacques Brel. Together since early 1999, John Miller, Ruthie Dornfeld, Laurie Andres, and Rayor have arranged a wide variety of French concert, café, folk, jazz, and cabaret tunes. While maintaining the song's vintage, Rouge brings its own inimitable style and taste to serve these great tunes and lyrics. Rouge released some of their most beloved arrangements of Piaf, Charles Aznavour, Kurt Weill, Brel, and Baker songs with "La Terre de Nos Desirs—Land of Our Desires."

5. Rayor, "La Foule," lyrics by Michel Rivgauche and Angel Cabral, trans. Janet Rayor, *Rouge*, Wordworks Music, n.d. My discussion is based on Rayor's translation and recording of this song.

6. This phrase is part of Janelle Reinelt's description of Walter Benjamin's notion of utopia in "Notes for a Radical Democratic Theater: Productive Crises and the Challenge of Indeterminacy," in *Staging Resistance: Essays on Political Theater*, ed. Jeanne Colleran and Jenny S. Spencer, 294 (Ann Arbor: University of Michigan Press, 1998). She writes, "The work of utopia is precisely to offer a horizon of possibility, a negative or empty space, an imaginary nowhere, as a provocation to desire."

7. Stewart, *Space on the Side of the Road*, 34, writes, "Imagine how narrator and audience find themselves in the space of a doubled, haunting epistemology that comes of speaking from within the object spoken of. How they find themselves both subject and object of story, both inside and outside storied events, simultaneously seduced and watchful, firmly placed in the immanence of remembered scenes and unfolding events."

8. Stewart, *Space on the Side of the Road*, 34.

9. Speaking of the irony invested in the "great American songs," Barber notes in an interview with Janet Seiz ("An Interview with the 'Queen of Cool'—Patricia Barber," *Jazz Review*, May 2000, www.jazzreview.com, par. 32 [accessed April 15, 2001]), "The form as it has been established demands a certain twist of lyric or perspective or poetry."

10. See Henry Pleasants, "The Great American Popular Singers," in *The Billie Holiday Companion: Seven Decades of Commentary*, ed. Leslie Gourse, 137 (New York: Schirmer, 1997), on Holiday; Anne Edwards, *Streisand: A Biography* (Boston: Little, Brown, 1997), 80, on Streisand; and Margaret Crosland, *Piaf* (New York: Fromm, 1987), 61, on Piaf.

11. Leslie Gourse, *Sassy: The Life of Sarah Vaughan* (New York: Da Capo, 1994), 90, writes that Vaughan's accompanists "often mentioned they felt as if eons were passing between each note."

12. Will Friedwald, *Jazz Singing: America's Great Voices from Bessie Smith to Bebop and Beyond* (New York: Da Capo, 1996), 276. See also Michael A. Gonzales, "Torch Song Soliloquy: One Man's Poetic Tribute to Ladies Who Sing the Blues," *Mode*, February 1998, 52, who writes that torch singing is "one of the few musical styles capable of transcending any limitations of genre."

13. Friedwald, *Jazz Singing*, 276.

14. Gary Giddens, *Visions of Jazz: The First Century* (New York: Oxford University Press, 1998), 301, writes that Vaughan's voice "had wings: [it was] luscious and tensile, disciplined and nuanced."

15. Giddens, *Visions of Jazz*, 276.

16. Giddens, *Visions of Jazz*, 301–3.

17. Harry J. Elam Jr., *Taking It to the Streets: The Social Protest Theater of Luis Valdez and Amiri Baraka* (Ann Arbor: University of Michigan Press, 1997), 79, writes that the "silences" in emotional space are "often taut, filled with anticipation."

18. Elam, *Taking It to the Streets*, 79. Elam also notes that these silences create "feelings of anxiousness and tension in audience members."

19. Elam, *Taking It to the Streets*, 80. Emotional space does not necessarily create tension or incite audience members to action. It can also function as a celebratory moment, a carnivalesque performance that breaks down the separation of performers and spectators.

20. Gourse, *Sassy*, 90, writes that Vaughan sang ballads "at exactly the right tempo to create the atmospheric sound she needed to express the full feeling of the lyrics."

21. Elam, *Taking It to the Streets*, 80, notes that even in the carnivalesque, celebratory articulations of emotional space, the status quo is not totally restored at the end of the performance (or the song). He notes, "The celebration of the carnival in its very composition entails excess, seepage, the permeation of existing boundaries."

22. Sandra L. Richards, "Writing the Absent Potential: Drama, Performance, and the Canon of African-American Literature," in *Performativity and Performance*, ed. Andrew Parker and Eve Kosofsky Sedgwick, 72 (New York: Routledge, 1995), writes that the central principle of emotional space is "the juxtaposition in performance of radical differences, oftentimes understood as binary oppositions, that generate deep emotional responses from those assembled, challenging them to imagine some interpretive resolution."

23. Elam, *Taking It to the Streets*, 79–80.

24. The critical potential of torch singing is better viewed as a space along a *continuum*—from performance as political intervention with specific grievances and remedies in mind to an underground, covert, open-ended commentary on oppression. Jeanne Colleran and Jenny S. Spencer, "Introduction," in *Staging Resistance: Essays on Political Theater*, ed. Jeanne Colleran and Jenny S. Spencer, 2 (Ann Arbor: University of Michigan Press, 1998), write, "political" theater exists on a continuum, from "theater as an action of political intervention taken on behalf of a designated population and having a specific political agenda; to theater that offers itself as a public forum through plays with overtly political content; to theater whose politics are covertly, or unwittingly, on display, inviting an actively critical stance from its audiences."

25. Stewart, *Space on the Side of the Road*, 38, writes, "The 'space on the side of the road' . . . becomes a space in which people literally 'find themselves' caught in space and time and watching to see what happens, and yet it also makes them irreducible subjects encountering a world. It places the storyteller on the same plane with the story and produces not meanings per se but points of view, voices, and tropes. It implies both the contingency of subject positions and the reversibility of things, the ability to turn time back on itself and to reinscribe events in distinct voices." Stewart's space on the side of the road is, literally and narratively, located in an "Other" America, the "hard-core Appalachian coal-mining region of southwestern West Virginia" (3). However, her notion of such space has clear and interesting resonance with "performance" space and "emotional" space.

26. Janet Rayor, personal interview, June 8, 2000.

27. Elaine Scarry, *On Beauty and Being Just* (Princeton, NJ: Princeton University Press, 1999), 109, asserts that beauty and ethical fairness (justice) are analogous, that they form a symmetrical relationship that models a just and symmetrical relationship among individuals. When justice is absent, or invisible, beauty—aesthetic practice—becomes "pressing, active, insistent, calling out for, directing our attention toward, what is absent . . . beauty is a call."

28. Rayor, personal interview.

29. Rayor, personal interview.

30. Pollock, "Introduction: Making History Go," in *Exceptional Spaces: Essays in Performance and History*, ed. Della Pollock, 23 (Chapel Hill: University of North Carolina Press, 1998). Drawing on Mikhail Bakhtin's emphasis on the dialogic nature of language, Pollock writes,

"Dialogue encompasses monologue. It simultaneously engages and disrupts efforts at closed and stable discourse."

31. Pollock, "Introduction," 23. Pollock notes that dialogue enacts "what Bakhtin calls the 'centripetal' and 'centrifugal' (the centralizing and disseminative, the colonizing and deconstructive) impulses in engaged politics."

32. Pollock, "Introduction," 23. Pollock writes, "The speaker who expresses her agency in the act of claiming rights and access to language use thus becomes the agent of her own transformation."

33. Rayor, personal interview.

34. Pollock, "Introduction," 23. Pollock argues that texts can become "intertexts" through the discourses of critique on and about other texts. Such intertexts are the "residue of performative pressures and exchange, as the messy noisy conjunction of multiple and competing voices."

35. Stewart, *Space on the Side of the Road*, 37, describes the space on the side of the road and the stories told there as a "scene that palpitates with vulnerability. Uncertainty and challenge, painful memory and self-parody, eccentric characters and unearthly voices all point to a world in which there is more to things than meets the eye and people are marked by events and drawn out of themselves. These are stories that dwell on what [Walter] Benjamin called the self-forgetfulness of the storyteller. They are opening stories that place the speaker in relation to others and the world and demonstrate an authority to speak as one who has 'been there' and been impacted or changed."

36. Janet Rayor, "T'es Beau," lyrics by Henri Contet, trans. Janet Rayor, *Rouge*, Wordworks Music, n.d. My discussion is based on this recording.

37. *The Random House Dictionary of the English Language*, 2nd ed. (New York: Random House, 1987), defines "engagement" (a noun) as "1. The act of engaging or the state of being engaged. 2. An appointment or arrangement. 3. Betrothal: *They announced their engagement.* 4. A pledge; an obligation or agreement. 5. Employment, or a period or post of employment, esp. in the performing arts. 6. An encounter, conflict, or battle. 7. *Mech.* The act or state of interlocking."

38. According to *The Random House Dictionary of the English Language*, "transcendence" (a noun) is "the quality or state of being transcendent." "Transcendent" (an adjective) is "1. going beyond ordinary limits; surpassing; exceeding. 2. Superior or supreme. 3. *Theol.* (of the Deity) transcending the universe, time, etc. . . . 4.b. *Philos. Kantianism.* transcending experience; not realizable in human experience."

39. My language is drawn from Chandra Talpade Mohanty's description and critique (*Feminism without Borders: Decolonizing Theory, Practicing Solidarity* [Durham, NC: Duke University Press, 2003], 114, 116) of a feminist politics of transcendence, which she asserts collapses difference in order to transcend barriers and oppression between and among women

based on race, class, gender, and sexual preference. A politics of transcendence constitutes the experience of women (as a unified category) as personal as "outside real politics or history" (114). Women are unified—an individual woman can identify with women as a category—by recognizing their common experience of oppression. However, this homogenizing unification neglects any specific, historically located notion of experience and creates a utopian vision of collective political action (while running the risk of undercutting struggle all together). As Mohanty puts it (and this is contained in her analysis of Robin Morgan's essay "Planetary Feminism: The Politics of the 21st Century" in Morgan's book *Sisterhood Is Global: The International Women's Movement Anthology*, 1–37 [New York: Anchor, 1994]), "Ultimately in this reductive utopian vision, men participate in politics while women can only hope to transcend. . . . Universal sisterhood does construct a unity. However, for me, the real challenge arises in being able to craft a political unity without relying on the logic of appropriation and, just as significant, a denial of agency" (116). Jill Dolan's materialist critique of liberal and cultural feminist approaches to performance raises similar questions. See *The Feminist Spectator as Critic* (Ann Arbor: University of Michigan Press, 1988).

40. Mohanty, *Feminism without Borders*, 118–19, contrasts a politics of transcendence with a politics of engagement (based on her reading of Bernice Johnson Reagon's essay "Coalition Politics: Turning the Century," in *Home Girls: A Black Feminist Anthology*, ed. Barbara Smith, 356–58 [New York: Kitchen Table, 1983]), which means working within existing racial, class, sexual, and gender relationships and structures in ways that recognize the differences among individuals and the particular *meanings* of these differences within various historical moments, while still striving to change these relationships/structures. Here, experience is not assumed or universal; it is discontinuous and fragmented, in history, politics, and experience. See also Dolan, *Feminist Spectator*, 121. She asserts that that materialist feminist approaches to performance imagine a "creative and critical project . . . located within . . . differences, which . . . demand[s] new forms and provoke[s] new meanings when they are inscribed in representation."

41. Avery F. Gordon, *Ghostly Matters: Haunting and the Sociological Imagination* (Minneapolis: University of Minnesota Press, 1997), 207.

42. Roland Barthes, *The Pleasure of the Text*, trans. Richard Miller (New York: Farrar, Straus and Giroux, 1975), 22.

43. Mohanty, *Feminism without Borders*, 114.

44. Mohanty, *Feminism without Borders*, 120.

45. Dwight Conquergood, "Performing as a Moral Act: Ethical Dimensions of the Ethnography of Performance," *Text and Performance Quarterly* 5, no. 2 (April 1985): 9, describes such performances as "dialogic," because they bring together different voices, experiences, and subject positions so that individuals might "question, debate, and challenge each other."

46. Discussing materialist perspectives on ideology and the critique of representation, Dolan, *Feminist Spectator*, 14, writes, "Cultural production is viewed as a framework for the imposition of ideology, a framework which can be dissected and exposed as complicit in the formation of systems of social relations."

47. Mohanty, *Feminism without Borders*, 226.

48. Stewart, *Space on the Side of the Road*, 5, writes that the space on the side of the road "is a space that marks the power of stories to re-member things and give them form."

49. Portions of this narrative are presented in revised form in Stacy Holman Jones, "The Way We Were, Are, and Might Be: Torch Singing as Autoethnography," in *Ethnographically Speaking*, ed. Arthur P. Bochner and Carolyn Ellis, 44–56 (Walnut Creek, CA: AltaMira, 2004).

50. Streisand, "The Way We Were," lyrics by Marvin Hamlisch, Alan Bergman and Marilyn Bergman, *Barbra Streisand: Just for the Record*, Columbia, 1991.

51. *The Way We Were*, videocassette, dir. Sydney Pollack, perf. Barbra Streisand and Robert Redford, prod. Ray Stark, Raystar, 1973.

52. Edwards, *Streisand*, 339, recounts how the crucial scene—a scene screenwriter Arthur Laurents believed was "the entire motivation for Katie's leaving Hubbell"—was cut from the film following a sneak preview at the Northpoint Theater in San Francisco.

53. Edwards, *Streisand*, 339, notes that this line was "So if we get a divorce and you don't have a subversive wife?"

54. Edwards, *Streisand*, 339. Edwards writes that producer "Ray Stark decided the audience was bored during [the] six-minute scene."

55. Edwards, *Streisand*, 339. Laurents complains that in the "revised" version, Streisand "has some line about how willy-nilly circumstances make one come to a decision, in her case to get a divorce. The audience seemed to have bought it."

56. Edwards, *Streisand*, 339, 342, quotes director Sydney Pollack, who cut the scene following an audience preview. He says, "I didn't even have the negative with me. I just made the cut with a razor blade on the positive print before previewing it the next night." Edwards does not discuss whether Streisand disagreed with the purging of the scene (though Laurents implied that she did). Further, Streisand was not fond of lyrics to "The Way We Were" which, according to Edwards, she thought were "too sentimental."

57. Michael Denning, *The Cultural Front: The Laboring of American Culture in the Twentieth Century* (London: Verso, 1997), traces the connections among music and the labor movement; Brian Ward's *Just My Soul Responding: Rhythm and Blues, Black Consciousness, and Race Relations* (Berkeley: University of California Press, 1998), explores the relationship among rhythm and blues and the civil rights movement; and Cynthia Lont's "Women's Music: No Longer a Small Private Party," in *Rockin' the Boat: Mass Music and Mass Movements*, ed. Reebee

Garofalo, 241–54 (Boston: South End, 1992), considers the role of women's music in the radical and cultural feminist movements.

58. Lewis A. Erenberg, *Swingin' the Dream: Big Band Jazz and the Rebirth of American Culture* (Chicago: University of Chicago Press, 1998), 24, makes such an argument about torch singers in the 1930s. He notes, "Torch singers expressed the torment that many women felt in the early 1930s: they were emotionally involved with men who could not provide or who did not see marriage in their future. In the depths of the depression, however, women found it difficult to leave these abusive situations since they had few resources. . . . The torch singers felt trapped in a world beyond their control. Their dreams dashed, they waited listlessly for the stormy weather to pass." See Timothy E. Scheurer, "Goddesses and Golddiggers: Images of Women in Popular Music of the 1930s," *Journal of Popular Culture* 24, no. 1 (1990): 23–38, for a similar characterization.

59. See Kathy E. Ferguson, *The Man Question: Visions of Subjectivity in Feminist Theory* (Berkeley: University of California Press, 1993), 161.

60. This topography of oppositional consciousness deploys forms of feminist consciousness that Chela Sandoval, *Methodology of the Oppressed*, foreword by Angela Y. Davis (Minneapolis: University of Minnesota Press, 2000), 54, identifies as "hegemonic feminist theory," which is atemporal, hierarchical, and modernist and as such fails to take into account the theorizing and actions of U.S. Third World feminists as well as postmodern "transnationalization [in which] new forms of resistance and opposition must be recognized." The "fifth" mode, a "differential coalitional consciousness," creates a "location wherein the aims of feminism, race, ethnicity, sex and marginality studies, and historical, aesthetic, and global studies can crosscut and join together in new relations through the recognition of a shared theory and method of oppositional consciousness" (64).

61. Sandoval, *Methodology of the Oppressed*, 56.

62. Sandoval, *Methodology of the Oppressed*, 56.

63. Sandoval, *Methodology of the Oppressed*, 57.

64. Sandoval, *Methodology of the Oppressed*, 57.

65. Sandoval, *Methodology of the Oppressed*, 58.

66. Sandoval, *Methodology of the Oppressed*, 62.

67. Chela Sandoval, "U.S. Third World Feminism: The Theory and Method of Oppositional Consciousness in the Postmodern World," *Genders* 19 (1991): 14. Where Mohanty is critical of a politics of transcendence and recommends a politics of engagement, Sandoval's topology suggests that separation—which shares many of the characteristics of a politics of transcendence as described by Mohanty—is a potentially useful strategy for feminist solidarity and struggle in particular instances, contexts, histories, and situations.

68. Sandoval, *Methodology of the Oppressed*, 58.

69. Sandoval's summary, "U.S. Third World Feminism," 14.

70. Gourse, *Sassy*, 56, 103, and James Haskins, *Lena: A Personal and Professional Biography of Lena Horne*, with Kathleen Benson (New York: Stein, 1984), 95, 98.

71. Lena Horne and Richard Schickel, *Lena* (Garden City, NY: Doubleday, 1965), 208.

72. Monique Lange, *Piaf* (New York: Seaver, 1981), 90, on Piaf; Haskins, *Lena*, 158, on Horne; and Donald Clarke, *Wishing on the Moon: The Life and Times of Billie Holiday* (New York: Viking, 1994), 164–65, on Holiday.

73. Crosland, *Piaf*, 198, on Piaf; Haskins, *Lena*, 154, on Horne; and Clarke, *Wishing on the Moon*, 165, on Holiday.

74. Denning, *Cultural Front*, 334, on Horne and Holiday's role in the Popular Front.

75. Billie Holiday, *Lady Sings the Blues*, with William Dufty (1956; New York: Penguin, 1992), 84. Citations are to the 1992 edition.

76. Crosland, *Piaf*, 194, on Piaf; Gourse, *Sassy*, 207, on Vaughan; and Edwards, *Streisand*, 374, on Streisand.

77. Crosland, *Piaf*, 117, on Piaf; Gourse, *Sassy*, 201, on Vaughan; and Camille Paglia, "The Way She Was," in *Diva: Barbra Streisand and the Making of a Superstar*, ed. Ethlie Ann Vare, 224 (New York: Boulevard, 1996), on Streisand.

78. Crosland, *Piaf*, 195, on Piaf; Friedwald, *Jazz Singing*, 276, on Vaughan; and Edwards, *Streisand*, 500, on Streisand.

79. Mim Udovitch, "k. d. lang: How Did a Lesbian, Feminist, Vegetarian Canadian Win a Grammy and the Hearts of America?" in *Rock She Wrote: Women Write about Rock, Pop, and Rap*, ed. Evelyn McDonnell and Ann Powers, 337 (New York: Delta, 1995).

80. Quoted in Brendan Lemon, "Virgin Territory: Music's Purest Vocalist Opens Up," *The Advocate* (June 16, 1992): 38.

81. Lemon, "Virgin Territory," 42.

82. Sandoval, "U.S. Third World Feminism," 14.

83. Mark Mattern, *Acting in Concert: Music, Community, and Political Action* (New Brunswick, NJ: Rutgers University Press, 1998), 26–28.

84. Mattern, *Acting in Concert*, 29–30. In addition, Mattern, *Acting in Concert*, 25–32, makes an argument about music and political action in keeping with Sandoval. He charts three forms of "acting in concert"—confrontational, deliberative, and pragmatic—resistive strategies that are used together and alone, depending on the context, situation, and setting of the performance. The confrontational form "occurs when members of one community use musical practices to resist or oppose another community. . . . Protest music is an example of

music used as a confrontational form of acting in concert" (25). The deliberative form "occurs when members of a community use musical practices to debate their identity and commitments or when members of different communities negotiate mutual relations. . . . The discovery, creation, and re-creation of community may themselves be a political process and form of political action marked by debate and deliberation over communal identity and commitments" (28). The pragmatic form "occurs when members of one or more communities use music to promote awareness of shared interests and to organize collaborative efforts to address them. . . . This form of political action is characterized by cooperative and collaborative efforts to engage in mutually beneficial problem solving" (30). However, he does not create a "differential" mode that works to create movement between and among these forms of acting in concert.

85. Fuoss, "Performance as Contestation," 109.

86. Stewart, *Space on the Side of the Road*, 34, writes, "Imagine how an interpretive space, a cultural epistemology, can be culled into a lyric image that gives pause, how it is these lyric images—this imaginary space—that seem to matter most, how this low point in action could become the high point of cultural practice: the place from which big meanings emerge."

87. Stewart, *Space on the Side of the Road*, 6.

88. Stewart, *Space on the Side of the Road*, 6.

# 8

# Circular Breathing

As it retells one story and in this way summons another, it . . . creat[es] a palimpsest, a document that has been inscribed several times, where remnants of earlier, imperfectly erased scripting is still detectable.

—*Avery Gordon,* Ghostly Matters[1]

Memories and events . . . mark my pursuit of understanding, turning this project into an act of deciphering a palimpsest.

—*Diane Losche, "The Impossible Aesthetic"*[2]

In an elaborate critical kind of circular breathing, the form is always simultaneously explaining and questioning itself.

—*Geoff Dyer,* But Beautiful[3]

---

**PALIMPSEST**

k. d. lang has big hair, a big band, and a big voice. She has a full house and a stage that looks like the set of the *Lawrence Welk Show.* She gives the signal for the bubble machine, and I am two years old, sitting too close to the set, murmuring, "Bubbles, bubbles," as Bobby and Sissy glide effortlessly in and out of view. This memory comes out of nowhere. Until now—until this moment in the Sacramento Community Theater when I am almost thirty—I had forgotten how much I loved the *Lawrence Welk Show.*

I usually watched the show at my grandparents' house.[4] My grandmother marveled at my early fixation on the set. At first, she thought it was the bubbles that held my attention, but I watched everything—the musical numbers, the singers, the dancing. I clapped in time with the movement of Bobby and Sissy. I clapped in time with my grandfather's typewriter click-clacking in the other room. My grandmother would call him in to see my performance and the typing—the writing of letters and essays and wild fictions—would stop. He would stroll into the living room to watch my performance. He would smile and pick me up, swinging me high over his head and onto his shoulders. He would hold my hands behind his ears and spin me in time to Bobby and Sissy's waltz or swing or foxtrot. And when the number was over, he would lift and float me down to my spot on the floor in front of the television and return to his typewriter. Out of sight, he would place his fingers on the keys, furiously tapping out his own rhythm and vision and story. And I would return to the dancing and the music and the singing and the bubbles.

Bubbles spin and hover around lang. She sings, "Just a kiss just a kiss/I have lived just for this,"[5] in a voice overflowing with want and mischief. The women in the audience—it seems we are all women here, there is not a man in sight—sigh and call her name. She sings, "She was a big boned gal . . . ain't no doubt she's a natural,"[6] yodeling and gyrating to bass drum pulses and trombone slides. The audience cheers. I sigh and call and cheer. I move and speak in the space of unlikely connections and the force of taking place.[7] Bubbles float into the darkened auditorium and touch my skin. My hands are saturated in the bursts of my applause. With each touch and crack and wet release, I write my desire.

This memory, too, comes out of nowhere, on a Monday morning as I sit down in my red bathrobe to write the latest chapter on torch singing. Before I begin, I check my e-mail and read the word for the day:

> palimpsest\PAL-ump-sest or puh-LIMP-sest\ (noun). 1. writing material (as a parchment or tablet) used one or more times after earlier writing has been erased. 2. something having usually diverse layers or aspects apparent beneath the surface.[8]

It comes out of nowhere, the idea that torch singing is a palimpsest, a layering of words and music and meanings only apparent beneath the surface. It comes out of nowhere, the thought that I've been writing this story, over and over, since I was two, sitting in front of the television and murmuring to the music and the magic of bubbles.

### GETTING CARRIED AWAY

The riding crop makes a whistling sound as it slices through the air in time with Holly Penfield's lashing rendition of "The Glory of Love." As she finishes the number, she pushes her way onto the lap of a red-faced man down front and caresses his cheek. She presses the microphone between his lips and her own and whispers, "Darling, where are you from?"

"Phoenix," the man says demurely.

"Phoenix!" she yells, leaping from his lap and bringing the riding crop crashing down on the white tablecloth. "I was just *in* Phoenix! We were traveling through Phoenix and Flagstaff and then on to that city of sin, Las Vegas!"

She spins and careens toward the stage and her piano player. She asks, "What should we do next?" Before he can answer, she says, "I know! 'I'm in the Mood for Love!'" The piano player begins the opening bars and Penfield whips around to face the audience. She smiles and swivels her hips. She strokes the riding crop and the audience giggles nervously.

Penfield is singing at Piaf's in San Francisco. It's been more than a year since my first visit. This time I'm here with Georgine, one of my closest friends. The diners have left for the evening, opening up the space in the back of the restaurant for the second show. A waiter clears away china and silverware, making room for martinis and Penfield's penchant for standing on tables. We choose seats near the bar and order glasses of champagne. Penfield is a jazz and cabaret performer who, as she puts it, cut her teeth on English audiences. Tonight she's returned to her hometown and she's ready to have some fun.

She leaves the riding crop on the piano and crawls onto a table left of the stage. Her knees make the tablecloth buckle and fold. The silverware clatters to the floor. Penfield stops, says, "*Oh my*," and steps down to pick up the cutlery. She stands and holds a butter knife up to the light. It flashes as she grins out at the audience. She turns back toward the table and climbs on. She holds the knife at the throat of the startled man seated there and asks, "Is this yours?"

Nervously, he plays along and says, "Yes."

"You must be Mack!"

The piano player begins an introduction to "Mack the Knife." Penfield releases the man and says to the audience, "I'm going to tell you a very, very sordid story about a guy named Mack. I think he was a *bad* man. I think he was a *hired killer*. Listen carefully. . . ."

She sings, "Oh, the shark has/pret-ty teeth dear/and he shows them/pear-ly white."[9] Her phrasing is breezy; the piano providing a staccato contrast to the sweet way she sings the menacing lyric.

Penfield jumps off the table and moves in close to a smiling woman in front of us. She places the knife alongside the woman's ear. "Just a jack knife/has Mac-heath dear/and he keeps it/out of sight." She sits on the woman's lap, then continues, "When the shark bites/with his teeth, dear/scar-let bil-lows/begin to spread." The woman throws back her head and laughs. Penfield begins, "Fancy gloves though/has Macheath dear," in this quiet tone, but then she belts out "so there's ne-ver/never a touch of red."

She backs away and thrusts the knife into the empty air in front of her. The pianist kicks up the pace and Penfield charges into, "Oh-oh one Sunday morning/on the side-walk/lies a bo-dy/oooooozin' life." She turns and points the knife at the man called Mack and sings her suspicions: "Someone's sneakin'/'round the corner/could that some-one/be Mack the Knife!" The accused smiles and lowers his eyes as Penfield sings of tugboats and cement bags "drrooop-in down" and her guess that Mackie's back in town.

She turns up the volume for "Ol' Louie Miller/dis-appeared dear/aft-er draw-ing out his cash from the cash machine."[10] And when she sings, "And Mac-heath spends/like a sai-lor," she takes blushing Mack's hand and drags him center stage. She asks us, "Did our boy do/some-thing rash?" Penfield turns our villain so that his back is to us. She tells him to, "Stay there and be good."

She sings, "Sukey Taw-dry/Jen-ny Di-ver/Pol-ly Peach-um/and Ol' Lucy Brown," pointing to several women in the audience as she names them. She tells us "Oh the line forms/on the right dear/Now that Mack-ie's/back in town." Then she repeats this verse, pointing—first to me on "Sukey Tawdry"—and then to Georgine on "Lucy Brown." She curves her fingers and waves us to the stage. Georgine and I look at each other, deciding without speaking that we'll stay where we are. But Penfield sings the verse again. Her voice is reckless, and I shift in my seat as she bounds toward me. She takes my hand and Georgine's, too, and pulls us up. We follow her to the stage. Then she pulls two other women out of their seats and to the stage. She positions the four of us in a single-file line to the right of Mack.

Penfield hands me the riding crop. She says, "Go ahead. Give him a good one!" I don't know this man, but I do know that I don't want to spank him.

Penfield has to repeat herself. "Go ahead. Give him a good one."

I look up, out at the audience. They are clapping and smiling. *Go ahead. Give him a good one.* I stand back and take aim. I swing and stop short, barely touching the target.

Penfield says, "Not nearly hard enough! Lucy, let's see if you can give him what he deserves." Georgine, too, has a soft touch. But the other women—Polly Peachum and Jenny Diver and Penfield herself—make the whip bend and snap. Mackie waves his arms and the audience cheers. At the end of the number, he takes a bow and a kiss on the cheek from Penfield.

I return to my seat. I feel a little dizzy. I remind myself that cabaret is part participation and part provocation, but I'm not sure what has just happened or what to think about the giddy shame I feel for my role in this drama. As Penfield passes out the wooden spoons that we'll use to accompany her on "It Don't Mean a Thing (If It Ain't Got That Swing),"[11] I think about the violence of torch lyrics and the responsibility of reciprocity, and I'm not sure I should join in. Still, I accept the spoon that Penfield offers, feeling the entanglement and antagonisms within this performance and the difficulty of opposing emotion and critique. And when it comes time to play, I tap my spoon on the table, quietly at first, afraid of repeating the sound of beatings and betrayals in an endless mimesis.[12] Soon the sounds of spoons fill the room with a pattern we recognize and repeat and reconstruct, beat by beat.[13] I try my spoon on a stray cup saucer, my champagne glass, the seat beneath me. I follow along, keeping time and taking pleasure in marking the rhythms of my listening. I get carried away.[14]

## PLAYING ALONG, PLAYING AGAIN

Thwap! Thwap! Thunk! Thwap! A simple form helps drill a torch lyric into the minds and hearts of an audience. Translated from confrontational cabaret stages to vaudeville and minstrel shows, sentimental torch songs became mass-produced accompaniment for an evening of comedy and diversion. They were instant entertainment for the girl singers who fronted big bands. Or so it seemed. The simple AABA form and sentimental content became a stage for an everyday sort of resistance spoken—in disguised form—in the spaces controlled by the powerful.[15] Holiday, Horne, Vaughan, and other singers used rhythm and tone to signify on the power relations that shaped their lives and their livelihood.

Thwap! Thwap! Thunk! I continue the rhythm, and then I miss the table and hit my thigh with the spoon. It makes a hollow Shusk sound. Shusk. Shusk. Shusk. Shusk. I continue in the void. The torch song is a frame for a performance of a singer—a star persona not to be confused with her biography or the discourses constructed to explain her life and her music. She uses her material to talk back—to the individual responsibility of an American Dream; victimhood; the failure to mention the larger historical, social, and political contexts in which she lives; to any certain or fixed characterization. She is not really there—in the song or on stage—at least not as I imagine her. I use the beat, the rhythm, the voicing of a torch song to create a lover's discourse in the intersections of memory and event. In the absence of a single, stable subject or singer, I write a kind of music as I listen, over and over.

Ping . . . ping . . . ping . . . I move the spoon from my body to the china saucer on the table. Each tap produces a siren's call that gives way to a new sound. Like an echo, a torch singer voices an ironic interpretation, embodying a multitude of characters and positions, creating pregnant silences around things not spoken, sounding difference as contention and connection. She uses her voice as counterpoint and campy retort to the tensions of class distinction, racial and gender inequity, and compulsory heterosexuality. That's what I hear in each note, line, and reverberation—in each ping . . . ping . . . ping . . .

CRASH. The china plate breaks. I stare at the fragments scattered on the table. I look around, but no one has noticed the results of my destructive playing. I watch the pieces dance and twist and clang into each other as the song—and my rhythm—marches on. A torch song is inscribed with violence—physical and emotional intrusions and abuses that sing love's wounds. Torch singing is a passionate and intellectual call and response that complicates easy identifications and quick fixes. It takes a stand within a "practical consciousness of a present kind."[16] Torch singing calls out this violence as a first step toward change.

A jagged piece of china bounces into my champagne flute and sets off a new chorus. I raise my spoon and tap the empty glass. Sing, sing, sing; it makes a high-pitched sound that quickly disappears, like the burst of a champagne bubble. I continue tapping and become accustomed to the tone. I hear, too, the spaces in between the beats of the spoon and the crowd and the blinking of an eye, an opening for engagement that disrupts the distinction between emotion and critical distance. In the moments when words, music, and performance collide, torch singing makes a space that makes room for the power of stories.

My spoon misses the glass and connects instead with a china shard. In the next beat, I tap the table and then my thigh and the china shard and the table and the glass and my body and on and on, combining all of the sounds: ping . . . Thwap! Shusk . . . ping . . . sing, sing, sing . . . I shift among instruments and locations, hearing the changes, hearing everything at once. And then I stop. I listen to the music in the room, to the dense beauty and cacophonous force of performance as a making. I watch Penfield move through the crowd, encouraging a raucous accompaniment. She takes the hand of the red-faced man and helps him pummel the table with his spoon. She dances to the beat of the woman down front. She laughs when she sees Mack using his butter knife to keep the beat. She shouts, "Do wap do wap do wap do wap do wap!"[17]

After the last "do wap," Penfield takes a break. Georgine and I stay in our seats, breathless and smiling after our wooden spoon recital. Georgine says, "So this is what you're writing about?"

"Yeah. I'm writing about torch singing as a sounding of desire, as a radical, hopeful politics."

Georgine raises her eyebrows. "Really?"

"I guess what I'm really doing is writing stories, lots of them."

"What kinds of stories?"

"Stories that tell another story of torch. Counterpoints, counterpoises."[18]

"*You* are writing *love* stories."

We turn our attention to our drinks and other topics, though I keep the conversation about torch stories and love stories going in my head.[19] They are stories about what happens in between binaries, about what occurs between participation and provocation, emotion and politics, music and language, subject and object, body and voice, intended and literal meaning, transcendence and engagement, form and function, sound and silence, monologue and dialogue, humble and superior irony, connection and distance, conclusions and possibilities.

These stories take their form and content—their very activity—from torch singing. They begin and end with the idea that performance, because it is imbricated in a culture and vast spiral of relationships, is necessarily and thoroughly *political*.[20] What torch singing creates in the gaps and fissures of cultural production and politics is *freedom* not just "*from* oppression, repression, exploitation . . . but also freedom *to reach beyond* existing systems of formalized power, freedom to create currently unimaginable forms of association and action,"[21] new "possibilities in performance."[22] For women who have been abused, discriminated against, looked over, and made invisible, torch singing becomes an active search for *hope* rather than despair.[23]

Torch singing is *radical* because it gestures toward "kinds of freedom that currently cannot be envisaged."[24] It "invites an ideological investment that it cannot itself determine"; it is a "performative process in need of direction."[25] One direction listeners take is to actively engage complex seeing and hearing within the tangle of identifications and differences, to build coalitions without forgetting the need to expose systems of oppression, to find new ways of being in the world.[26] Torch singing promises audiences and singers a performative field of dreams—if you want to hear and voice a critique, it can be done.

Because torch singing creates an open, indeterminate space for interpretation and action, tracing the political efficacy of a performance is something like creating a map of a feeling or tracking the movement of an unspoken idea. I began with my own location and the inspiration that when I listen to Holiday and Piaf and Horne and Vaughan and Streisand and lang and the others, something *radical* happens. I allowed myself to imagine that when you listen to these women and others, something radical could happen for you, too.

The directions I have taken and the determinations I have tried to make in this story are as ideologically itinerant as torch singing itself.[27] The points of contact in my story do not connect in a predictable route or on a hierarchical course. They are destinations that can be arrived at from any number of locations, and it is easy to get carried away. Like every instance of listening and playing and writing I have undertaken, these stories leave me asking, "Has anything *radical* happened? How was it done?"[28]

## SILENT SONG

Penfield begins the second set with a story. She says that at Piaf's, Edith lives on. She points at a black and white photo of Piaf with her eyes closed and her mouth wide open, singing. She says if you look at Piaf's face, you'll see a woman who lived intensely, passionately. She says Piaf had a life most of us could not imagine, abandoned by her mother and forced to sing in the streets. But her voice and her heart were strong, so strong, and she became a . . . *star*. Penfield pulls out a chair, steps up onto it, and begins to sing "La Vie en Rose."

She sings "La Vie en Rose" in French, though her rendition doesn't sound like Piaf's playful and languorous version. Instead, her voice takes up Streisand's pleasurable and unabashed belting. During the saxophone solo, her mouth continues to work, silently singing the verse again, with all the fervent emotion of the fully sounded lyrics. Watching Penfield standing on a chair, mouthing the words does not seem odd or out of place. It is as if she can't convey the force and passion of the song without continuing, silently, into the instrumental. And somehow, in her empty words and wanting gestures, Penfield gets closer to the Piaf photographed and framed behind glass all around us. Somehow, this is where her story of Piaf generates its force and passion.

The solo is complete and Penfield comes in again for the final verse. She sings "Alors je sens dans moi/Mon coeur qui bat"[29] in round, sustained notes and then bows deeply. The audience responds with quick applause and whistles. Penfield says, "Thank you," then steps down from the chair. She sighs and says, "Thank you, Edith Piaf." She pauses for a moment, waiting for the crowd to quiet. Then it's time for another story. . . .

## WRITING PERFORMANCE

When I got a little older, my Saturday night stays with my grandparents in the company of Lawrence Welk were extended to weeklong visits over summer vacation. I would visit them at their lake house, with its screened porch and sloping lawn and dense stand of trees out back. Inside the house there was a guest bedroom with a white iron twin bed, just for me. There was grandma's electric organ, with its waltz and foxtrot and bossa nova accompaniment. I liked to play "Silent Night" with a bossa nova beat. There were shelves of books and stacks of board games—Monopoly and Scrabble and Parcheesi. There were all of these things to keep my hands and thoughts busy, and after about twenty minutes I would whine that there was "absolutely nothing to do!"

I'd start wondering how long until my parents would come to pick me up.

I'd sprawl on the couch and sulk.

I'd wander into the kitchen and watch my grandma peeling potatoes. I'd watch her so intently that she'd turn around and ask, "What's the matter?"

"I'm *bored*."

"Do you want to read?"

"No."

"Want to go outside and play?"

"Nope."

"Want to play Scrabble?"

"No."

"Well, then, dear, what *do* you want to do?"

I would stare back at her, expressionless. She'd return to peeling the potatoes.

We enacted this scene almost every day on my visits. But one summer, as my grandmother was peeling potatoes and I was slumped in a chair at the kitchen table, watching her, she turned to me and said, "Why don't you write something?"

"*What*?" I hadn't heard this one before.

"Why don't you pretend you're a reporter and you're going to write a story for the evening edition?"

"But I don't know how to be a reporter."

"I'll show you how."

And with that, grandma set off to look for my costume. She gave me a small pad and pencil. She gave me an old hat of grandpa's. She wrote *Press* on a slip of paper and stuck it in the hatband. Then she said, "Why don't you interview grandpa?"

At least I think that's what she said. I was already looking for grandpa.

He was sitting at the dining room table, staring at his typewriter. His hands were clasped behind his head. He was reading the newly typed sheet in front of him, silently mouthing the words. He looked up from his work and said, "Well, what have we got here?"

"I'm a reporter and I'm here to interview you for the evening edition!"

"Sure. Pull up a chair. Care for a drink?"

"Can't. I'm on the job."

"Very well, then. What can I do for you?"

I asked grandpa how old he was, how much he weighed, how tall.

I asked about his favorite color and record and book. I asked him why he loved grandma and whether he wished he could live forever. I asked him why he sat at his typewriter all afternoon and into the darkness, typing.

He said he typed because he was writing stories.

"Stories about what?"

"Stories about what I see when I close my eyes and listen very, very carefully."

"Listen to what?"

"To the radio. To the mourning doves. To you playing the organ. To the beating of my own heart."

He smiled and asked me if I had any other questions. I said, "No, that does it."

He went back to staring at the page and reading his words to himself. And then he put his fingers on the keys and began writing.

I stayed there, very still in my chair and wrote down the things I noticed about grandpa as he worked—the way his glasses glinted when the light hit them just so, the way his right hand would raise up from the keys and push the return and land back on the keys in one fluid motion, the way he smiled at being watched and documented.

I worked on my story for several days. When I was done, grandma pasted it onto a large sheet of construction paper with a masthead that read, *Stacy Times.* Both grandma and grandpa said they liked my story very much.

## PERFORMING WRITING, PERFORMING ETHNOGRAPHY

The story I wrote at my grandparents' house that summer did not come out of nowhere. I intended to write it. I donned the costume of a reporter and I played the role as I remembered it—watching carefully, asking questions, and writing things down. I don't recall how the story went, but I do know that it was about grandpa's performance as a writer. It was about music and movement and the beating of his heart. It was my first attempt at writing a text that enacted the very art it sought to inscribe. It was my first experience with the performance and unrequited desires of ethnography.

Like the torch song, ethnography is a storytelling institution that is lyrical, verbose.[30] Ethnographies often take the form of a "postmodern lament" that evokes melancholy, mourning, nostalgia, and release in the intersections of writers and readers.[31] And like torch songs, the stories of ethnography seek to create a highly charged, emotional atmosphere that encourages the participation of readers.[32]

Ethnographic representations are also processes and productions of *desire.*[33] Like the desire to love and be loved expressed in the torch song, ethnographers and their subjects engage in a lover's discourse, a "charged exchange of presence—or mutual presentness."[34] Like torch singing, ethnography is a love story, an intimate provocation.

Ethnographers try to make points of contact between authors, texts, performances, and contexts. In doing so, we must address the impossibility of "capturing" lived experience, the difficulty of establishing textual authority and the conditions for its interpretation and evaluation, and the challenge of creating change outside of texts and discursive practices.[35]

One possible way to connect is through performance—through practicing and understanding ethnography *as a performance* as well as practicing and understanding performance as a *means* for creating and embodying cultural meanings.[36] With its focus on specificity and the permeable and partial nature of experience and context, intimacy and emotion, and participation and provocation, performance highlights the intersubjective practices of culture and ethnography.[37] And rather than view subjectivity as a stable, coherent force that enhances or detracts from objectively valid ethnographic data and claims about social and cultural knowledge, performance ethnography seeks to show how multiple and shifting subjectivities are constructed in and constructive of their representations.[38] The power and presence of these representations are not contained in the "object" of a story, but in the interaction of performers and audience members.[39]

Performance also underscores how ethnographic representations are not merely "carriers" of ideological narratives, but "sites of political negotiation."[40] Using a storied, performative approach to representation enables us to "locate specific sites at which change can be produced" and to "employ participatory forms that bring persons from the everyday world directly into the narrative, storytelling process."[41] In other words, performing ethnographic stories not only provides the process, form, and context for critique, but also constitutes its very activity. Whatever truth claims emerge in the collision of conversation and meaning and the connection of text and performance are "the very motive for telling the story and its point in the end."[42]

There is never a complete or final textual or performative "solution, no way of resolving the dialogic of the interpreter/interpreted or subject/object through efforts to 'place' ourselves in the text, or to represent 'the fieldwork experience' or to gather up the voices of the other as if they could speak for themselves."[43] Instead, writing performance and writing ethnography practice an ethics of "nonmastery, a recognition that we often do not know what we are seeing, how much we are missing, what we are not understanding."[44] They are open-ended and ongoing, "point[s] of entry to experience, to culture, to power, to history."[45]

Creating these points of entry—these open-ended, responsible, and free representations—requires a radical form of textuality.[46] It is a textuality that urges authors to assemble hybrid, "multigenre texts" that nervously juxtapose "interruptions, amassed densities of description, evocations of voices and the conditions of their possibility, and lyrical, ruminative aporias that give pause."[47] This textuality is "organized by the principle that even if something did not happen, it could have happened," while striving for a "fundamental accuracy about what is heard and felt."[48] It approaches understanding as sensual and somatic, informed not by vision alone, but by all the senses.[49] It is musical—aurally, melodically, and rhythmically "stressing the sound and feel of worlds."[50] It traces the path of feeling and the movement of an unspoken idea; it "maps a territory not yet seen."[51] It *creates* a performance, rather than describes one.

## CIRCULAR BREATHING

This is the kind of text I have created in my love stories about torch singing. I have taken the responsibilities and challenges of writing performance and writing ethnography to heart. I have sketched a poetics and politics of torch that performs the radical potential it seeks to discover. Like torch singing, my performance requires an audience, readers willing to embrace an experimental, experiential, and critical encounter with a text.[52] The meaning of these stories inheres in the generative processes of listening, hearing, playing, and reading into everyday instances of conflict and struggle. This text—our performance—is a kind of critical circular breathing, a simultaneous explaining and questioning that hears an unexpected critique inside a recognizable melody.[53] Do you hear it, too?

Though maybe the question isn't whether you hear an unexpected critique inside a torch song, inside this text. Maybe the question is, What do these stories, my love stories, do? Who or what are they for?[54]

## FOOTNOTES, AND THE HABIT OF TURNING BACK IN ORDER TO CHECK A POINT, NEED TO BE INTRODUCED INTO PLAY WRITING, TOO[55]

1. Avery F. Gordon, *Ghostly Matters: Haunting and the Sociological Imagination* (Minneapolis: University of Minnesota Press, 1997), 146.

2. Diane Losche, "The Impossible Aesthetic: The Abelan, the Moa Bird and Me," *Oceana* 66 (1996): 309.

3. Geoff Dyer, *But Beautiful: A Book About Jazz* (New York: North Point, 1996), 190.

4. Portions of the stories about watching Lawrence Welk and my grandparents appear in revised form in Stacy Holman Jones, "Autoethnography: Making the Personal Political," in *The Sage Handbook of Qualitative Research*, 3rd ed., ed. Norman K. Denzin and Yvonna S. Lincoln, 777, 779–80 (Thousand Oaks, CA: Sage, 2005).

5. k. d. lang, "Miss Chatelaine," lyrics by k. d. lang and Ben Mink, *Ingénue*, Sire, 1992. My discussion is based on this recording.

6. k. d. lang, "Big Boned Gal," by k. d. lang and Ben Mink, *Absolute Torch and Twang*, Sire, 1989. My discussion is based on this recording.

7. Janelle Reinelt, "Notes for a Radical Democratic Theater: Productive Crises and the Challenge of Indeterminacy," in *Staging Resistance: Essays on Political Theater*, ed. Jeanne Colleran and Jenny S. Spencer, 283–300 (Ann Arbor: University of Michigan Press, 1998), 292, 291. I am borrowing Reinelt's description of Anna Deavere Smith's performance technique in which she interviews individuals involved in specific social, cultural, and political events (for example, *Twilight—Los Angeles 1992* explores events surrounding the beating of Rodney King) and then embodies their words, gestures, and individual style in her performance. Reinelt writes that "Smith's performance technique [is] a bridge that makes unlikely things seem connected." Reinelt also asserts that performance asks people to "choose to participate in an event that recognizes the marginality of some members of the society and strengthens that group by force of taking place."

8. "Palimpsest," *Merriam-Webster Online*, n.d., www.merriam-webster.com.

9. Kurt Weill and Bertolt Brecht, lyrics for "Mack the Knife," BobbyDarin.net, n.d., www.bobbydarin.net/macklyrics.html (accessed June 6, 2005).

10. Penfield adds "from the cash machine" to the lyrics.

11. Duke Ellington and Irving Mills, lyrics for "It Don't Mean a Thing (If It Ain't Got That Swing)," Heptune, n.d., www.heptune.com/lyrics/itdontme (accessed June 6, 2005).

12. I am borrowing from Josephine Lee's description ("Pity and Terror as Public Acts: Reading Feminist Politics in the Plays of Maria Irene Fornes," in *Staging Resistance: Essays on Political Theater*, edited by Jeanne Colleran and Jenny S. Spencer, 183 [Ann Arbor: University of Michigan Press, 1998]), of Maria Irene Fornes's work, which she argues forces performance critics to reconsider Brecht's assumption that dramatic theater "automatically results in a simple mimetic process, with the spectator compelled to repeat ideological patterns imprinted on her by the [theater] events she witnesses."

13. Lee, "Pity and Terror," 176, writes, "Emotional empathy—the recognition experienced in familiar, repeated action—is emphasized as pleasurable as well as necessary."

14. I am referencing Lee's writing ("Pity and Terror," 168, 169) about the difficulty in achieving the alienation and critical distance of Brecht's epic theater and the inadvisability of working against emotional identification and entanglement in performance. Lee notes that Brecht's epic theater "interrupts the illusion of reality and prevents the spectator's being 'carried away.' . . . Agency might be conceived of as control over empathic identifications." Writing about the music in *The Threepenny Opera* (which includes "Mack the Knife"), Bertolt Brecht, *Brecht on Theatre*, ed. John Willett, 44–45 (New York: Hill, 1991), instructs that "the actor must not only sing but show a man singing." This prevents the spectator from being carried away by a full identification with the performer or the song. He also asserts that "the music, just because it took up a purely emotional attitude and spurned none of the stock narcotic attractions, became an active collaborator in the stripping bare of the middleclass corpus of ideas" (85).

15. Robin D. G. Kelley, *Race Rebels: Culture, Politics, and the Black Working Class* (New York: Free Press, 1994), 8.

16. Raymond Williams, *Marxism and Literature* (Oxford: Oxford University Press, 1977), 132.

17. Ellington and Mills, "It Don't Mean a Thing."

18. Sandoval, *Methodology of the Oppressed*, foreword by Angela Y. Davis (Minneapolis: University of Minnesota Press, 2000), 62, writes that differential oppositional consciousnesses are "composed of narratives worked self-consciously. Its processes generate the other story—the counterpoise."

19. Portions of this analysis appear in revised form in Holman Jones, "Autoethnography," 782–83.

20. Colleran and Spencer, "Introduction," 1. See also Baz Kershaw, *The Radical in Performance: Between Brecht and Baudrillard* (London: Routledge, 1999).

21. Kershaw, *Radical in Performance*, 18.

22. Kershaw, *Radical in Performance*, 19.

23. This line is inspired by a comment made by Arthur Laurents in the film *The Celluloid Closet*, dir. and prod. Rob Epstein and Jeffrey Friedman, Telling Pictures, 1995. Laurents observes that "all minority audiences watch movies with hope."

24. Kershaw, *Radical in Performance*, 18. Kershaw prefers the term radical to political, basing his usage of radical on Williams's definition, which, beginning in the midtwentieth century, "seemed to offer a way of avoiding dogmatic and factional association while reasserting the need for vigorous and fundamental change." See Raymond Williams, *Keywords: A Vocabulary of Culture and Society*, rev. ed. (London: Fontana, 1983), 252.

25. Kershaw, *Radical in Performance*, 20.

26. Brecht, *Brecht on Theatre*, 44.

27. I have located torch singing in the context of its first performances in the United States while considering contemporary incarnations of musical genres and performance styles that do not neatly fit into these social, cultural, and political frames. I have written about performances I experience on record or film or in photographs alongside those that I participate in, live, in person. I have drawn inspiration and explanations from performers, music critics, linguists, political theorists, feminists, musicologists, fans, anthropologists, performance scholars, literary theorists, sociologists, friends, and musicians. I have sampled and cited and combined and repeated ideas about hidden transcripts; everyday politics; haunting; fandom; star discourses and lover's discourses; autobiographics; modern and postmodern irony; silence; visibility and surveillance; structures of feeling; consciousness-raising; spectatorship; reciprocity; standpoints and situated knowledges; emotional, cultural, political, and ideological space; shared agency; differential oppositional consciousness; and resistive and radical performance.

28. Kershaw, *Brecht on Theatre*, 218.

29. Edith Piaf and Louis Guglielmi, lyrics for "La Vie en Rose," http://home.earthlink.net/~tenspeed/SimonaSara/rose (accessed April 15, 2001).

30. John Van Maanen, "An End to Innocence: The Ethnography of Ethnography," *Representation in Ethnography*, ed. John Van Maanen, 3 (Thousand Oaks, CA: Sage, 1995).

31. Carolyn Ellis and Michael G. Flaherty, "An Agenda for the Interpretation of Lived Experience," in *Investigating Subjectivity: Research on Lived Experience*, ed. Carolyn Ellis and Michael G. Flaherty, 35 (Newbury Park, CA: Sage, 1992).

32. Norman K. Denzin, *Interpretive Ethnography: Ethnographic Practices for the 21st Century* (Thousand Oaks, CA: Sage, 1997), 209, 246.

33. Lyall Crawford, "Personal Ethnography," *Communication Monographs* 63 (1996): 167, wonders whether the "experience of falling in love with the people about whom one is curious" might be a way to avoid appropriating the lives and experiences of others for one's own purposes. Barbara Tedlock, "From Participant Observation to the Observation of Participation: The Emergence of Narrative Ethnography," *Journal of Anthropological Research* 47 (1991): 82, characterizes the process of the ethnographer as that of an amateur, which derives from the Latin *amatus*, or "to love." See also Sandoval's discussion of differential consciousness and love in *Methodology of the Oppressed.*

34. Jill Dolan, *Presence and Desire: Essays on Gender, Sexuality, Performance* (Ann Arbor: University of Michigan Press, 1993), 151.

35. Denzin, *Interpretive Ethnography*, 3–4. These challenges are often termed the crises of representation, legitimation, and praxis. Laurel Richardson, *Writing Strategies: Reaching Diverse Audiences*, Sage University Paper Series on Qualitative Research Methods, vol. 21 (Newbury Park, CA: Sage, 1990), 12, writes that the crisis of representation in ethnography

grows out of an "uncertainty about what constitutes adequate depiction of social reality." Andrew C. Sparkes, "Writing People: Reflections on the Dual Crises of Representation and Legitimation in Qualitative Inquiry," *Quest* 47 (1995): 159, writes that the crisis of representation problematizes and politicizes the nature of authorship and asks scholars to confront the impossibility of directly and completely capturing lived experience. Sparkes also asserts that the crisis of legitimation in ethnography problematizes and politicizes the traditional criteria used to evaluate scholarship and calls for a rethinking of notions of truth, validity, generalizability, reliability, and meaning. Denzin, *Interpretive Ethnography*, 4, characterizes the crisis of praxis as questioning whether it is "possible to effect change in the world, if society is only and always a text." These crises have prompted ethnographers to investigate new critical theoretical perspectives that denaturalize and deconstruct the nature and purpose of scholarship (feminist theory, cultural studies, queer theory, postcolonial studies), as well as forms of scholarly representation and the criteria by which scholarship is judged to be responsible, rigorous, and effective.

36. Joni L. Jones, "Performance Ethnography: The Role of Embodiment in Cultural Authenticity," *Theatre Topics* 21 (2002): 7, writes that performance ethnography is "most simply, how culture is done in the body." See also Norman K. Denzin, *Performance Ethnography: Critical Pedagogy and the Politics of Culture* (Thousand Oaks, CA: Sage, 2003), 2, who writes, we are "performing culture as we write it."

37. This statement draws heavily from Dwight Conquergood's writing about performance ethnography. In "Rethinking Ethnography: Towards a Critical Cultural Politics," *Communication Monographs* 58 (June 1991): 187, he notes, "The performance paradigm privileges particular, participatory, dynamic, intimate, precarious, embodied experience grounded in historical process, contingency, and ideology. . . . Performance-centered research takes as both its subject matter and method the experiencing body situated in time, place, and history. The performance paradigm insists on face-to-face encounters instead of abstractions and reductions."

38. Shannon Jackson, "Ethnography and the Audition: Performance as Ideological Critique," *Text and Performance Quarterly* 13, no. 1 (1993): 25.

39. Henry M. Sayre, *The Object of Performance: The American Avant-Garde since 1970* (Chicago: University of Chicago Press, 1989), 6. See also Denzin, *Interpretive Ethnography*, 94–95, who writes that performance texts and "ethnographic stagings" can "undo the voyeuristic, gazing eye of the ethnographer, bringing audiences and performers into a jointly felt and shared field of experience. These works also unsettle the writer's place in the text, freeing the text and the writer to become interactional productions. The performance text is the single, most powerful way for ethnography to recover yet interrogate meanings of lived experience."

40. Denzin, 247. See also Elin Diamond, "Introduction," in *Performance and Cultural Politics*, ed. Elin Diamond, 2 (London: Routledge, 1996), who writes, "Viewing performance within a

complex matrix of power, serving diverse cultural desires, encourages a permeable understanding of history and change."

41 Denzin, 248.

42. Kathleen Stewart, *A Space on the Side of the Road: Cultural Poetics in an "Other" America* (Princeton, NJ: Princeton University Press, 1996), 211. Of course, performers and ethnographers must take responsibility for their interpretations and representations. Dwight Conquergood, "Performing as a Moral Act: Ethical Dimensions of the Ethnography of Performance," *Text and Performance Quarterly* 5, no. 2 (April 1985): 1–13, cautions ethnographers to avoid several ethical "pitfalls" that can lead to abuses of the performer's authority, disregard for the subject's humanity, and a shirking of responsibility for the audience's experience and understanding of the performance. These pitfalls include "The Custodian's Rip-Off," "The Enthusiast's Infatuation," "The Curator's Exhibitionism," and "The Skeptic's Cop-Out." The Custodian, or cultural imperialist, enters the field in order to find and appropriate material for a performance, often denigrating sacred cultural texts in the process (4). The Enthusiast blindly forges an easy and superficial identification with the "other," refusing to become deeply engaged and thus trivializing the experience (and performance) of the other (6–7). The Curator or tour guide is committed to the absolute difference of the other, so much so that she sensationalizes the performance and exoticizes the other (7–8). Curators fail to recognize that it's not polite to stare. Finally, ever the cynic, the Skeptic throws her hands up and declares it impossible to perform an "other" (7). What the Skeptic fails to note is that only the voice of privilege can enjoy such an easy out. Conquergood also outlines a morally responsible stance, which he terms dialogic performance. Here, different experiences, viewpoints, and subjectivities—those of the performer and her subject(s)—are brought together so they can "question, debate, and challenge one another" (9). See also Joni L. Jones, "The Self as Other: Creating the Role of Joni the Ethnographer for *Broken Circles*," *Text and Performance Quarterly* 16 (1996): 134–37, and Kamala Visweswaran, *Fictions of Feminist Ethnography* (Minneapolis: University of Minnesota Press, 1994), 48.

43. Stewart, *Space on the Side of the Road*, 210.

44. Patti Lather, "Postbook: Working the Ruins of Feminist Ethnography," *Signs* 26, no. 4 (2001): 216.

45. Stewart, *Space on the Side of the Road*, 211.

46. This textuality has been given many names, including (but by no means limited to) imaginative criticism, experimental texts, experimental critical writing, performative writing, and cultural poesis. See G. Dyer, *But Beautiful*, vii; Denzin, *Interpretive Ethnography*, 44–48; Eve Kosofsky Sedgwick, "Teaching 'Experimental Critical Writing,'" in *The Ends of Performance*, ed. Peggy Phelan and Jill Lane, 104–15 (New York: New York University Press, 1998); Della Pollock, "Performative Writing," in Phelan and Lane, *Ends of Performance*, 73–103; and Kathleen Stewart, "Cultural Poesis: The Generativity of Emergent Things," in Denzin and Lincoln, *Sage Handbook of Qualitative Research*, 3rd ed., 1027–28, respectively. As their naming implies, these texts are

disparate and complex, though each centers on discursive *practice*, rather than establishing a specific form or genre of writing (Pollock, "Performative Writing," 75).

47. Stewart, *Space on the Side of the Road*, 7. See also Lather, "Postbook," 206, and Paul Stoller, *Sensuous Scholarship* (Philadelphia: University of Pennsylvania Press, 1997), 42.

48. Denzin, *Interpretive Ethnography*, 46.

49. Denzin, *Interpretive Ethnography*, 46. See also Stoller, *Sensuous Scholarship*, xv–xvi.

50. Denzin, *Interpretive Ethnography*, 46. Many of the characteristics of performative texts are hallmarks of feminist approaches to ethnography and performance. See, for example writing about feminist ethnography including Lila Abu-Lughod, "Can There Be a Feminist Ethnography?" *Women and Performance* 5, no. 1 (1990): 7–27; Elspeth Pobryn, "Moving Selves and Stationary Others: Ethnography's Ontological Dilemma," in *Sexing the Self: Gendered Positions in Cultural Studies*, 58–81 (New York: Routledge, 1993); and Visweswaran, *Fictions of Feminist Ethnography*. In performance studies see, for example, Jeanie Forte, "Women's Performance Art: Feminism and Postmodernism," in *Performing Feminisms: Feminist Critical Theory and Theater*, ed. Sue-Ellen Case, 251–69 (Baltimore: Johns Hopkins University Press, 1990); Peggy Phelan, *Unmarked: The Politics of Performance* (New York: Routledge, 1993); and Jill Dolan, *Geographies of Learning: Theory and Practice, Activism and Performance* (Middletown, CT: Wesleyan University Press, 2001).

51. Peggy Phelan, "Introduction: The Ends of Performance," in Phelan and Lane, *Ends of* Performance, 14.

52. Denzin, *Interpretive Ethnography*, 246.

53. Stacy Wolf, *A Problem Like Maria: Gender and Sexuality in the American Musical* (Ann Arbor: University of Michigan Press, 2002), 38, writes of lesbian readings of performance that "finding a lesbian in representation requires a certain circular knowledge."

54. This line is borrowed from Pollock, "Performative Writing," 98, who writes of an author who asks, "'What is [performative writing]?' and finds [her]self now reading writing, writing reading, touching pages touching me, drawing me into mutual desire for—what? what is it for? The question moves as does the writing, forward, into exigency. Performative writing is what it is not in itself but for . . . for what? . . . It is for writing, for writing ourselves out of our-selves, for writing our-selves into what (never) was and may (never) be. It is/is it for love?"

55. Brecht, *Brecht on Theatre*, 44.

# 9

# Music for Torching

Like Alice, wherever [she] goes she gets there only by proceeding in a different direction.

—*Richard Eder, "To Understand Is to Be Perplexed"*[1]

Moments of being pierced, being surrounded by sound, being called, are worth collecting.

—*Wayne Koestenbaum,* The Queen's Throat[2]

Billie Holiday started to sing, hauntingly, and an indefinable electricity touched the audience. Billie was singing . . . with an infinite tenderness and warmth, with infinite heartbreak in every phrase. Billie Holiday, on this night, was singing her songs—music for torching.

—*Liner notes,* Music for Torching with Billie Holiday[3]

---

**AND FIRES BURN**

I kept the rented piano. And I kept practicing my torch songs—listening carefully, picking out notes, and playing by ear. Ignoring the humid August air that seeps in under loose floorboards and the roar of an afternoon thunderstorm, I place my fingers on the keys. Inspired, I tap out first "Stormy Weather" and then "My Man." I begin "Not to Worry," deciding to sing along. Rain beats down on my tiny rented house and the first drops fall from a leak that resists repair. As the water finds its way through the small opening and marks time on the floor, I sing, "Never mind a sad romance. A time has come. A corner turned. It's clearer now. The lessons learned. And time will tell. And fires burn . . ."[4]

**AND SUNSHINE, TOO**

Alice imagines that she is dancing, spinning into a shimmering, light-filled place. Colors flash before her eyes—crimson, ochre, scarlet, saffron, garnet, burnt orange. These are the colors of fire, the colors of passion for a form, a lyric, a space of possibility and hope. Heat pulses around her and Alice hears the first tentative notes. She takes her seat and waits for the curtain to draw into her longing—for recognition, for pleasure and, yes, for freedom. Horns, strings, and a lone bass create a stage for her voice, for the voices of yearning and movement. Alice imagines herself in the sounding of desire.

Alice imagines this as she files into the theater in another town, on the threshold of another concert. This theater is red like the others, with a peeling and faded grandness. Tonight she wants a more expansive view of the stage and the audience, so she chooses a seat in the balcony. She sinks into the stiff velvet and runs her hands along the armrests. She leans back and thinks of other seats in other venues—waiting, open, full of anticipation. She begins her preshow ritual, folding a single sheet of notebook paper in half and then in half again, creating a small book in which she will record song titles and musical details and fleeting observations. She pins the book closed with the clasp of her pen and covers it with her hand.

Alice watches the theater fill with people. She reminds herself to look for demographic clues—ages, genders, races, ethnicities, sexualities. But as she looks into the faces of the men and women who spread into the theater, what she notices is their parted lips, their searching eyes. What she notices is that the people here are looking for something, too, waiting for something to happen.

Alice shifts in her seat. The theater is warm and as more and more people crowd through the doors and into the aisles, the temperature climbs until Alice is sticky with sweat. She fans herself with the blank notebook paper and wonders how long until the music begins. She closes her eyes and imagines that the lights are dimming and the curtain is swinging open.

The applause begins and Alice opens her eyes. The announcer says, "Patricia Barber might just be the coolest singer-songwriter around. She has really paid her dues, enduring slights from the musical establishment until the world caught up with her and realized what an amazing talent she is. Fans who saw her at last year's festival certainly seem to think so. She's back again to dazzle us with her mix of jazz, minimalism, and torch song sensuality." Then the announcer says, "Ladies and gentlemen, Patricia Barber!"

A tide of applause moves through the audience and Barber, along with a stand-up bass player and drummer, walks into the spotlight. Barber sits behind the shimmering piano and places her fingers on the keys. She plays a single chord, a siren note. She sings, "I fall in love too easily/I fall in love too fast."[5] Her voice is sparse, almost a whisper. She closes her eyes and bows her head. Alice's blood pulses in her ears. Her breath comes fast.

She sings, "I fall in love too terribly hard/for love ever to last." She takes her fingers from the keys and lays them over her heart. She taps out a beat as her voice holds the note. Alice feels a space inside her chest open up. She sighs and leans in, trying to absorb every sound, every movement, every hidden promise.

She sings, "My heart should be well schooled/'cause I've been fooled in the past," and Alice's eyes are wet. She is pierced by a voice, by a sentimental song. She is surprised by this naked need, so close to the surface.

She sings, "I fall in love too easily/I fall in love too fast," slowly, each note a photograph of loss and regret. Alice closes her eyes, the tears stinging and spilling over. She imagines her own hands on the keys, trying to write this feeling. She imagines saying that performance itself—ephemeral, impossible to capture or record or re-create—is hopefulness in the moment of loss. She imagines that listening to Patricia Barber sing "I Fall in Love Too Easily" in a humid theater packed tight with lovers is to witness the power of desire and want, the hungry willingness to follow a voice wherever it leads. She imagines that the deepest desire is the desire to give responsibility for our own desire to someone, somebody else.[6] She imagines such a desire as an ironic investment in (an)other, a play of opposites, an explosion of ideas and categories from the inside out, from below and around the beat. Alice imagines she can story this moment in a word, on a page. She reaches for her empty book and slides the pen from the paper.

But it is too hot. My fingers are stiff and swollen, unwilling to write. I push the pen and the blank page down into the seat, deciding to take a different direction. I decide to just listen, to try and hear and see and feel the music. I imagine that the deepest desire is the desire to listen to our own desires, in all of their contradictions and failings and hopeful delays. I imagine that being pierced by a voice and surrounded by sound and called to the stage are worth paying attention to, worth collecting. I imagine that *this* is the art of torch singing. It is a reimagining of the torch song—that sentimental ballad of unrequited love, victimhood, and the pleasure of pain—into a space for the sounding of desire and the performance of possibility.

Barber closes the show with "You Are My Sunshine."[7] Her voice is raspy, vague. Her sound reminds me of words critics used to describe Billie Holiday's mature voice—the voice marked by excess. It was diminished, ravaged, *burnt*. It lacked materiality. It was over, destroyed.[8] This isn't true. In quiet tones and whispered notes, Holiday's voice—a torch singer's voice—is utterly there, on record, and, hopefully, here in these pages. She sings not a fictional but a *live* and *alive* body, an unforgettable circumstance and history, an honest and ironic account, a grainy love song. She sings—*just sings*—sharpening love in the service of myth.[9] Her sound, her body, and her language tell (an)other story. Her burnt, torched voice isn't (only) evidence of her surrender to a destined decimation, but (also) the promise of new growth after the fire.

Barber places her hand over her heart, speaking to us in the pause; waiting, deciding. She takes a breath and begins again, "You are my sunshine . . ." Her voice is crimson, scarlet, burnt-orange. Alice is seeing red. I see it, too. We follow, deeply inside the power of stories. We hear the shifting, humming shades of fire. It is music for torching.

## SEEING RED AND OTHER SHADES, SHADOWS, AND LIGHTS

1. Richard Eder, "To Understand Is to Be Perplexed: The Life's Work of the Shape-Shifting Paul Muldoon, a Poet at Large in a Universe That Won't Hold Still," *New York Times Book Review*, June 10, 2001, 14.

2. Wayne Koestenbaum, *The Queen's Throat: Opera, Homosexuality, and the Mystery of Desire* (New York: Poseidon, 1993), 16.

3. *Music for* Torching *with Billie Holiday*, liner notes, Verve, 1995.

4. Abbey Lincoln, "Not to Worry," *A Turtle's Dream*, Verve, 1995.

5. Patricia Barber, "I Fall in Love Too Easily," lyrics by Sammy Cahn and Jule Styne, *Nightclub*, Premonition, 2000. My discussion is based on this recording.

6. Jean Baudrillard, *Selected Writings*, ed. with an introduction by Mark Poster (Stanford, CA: Stanford University Press, 1988), 215.

7. Jimmie Davis and Charles Mitchell, lyrics for "You Are My Sunshine," n.d., www.geocities.com/holidaysfun/sunshine (accessed June 6, 2005).

8. See Leslie Gourse, "Preface," in *The Billie Holiday Companion: Seven Decades of Commentary*, ed. Leslie Gourse (New York: Schirmer, 1997), xxii, who writes, "Around 1950, her voice took on a subtly dismaying hue. Her undertones and low notes began to sound almost *burnt*; they took on an acrid quality." See also Farah Jasmine Griffin's description (*If You Can't Be Free, Be a Mystery: In Search of Billie Holiday* [New York: Free Press, 2001], 156–58) of Holiday's voice in terms of the open stanza of Rita Dove's poem on Holiday, "Canary": "Billie Holiday's burned voice/had as many shadows as lights,/a mournful candelabra against a sleek piano,/the gardenia her signature under that ruined face" (poem reprinted in Griffin, *If You Can't Be Free*, 156). Griffin notes, "In this stanza, her voice and her signature gardenia are the things by which we remember her, the sound and image that can invoke her presence. The voice is burned—it lacks materiality. The face is ruined. Both 'ruined' and 'burned' are verbs in the past tense. They are also adjectives that suggest things are over, past and destroyed" (156). The final line of the poem "stands free from the other stanzas." It reads, "If you can't be free, be a mystery" (157). Griffin argues that this line "is a directive to the readers, one learned from Holiday. It opens out, telling others to choose mystery if you cannot have freedom. . . . Choosing to be a mystery is the one way to maintain a semblance of control, to keep your inner self to yourself. This is an act of agency from the unfree . . . . [Holiday] is what Lewis Turco describes as 'an unanchored abstraction,' that which means nothing and therefore can mean anything" (157–58). I would suggest that Holiday's voice (and the voices of the other torch singers I write about here) do not lack materiality; that they are not over, past, and destroyed. Torch singing might be one way (though not the only way) to exercise control over music and language and meaning because it is a *source of freedom*.

9. Dove, "Canary," reprinted in Griffin, *If You Can't Be Free*, 156. The third stanza of the poem reads, "Fact is, the invention of women under siege/has been to sharpen love in the service of myth."

# Bibliography

Abbate, Carolyn. "Opera; Or, the Envoicing of Women." In *Musicology and Difference: Gender and Sexuality in Music Scholarship*, edited by Ruth A. Solie, 225–58. Berkeley: University of California Press, 1993.

"Abbey Lincoln, Biography." bsonic.com, n.d. www.bsoinc.com/AbbeyLincoln.html (accessed April 20, 2001).

Abu-Lughod, Lila. "Can There Be a Feminist Ethnography?" *Women and Performance* 5, no. 1 (1990): 7–27.

Acker, Kathy. "Seeing Gender." *Critical Quarterly* 37, no. 4 (1995): 78–85.

Adams, Alice. *Listening to Billie.* New York: Knopf, 1978.

Albertson, Chris. "Abbey Lincoln: A Singer in a Class Lyrics by Herself." *Stereo Review* 60, no. 8 (August 1995). www.infotrac.com (accessed April 20, 2001).

Appignanesi, Lisa. *The Cabaret.* 2nd ed. New York: Grove, 1984.

Auslander, Philip. "Performance Analysis and Popular Music: A Manifesto." *Contemporary Theatre Review* 14, no. 1 (2004): 1–13.

Austin, J. L. *How to Do Things with Words.* Cambridge, MA: Harvard University Press, 1962.

Bacon, Nicholas, Libby Holmes, and Josh White. Lyrics for "The House of the Rising Sun." DigitalDreamDoor.com, n.d. www.digitaldreamdoor.com/pages/lyrics/house_rising.html (accessed July 8, 2005).

Baraka, Amiri. "Dark Lady of the Sonnets." In *The Billie Holiday Companion: Seven Decades of Commentary*, edited by Leslie Gourse, 182. New York: Schirmer, 1997.

Barber, Patricia. "I Fall in Love Too Easily." Lyrics by Sammy Cahn and Jule Styne. *Nightclub.* Premonition, 2000.

———. "Company." *Modern Cool.* Premonition Records, 1998.

"Barbra Streisand." N.d. www.music.excite.com/artist/biography/22897 (accessed April 15, 2001).

"Barbra Streisand, Biography." Barbra Streisand website, n.d. www.barbrastreisand.com/bio_bio_pg2.html (accessed June 6, 2005).

Barthes, Roland. *Camera Lucida: Reflections on Photography.* Translated by Richard Howard. London: Fontana, 1986.

———. *Image-Music-Text.* Translated by Stephen Heath. New York: Hill, 1977.

———. *A Lover's Discourse: Fragments.* Translated by Richard Howard. New York: Hill, 1978.

———. *The Pleasure of the Text.* Translated by Richard Miller. New York: Farrar, Straus and Giroux, 1975.

———. *The Responsibility of Forms: Critical Essays on Music, Art, and Representation.* Translated by Richard Howard. Berkeley: University of California Press, 1985.

Bartky, Sandra Lee. "Foucault, Femininity, and the Modernization of Patriarchal Power." In *Femininity and Domination: Studies in the Phenomenology of Oppression*, 63–82. New York: Routledge, 1991.

Baudrillard, Jean. *Selected Writings.* Edited with an introduction by Mark Poster. Stanford, CA: Stanford University Press, 1988.

Bedoian, Jim. Liner notes. *The First Torch Singers.* Vol. 1, *The Twenties.* Take Two Records, 1992.

Behler, Ernst. *Irony and the Discourse of Modernity.* Seattle: University of Washington Press, 1990.

Benterrak, Krim, Stephen Muecke, and Paddy Roe. *Reading the Country: Introduction to Nomadology.* Fremantle, Australia: Fremantle Arts, 1984.

Berlant, Lauren. "Intimacy: A Special Issue." In *Intimacy*, edited by Lauren Berlant, 1–8. Chicago: University of Chicago Press, 2000.

Biesecker, Barbara. "Coming to Terms with Recent Attempts to Write Women into the History of Rhetoric." *Philosophy and Rhetoric* 25, no. 2 (1992): 140–61.

"Billie Holiday." N.d. www.music.excite.com/artist/biography/33213 (accessed April 15, 2001).

"Billie Holiday, Biography." *DownBeat*, n.d. www.downbeat.com/default.asp?sect=artists (accessed June 3, 2005).

Blair, Gwenda. "Jazz Bird." *New York* magazine, June 3, 2002. www.newyorkmetro.com/nymetro/arts/music/jazz/reviews/6064 (accessed June 16, 2005).

Booth, Wayne C. *A Rhetoric of Irony.* Chicago: University of Chicago Press, 1974.

Brackett, David. *Interpreting Popular Music.* New York: Cambridge University Press, 1995.

Brecht, Bertolt. *Brecht on Theatre,* edited by John Willett. New York: Hill, 1991.

Bret, David. *The Mistinguett Legend.* London: Robson, 1990.

Brooks, Michael. Liner notes. *Billie Holiday—The Legacy (1933–1958).* Columbia/Legacy, 1991.

Bryson, Valerie. *Feminist Political Theory: An Introduction.* New York: Paragon House, 1992.

Burke, Kenneth. *A Grammar of Motives.* 1945. Berkeley: University of California Press, 1969. Page references are to the 1969 edition.

Butler, Judith. *Gender Trouble: Feminism and the Subversion of Identity.* New York: Routledge, 1990.

———. "Performative Acts and Gender Constitution: An Essay in Phenomenology and Feminist Theory." In *Performing Feminisms: Feminist Critical Theory and Theatre,* edited by Sue-Ellen Case, 270–82. Baltimore: Johns Hopkins University Press, 1990.

Carver, Raymond. *Call If You Need Me: The Uncollected Fiction and Other Prose.* 1991. New York: Vintage, 2000.

*The Celluloid Closet.* Videocassette. Directed and produced by Rob Epstein and Jeffrey Friedman. Telling Pictures, 1995.

Clarke, Donald. *Wishing on the Moon: The Life and Times of Billie Holiday.* New York: Viking, 1994.

Clements, Marcelle. "Sighing, a French Sound Endures." *New York Times,* October 18, 1998, AR2, 33–36.

Cloud, Dana L. *Control and Consolation in American Culture and Politics: Rhetorics of Therapy.* Thousand Oaks, CA: Sage, 1998.

———. "The Null Persona: Race and the Rhetoric of Silence in the Uprising of '34." *Rhetoric & Public Affairs* 2, no. 2 (1999): 177–209.

Colleran, Jeanne, and Jenny S. Spencer. "Introduction." In *Staging Resistance: Essays on Political Theater,* edited by Jeanne Colleran and Jenny S. Spencer, 1–10. Ann Arbor: University of Michigan Press, 1998.

Collis, Rose. *k.d. lang.* Somerset, England: Absolute Press, 1999.

"Coming Star." In *Diva: Barbra Streisand and the Making of a Superstar*, edited by Ethlie Ann Vare, 16–20. New York: Boulevard, 1996.

Conquergood, Dwight. "Performing as a Moral Act: Ethical Dimensions of the Ethnography of Performance." *Text and Performance Quarterly* 5, no. 2 (April 1985): 1–13.

———. "Rethinking Ethnography: Towards a Critical Cultural Politics." *Communication Monographs* 58 (June 1991): 179–94.

Crawford, Lyall. "Personal Ethnography." *Communication Monographs* 63 (1996): 158–70.

Crosland, Margaret. *Piaf.* New York: Fromm, 1987.

Daubney, Kate. "Songbird or Subversive? Instrumental Vocalisation Technique in the Songs of Billie Holiday." *Journal of Gender Studies* 11, no. 1 (2002): 17–28.

Davis, Angela Y. *Blues Legacies and Black Feminism: Gertrude "Ma" Rainey, Bessie Smith, and Billie Holiday.* New York: Pantheon, 1998.

Davis, Jimmie. Lyrics for "You Are My Sunshine." Music by Charles Mitchell. N.d. www.geocities.com/holidaysfun/sunshine (accessed June 6, 2005).

Davis, Ronald L. *A History of Music in American Life.* Vol. 3, *The Modern Era, 1920–Present.* Huntington, NY: Krieger, 1981.

Deleuze, Gilles. *Proust and Signs.* Translated by Richard Howard. New York: Braziller, 1972.

Denning, Michael. *The Cultural Front: The Laboring of American Culture in the Twentieth Century.* London: Verso, 1997.

Denzin, Norman K. *Interpretive Biography.* Sage University Paper Series on Qualitative Research Methods. Vol. 17. Newbury Park, CA: Sage, 1989.

———. *Interpretive Ethnography: Ethnographic Practices for the 21st Century.* Thousand Oaks, CA: Sage, 1997.

———. *Performance Ethnography: Critical Pedagogy and the Politics of Culture.* Thousand Oaks, CA: Sage, 2003.

Derrida, Jacques. *Speech and Phenomena and Other Essays on Husserl's Theory of Signs.* Translated by David B. Allison and Newton Garver. Evanston, IL: Northwestern University Press, 1973.

———. *Writing and Difference.* Translated by Alan Bass. Chicago: University of Chicago Press, 1978.

Diamond, Elin. "Introduction." In *Performance and Cultural Politics*, edited by Elin Diamond, 1–12. London: Routledge, 1996.

Dolan, Jill. "The Discourse of Feminisms: The Spectator and Representation." In *The Routledge Reader in Gender and Performance*, edited by Lizbeth Goodman, with Jane de Gay, 288–94. London: Routledge, 1998.

———. *The Feminist Spectator as Critic.* Ann Arbor: UNI Research, 1988.

———. *Geographies of Learning: Theory and Practice, Activism and Performance* (Middletown, CT: Wesleyan University Press, 2001).

———. *Presence and Desire: Essays on Gender, Sexuality, Performance.* Ann Arbor: University of Michigan Press, 1993.

———. "Rehearsing Democracy: Advocacy, Public Intellectuals, and Civic Engagement in Theatre and Performance Studies." *Theatre Topics* 11, no. 1 (2001): 1–17.

Du Bois, W.E.B. *The Souls of Black Folk: Essays and Sketches.* New York: Fawcett, 1961.

Dyer, Geoff. *But Beautiful: A Book about Jazz.* New York: North Point, 1996.

Dyer, Richard. *Heavenly Bodies: Film Stars and Society.* New York: St. Martin's, 1986.

Eagleton, Terry. *Ideology: An Introduction.* London: Verso, 1991.

———. *Walter Benjamin; or, Towards a Revolutionary Criticism.* London: Verso, 1981.

Ebert, Teresa. *Ludic Feminism and After: Postmodernism, Desire, and Labor in Late Capitalism.* Ann Arbor: University of Michigan Press, 1996.

Eder, Richard. "To Understand Is to Be Perplexed: The Life's Work of the Shape-Shifting Paul Muldoon, a Poet at Large in a Universe That Won't Hold Still." *New York Times Book Review,* June 10, 2001, 14.

"Edith Piaf." N.d. www.music.excite.com/artist/biography/18980 (accessed April 15, 2001).

*Edith Piaf: La Vie en Rose.* Videocassette. New River Media, 1985.

Edwards, Anne. *Streisand: A Biography.* Boston: Little, Brown, 1997.

Elam, Harry J., Jr. *Taking It to the Streets: The Social Protest Theater of Luis Valdez and Amiri Baraka.* Ann Arbor: University of Michigan Press, 1997.

Ellington, Duke, and Irving Mills. Lyrics for "It Don't Mean a Thing (If It Ain't Got That Swing)." Heptune, n.d. www.heptune.com/lyrics/itdontme (accessed June 6, 2005).

Ellis, Carolyn, and Michael G. Flaherty. "An Agenda for the Interpretation of Lived Experience." In *Investigating Subjectivity: Research on Lived Experience,* edited by Carolyn Ellis and Michael Flaherty, 1–13. Newbury Park, CA: Sage, 1992.

"Engagement." *The Random House Dictionary of the English Language.* 2nd ed. New York: Random House, 1987.

Engh, Barbara. "Loving It: Music and Criticism in Roland Barthes." In *Musicology and Difference: Gender and Sexuality in Music Scholarship,* edited by Ruth A. Solie, 66–79. Berkeley: University of California Press, 1993.

Erenberg, Lewis A. *Swingin' the Dream: Big Band Jazz and the Rebirth of American Culture.* Chicago: University of Chicago Press, 1998.

Farley, Reynolds, and Walter R. Allen. *The Color Line and the Quality of Life in America.* New York: Sage Foundation, 1987.

Farnsworth, Marjorie. *The Ziegfeld Follies.* New York: Bonanza, 1956.

Feather, Leonard. "Lady Day." In *The Billie Holiday Companion: Seven Decades of Commentary,* edited by Leslie Gourse, 3–17. New York: Schirmer, 1997.

———. "Lady Day Has Her Say." In *The Billie Holiday Companion: Seven Decades of Commentary,* edited by Leslie Gourse, 57–61. New York: Schirmer, 1997.

Ferguson, Kathy E. *The Man Question: Visions of Subjectivity in Feminist Theory.* Berkeley: University of California Press, 1993.

Friedman, Michael. "Patricia Barber on 'Modern Cool.'" *All about Jazz,* November 1998. www.allaboutjazz.com/iviews/pbarber.htm (accessed April 12, 2001).

Friedwald, Will. *Jazz Singing: America's Great Voices from Bessie Smith to Bebop and Beyond.* New York: Da Capo, 1996.

Forte, Allen. *The American Popular Ballad of the Golden Era, 1924–1950.* Princeton, NJ: Princeton University Press, 1995.

Forte, Jeanie. "Women's Performance Art: Feminism and Postmodernism." In *Performing Feminisms: Feminist Critical Theory and Theater,* edited by Sue-Ellen Case, 251–69. Baltimore: Johns Hopkins University Press, 1990.

Frith, Simon. "The Body Electric." *Critical Quarterly* 37, no. 2 (1995): 1–9.

———. *Performing Rites: On the Value of Popular Music.* Cambridge, MA: Harvard University Press, 1996.

*Funny Girl.* Videocassette. Directed by William Wyler. Performed by Barbra Streisand, Omar Sharif, and Kay Medford. Columbia/Tristar, 1968.

Fuoss, Kirk W. "Performance as Contestation: An Agonistic Perspective on the Insurgent Assembly." In *Exceptional Spaces: Essays in Performance and History,* edited by Della Pollock, 98–117. Chapel Hill: University of North Carolina Press, 1998.

Gates, Henry Louis, Jr. *The Signifying Monkey: A Theory of African-American Literary Criticism.* New York: Oxford University Press, 1988.

Gershwin, George, and Ira Gershwin. Lyrics for "They Can't Take That Away from Me." LyricsFreak, n.d. www.lyricsfreak.com/b/billie-holiday/18026.html (accessed June 3, 2005).

Giddens, Gary. *Visions of Jazz: The First Century.* New York: Oxford University Press, 1998.

Gilmore, Leigh. "The Mark of Autobiography: Postmodernism, Autobiography, and Genre." In *Autobiography and Postmodernism,* edited by Kathleen Ashley, Leigh Gilmore, and Gerald Peters, 3–18. Amherst: University of Massachusetts Press, 1994.

———. "Policing Truth: Confession, Gender, and Autobiographical Authority." In *Autobiography and Postmodernism*, edited by Kathleen Ashley, Leigh Gilmore, and Gerald Peters, 54–78. Amherst: University of Massachusetts Press, 1994.

———. *Autobiographics: A Feminist Theory of Women's Self-Representation*. Ithaca, NY: Cornell University Press, 1994.

Gonzales, Michael A. "Torch Song Soliloquy: One Man's Poetic Tribute to Ladies Who Sing the Blues." *Mode*, February 1998, 52–55.

Gordon, Avery F. *Ghostly Matters: Haunting and the Sociological Imagination*. Minneapolis: University of Minnesota Press, 1997.

Gourse, Leslie. "Preface." In *The Billie Holiday Companion: Seven Decades of Commentary*, edited by Leslie Gourse, ix–xxii. New York: Schirmer, 1997.

———. *Sassy: The Life of Sarah Vaughan*. New York: Da Capo, 1994.

———. "There Was No Middle Ground with Billie Holiday." In *The Billie Holiday Companion: Seven Decades of Commentary*, edited by Leslie Gourse, 139–50. New York: Schirmer, 1997.

Granger, Percival, Robert Prince, and Clarence Williams. Lyrics for "Ain't Nobody's Business If I Do." Running Horse Lyrics Page, n.d. ww.therunninghorse.ukpub.net/lyrics.html (accessed June 3, 2005).

Griffin, Farah Jasmine. *If You Can't Be Free, Be a Mystery: In Search of Billie Holiday*. New York: Free Press, 2001.

Grumet, Madeline. "Scholae Personae: Masks for Meaning." In *Pedagogy: The Question of Impersonation*, edited by Jane Gallop, 36–45. Bloomington: Indiana University Press, 1995.

Guillaumin, Colette. *Racism, Sexism, Power and Ideology*. London: Routledge, 1995.

Hamm, Charles. *Yesterdays: Popular Song in America*. New York: Norton, 1979.

Haraway, Donna J. *How Like a Leaf: An Interview with Thyrza Nichols Goodeve/Donna J. Haraway*. New York: Routledge, 2000.

———. "Situated Knowledges: The Science Question in Feminism and the Privilege of Partial Perspective." *Feminist Studies* 14, no. 3 (1988): 575–99.

Hardin Armstrong, Lilla, and Don Raye. Lyrics for "Just for a Thrill." Todd and Sharon Peach's website, n.d. www.thepeaches.com/music/randb/JustForaThrill.txt (accessed June 3, 2005).

Hardwick, Elizabeth. "Billie Holiday: Sleepless Nights." In *The Billie Holiday Companion: Seven Decades of Commentary*, edited by Leslie Gourse, 160–67. New York: Schirmer, 1997.

Hartsock, Nancy C. M. "Comment on Hekman's 'Truth and Method: Feminist Standpoint Theory Revisited': Truth or Justice." *Signs: Journal of Women in Culture and Society* 22, no. 2 (Winter 1997): 367–75. http://sbweb2.med.icanet.com/infotrac (accessed June 4, 2005).

Haskins, James. *Lena: A Personal and Professional Biography of Lena Horne.* With Kathleen Benson. New York: Stein, 1984.

Hentoff, Nat. "The Real Lady Day." In *The Billie Holiday Companion: Seven Decades of Commentary*, edited by Leslie Gourse, 153–60. New York: Schirmer, 1997.

Hirschman, Alli. "Q & Alli: A Modern Cool Companion." October 25, 1999. www.premonitionandmusic.com/artists/barber/interviews (accessed April 15, 2001).

Holiday, Billie. *All or Nothing at All.* LP. Verve, n.d.

———. *Lady Sings the Blues.* With William Dufty. 1956. New York: Penguin, 1992. Page references are to the 1992 edition.

———. "My Man." Lyrics by Albert Willemetz and Jacques Charles. Music by Maurice Yvain. Translated by Channing Pollock. *The Essential Billie Holiday at Carnegie Hall.* Recorded November 1956. Verve, 1989.

———. "Strange Fruit." *Billie Holiday: Ken Burns Jazz.* Verve, 2000.

———. "They Can't Take That Away from Me." Lyrics by George Gershwin and Ira Gershwin. *Billie Holiday—The Legacy (1933–1958).* Columbia/Legacy, 1991.

Holman Jones, Stacy. "Autoethnography: Making the Personal Political." In *The Sage Handbook of Qualitative Research*, 3rd ed., edited by Norman K. Denzin and Yvonna S. Lincoln, 763–91. Thousand Oaks, CA: Sage, 2005.

———. "Emotional Space: Performing the Resistive Possibilities of Torch Singing." *Qualitative Inquiry* 8, no. 6 (2002): 738–59.

———. "Listening to the Bones: A Meditation on Torch Singers and Ghost Stories." In *The Green Window: Proceedings of the Giant City Conference on Performative Writing*, edited by Lynn C. Miller and Ronald J. Pelias, 8–18. Carbondale: Southern Illinois University Press, 2001.

———. "Torch." *Qualitative Inquiry* 5, no. 2 (June 1999): 280–304.

———. "The Way We Were, Are, and Might Be: Torch Singing as Autoethnography." In *Ethnographically Speaking: Autoethnography, Literature, and Aesthetics*, edited by Arthur P. Bochner and Carolyn Ellis, 44–56. Walnut Creek, CA: AltaMira, 2001.

hooks, bell. "Gangsta Culture—Sexism and Misogyny: Who Will Take the Rap?" In *Outlaw Culture: Resisting Representations*, 115–24. New York: Routledge, 1994.

———. "Performance Practice as a Site of Opposition." In *Let's Get It On: The Politics of Black Performance*, edited by Catherine Ugwu, 210–21. Seattle: Bay, 1995.

———. *Yearning: Race, Gender, and Cultural Politics.* Boston: South End, 1990.

Horkheimer, Max, and Theodor Adorno. *Dialectic of Engagement.* 1944. New York: Herder, 1972. Page references are to the 1972 edition.

Horne, Lena. "Bewitched, Bothered, and Bewildered." Lyrics by Lorenz Hart and Richard Rodgers. *Lena Horne—The Lady and Her Music: Live on Broadway.* Warner Brothers, 1995.

———. *Stormy Weather.* LP. RCA/Victor, n.d.

———. "Stormy Weather." Lyrics by Ted Koehler and Harold Arlen. *Lena Horne: Stormy Weather.* BMG, 1990.

Horne, Lena, and Richard Schickel. *Lena.* Garden City, NY: Doubleday, 1965.

Hunter, Anne Marie. "Numbering the Hairs of Our Heads: Male Social Control and the All-Seeing Male God." *Journal of Feminist Studies in Religion* 8, no. 2 (1992): 7–23.

Hutcheon, Linda. "Introduction." In *Double-Talking: Essays on Verbal and Visual Ironies in Contemporary Canadian Art,* ed. Linda Hutcheon, 11–31. Toronto: ECW, 1992.

Hyland, William G. *The Song Is Ended: Songwriters and American Music, 1900–1950.* New York: Oxford University Press, 1995.

Jackson, Shannon. "Ethnography and the Audition: Performance as Ideological Critique." *Text and Performance Quarterly* 13, no. 1 (1993): 21–43.

Jaworski, Adam. *The Power of Silence: Social and Pragmatic Perspectives.* Newbury Park, CA: Sage, 1993.

Jelavich, Peter. *Berlin Cabaret.* Cambridge, MA: Harvard University Press, 1993.

Johnson, Robert E. "Lena Horne Burns Broadway with Hot Songs and Biting Rap." *Jet,* July 23, 1981, 54–57, 60.

Jones, Joni L. "Performance Ethnography: The Role of Embodiment in Cultural Authenticity." *Theatre Topics* 21 (2002): 1–15.

———. "The Self as Other: Creating the Role of Joni the Ethnographer for *Broken Circles.*" *Text and Performance Quarterly* 16 (1996): 131–45.

Joyner, David Lee. *American Popular Music.* Madison, WI: Brown & Benchmark, 1993.

Kafka, Franz. "A Hunger Artist." In *Fiction 100: An Anthology of Short Stories,* 4th ed., edited by James H. Pickering, 642–47. New York: Macmillan, 1985.

"k.d. lang." N.d. www.music.excite.com/artist/biography/13521 (accessed April 15, 2001).

"k.d. lang, Biography." k. d. lang website, n.d. www.kdlang.com/biography2.htm (accessed June 15, 2005).

Keepnews, Orrin. "Lady Sings the Blues." In *The Billie Holiday Companion: Seven Decades of Commentary*, edited by Leslie Gourse, 110–14. New York: Schirmer, 1997.

Kelley, Robin D. G. *Race Rebels: Culture, Politics, and the Black Working Class.* New York: Free Press, 1994.

Kenney, William Howard. *Recorded Music in American Life: The Phonograph and Popular Memory, 1890–1945.* New York: Oxford University Press, 1999.

Kershaw, Baz. *The Radical in Performance: Between Brecht and Baudrillard.* London: Routledge, 1999.

Kibler, Alison M. *Rank Ladies: Gender and Cultural Hierarchy in American Vaudeville.* Chapel Hill: University of North Carolina Press, 1999.

Kipnis, Laura. "Feminism: The Political Consequence of Postmodernism?" *Universal Abandon? The Politics of Postmodernism*, edited by Andrew Ross, 149–66. Minneapolis: University of Minnesota Press, 1988.

Koestenbaum, Wayne. *The Queen's Throat: Opera, Homosexuality, and the Mystery of Desire.* New York: Poseidon, 1993.

Kristeva, Julia. "Tales of Love." In *The Portable Kristeva*, edited by Kelly Oliver, 137–79. New York: Columbia University Press, 1997.

*The Ladies Sing the Blues.* Videocassette. V.I.E.W. Video, 1988.

*Lady Day: The Many Faces of Billie Holiday.* Videocassette. Kulture, 1990.

lang, k. d. *Absolute Torch and Twang.* Sire, 1989.

———. "Big Boned Gal." Lyrics by k. d. lang and Ben Mink. *Absolute Torch and Twang.* Sire, 1989.

———. "Love's Great Ocean." Lyrics by Ben Mink and k. d. lang. *Invincible Summer.* Warner Brothers, 2000.

———. "Miss Chatelaine." Lyrics by k. d. lang and Ben Mink. *Ingénue.* Sire, 1992.

———. "Pullin' Back the Reins." Performed on *Saturday Night Live.* 1992.

———. "Save Me." Lyrics by k. d. lang and Ben Mink. *Ingénue.* Sire, 1992.

———. "Summerfling." Performed on *The Tonight Show.* June 2000.

———. "What Better Said." Lyrics by Abe Laboriel Jr. and k. d. lang. *Invincible Summer.* Warner Bros., 2000.

Lange, Monique. *Piaf.* New York: Seaver, 1981.

Lather, Patti. "Postbook: Working the Ruins of Feminist Ethnography. *Signs* 26, no. 4 (2001): 199–227.

Lee, Josephine. "Pity and Terror as Public Acts: Reading Feminist Politics in the Plays of Maria Irene Fornes." In *Staging Resistance: Essays on Political Theater*, edited by Jeanne Colleran and Jenny S. Spencer, 166–85. Ann Arbor: University of Michigan Press, 1998.

Lees, Gene. *Singers and the Song*. New York: Oxford University Press, 1987.

Lemon, Brendan. "Virgin Territory: Music's Purest Vocalist Opens Up." *Advocate*, June 16, 1992, 34–36, 38, 40, 42, 44, 46.

"Lena Horne." N.d. www.music.excite.com/artist/biography/11153 (accessed April 15, 2001).

"Lena Horne, Biography." *DownBeat*, n.d. www.downbeat.com/default.asp?sect=artists (accessed June 3, 2005).

Lhamon Jr., W. T. *Raising Cain: Blackface Performance from Jim Crow to Hip Hop*. Cambridge, MA: Harvard University Press, 1998.

Lincoln, Abbey. "Come Sunday." Lyrics by Duke Ellington. *Abbey Is Blue*. Recorded 1959. Fantasy, 1987.

———. "Hey Lordy Mama." Lyrics by Abby Lincoln and Nina Simone. *A Turtle's Dream*. Verve, 1995.

———. "Lonely House." Lyrics by Langston Hughes and Kurt Weill. *Abbey Is Blue*. Recorded 1959. Fantasy, 1987.

———. "My Man." Lyrics by Albert Willemetz and Jacques Charles. Music by Maurice Yvain. Translated by Channing Pollock. *That's Him*. Recorded 1958. Fantasy, 1988.

———. "Not to Worry." Written by Abbey Lincoln. *A Turtle's Dream*. Verve, 1995.

———. "Who Will Revere the Black Woman?" In *Black Woman*, edited by Toni Cade, 82–87. New York: New American Library, 1970.

*The Long Night of Lady Day*. Videocassette. Directed by John Jeremy. TCB/BBC-TV, 1984.

Lont, Cynthia M. "Women's Music: No Longer a Small Private Party." In *Rockin' the Boat: Mass Music and Mass Movements*, edited by Reeebee Garofalo, 241–54. Boston: South End, 1992.

Losche, Diane. "The Impossible Aesthetic: The Abelan, the Moa Bird and Me," *Oceana* 66 (1996): 305–10.

Lott, Eric. *Love and Theft: Blackface Minstrelsy and the American Working Class*. New York: Oxford University Press, 1993.

Lumet Buckley, Gail. *The Hornes: An American Family*. New York: Knopf, 1986.

Marchois, Bernard. Personal interview. June 30, 2000.

Margolick, David. *Strange Fruit: Billie Holiday, Café Society, and an Early Cry for Civil Rights*. Foreword by Hilton Als. Philadelphia: Running Press, 2000.

Marshall, P. David. *Celebrity and Power: Fame in Contemporary Culture.* Minneapolis: University of Minnesota Press, 1997.

Mattern, Mark. *Acting in Concert: Music, Community, and Political Action.* New Brunswick, NJ: Rutgers University Press, 1998.

McClary, Susan. *Feminine Endings: Music, Gender, and Sexuality.* Minneapolis: University of Minnesota Press, 1991.

McCorkle, Susannah. "'I Swear I Won't Call No Copper If I'm Beat Up by My Poppa.'" *New York Times Magazine,* January 9, 1994, 32–33.

Millstein, Gilbert, narrator. *The Essential Billie Holiday Carnegie Hall Concert.* Recorded November 1956. Verve, 1989.

Mohanty, Chandra Talpade. *Feminism without Borders: Decolonizing Theory, Practicing Solidarity.* Durham, NC: Duke University Press, 2003.

Moore, John. "'The Hieroglyphics of Love': The Torch Singers and Interpretation." *Popular Music* 8, no. 1 (1989): 31–57.

Morehead, Philip D. "Torch Song." With Anne MacNeil. In *The New American Dictionary of Music* (New York: Dutton, 1991).

Morgan, Robin. "Planetary Feminism: The Politics of the 21st Century." In *Sisterhood Is Global: The International Women's Movement Anthology,* 1–37. New York: Anchor, 1984.

Mowry, George E. *The Urban Nation, 1920–1960.* New York: Hill, 1965.

Muñoz, José Esteban. *Disidentifications: Queers of Color and the Performance of Politics.* Minneapolis: University of Minnesota Press, 1999.

*Music for Torching with Billie Holiday.* Liner notes. Verve, 1995.

Nelson, J. "Abbey Lincoln." *Essence* 22, no. 12 (1992): 72.

Nicholson, Stuart. *Billie Holiday.* Boston: Northeastern University Press, 1995.

O'Brien, Lucy. *She Bop: The Definitive History of Women in Rock, Pop, and Soul.* New York: Penguin, 1995.

Ogunba, Oyin. "Traditional African Festival Drama." In *Theatre in Africa,* edited by Oyin Ogunba and Abiola Irele. Ibadan, Nigeria: Ibadan University Press, 1978.

O'Meally, Robert. *Lady Day: The Many Faces of Billie Holiday.* New York: Arcade, 1991.

Paglia, Camille. "The Way She Was." In *Diva: Barbra Streisand and the Making of a Superstar,* edited by Ethlie Ann Vare, 221–26. New York: Boulevard, 1996.

"Palimpsest." *Merriam-Webster Online,* n.d. www.merriam-webster.com.

Panish, Jon. *The Color of Jazz: Race and Representation in Postwar American Culture.* Jackson: University of Mississippi Press, 1997.

Phelan, Peggy. "Introduction: The Ends of Performance." In *The Ends of Performance*, edited by Peggy Phelan and Jill Lane. New York: New York University Press, 1998.

———. *Unmarked: The Politics of Performance.* New York: Routledge, 1993.

Piaf, Edith. *La Vie en Rose.* LP. Columbia, n.d.

———. "*La Vie en Rose.*" Lyrics by Edith Piaf and Louis Guglielmi. Translated by Mack David. *Sirens of Song: Classic Torch Singers.* Rhino, 1997.

———. *My Life.* Translated and edited by Margaret Crosland. London: Owen, 1990.

Piaf, Edith, and Louis Guglielmi. Lyrics for "*La Vie en Rose.*" N.d. http://home.earthlink.net/~tenspeed/SimonaSara/rose (accessed April 15, 2001).

Pleasants, Henry. "The Great American Popular Singers." In *The Billie Holiday Companion: Seven Decades of Commentary*, edited by Leslie Gourse, 131–38. New York: Schirmer, 1997.

Pobryn, Elspeth. "Moving Selves and Stationary Others: Ethnography's Ontological Dilemma." In *Sexing the Self: Gendered Positions in Cultural Studies*, 58–81. New York: Routledge, 1993.

Pollock, Della. "Introduction: Making History Go." In *Exceptional Spaces: Essays in Performance and History*, 1–45. Chapel Hill: University of North Carolina Press, 1998.

———. "Performative Writing." In *The Ends of Performance*, edited by Peggy Phelan and Jill Lane, 73–103. New York: New York University Press, 1998.

Priestley, Brian. *Jazz on Record: A History.* London: Elm Tree, 1988.

Rayor, Janet. "La Foule." Lyrics by Michel Rivgauche and Angel Cabral. Translated by Janet Rayor. *Rouge.* Wordworks Music, n.d.

———. Personal interview. 8 June 2000.

———. "T'es Beau." Lyrics by Henri Contet and Joseph Mustacchi. Translated by Janet Rayor. *Rouge.* Wordworks Music, n.d.

Reagon, Bernice Johnson. "Coalition Politics: Turning the Century." In *Home Girls: A Black Feminist Anthology*, edited by Barbara Smith, 356–68. New York: Kitchen Table, 1983.

Reich, Howard. "Her Way—Patricia Barber Continues to Evolve with Soft Sounds on Ravishing 'Nightclub.'" *Chicago Tribune*, September 24, 2000. www.patriciabarber.com/press/chicagotribune (accessed June 3, 2005).

Reinelt, Janelle. "Beyond Brecht: Britain's New Feminist Drama." In *Performing Feminisms: Feminist Critical Theory and Theatre*, edited by Sue-Ellen Case, 150–59. Baltimore: Johns Hopkins University Press, 1990.

———. "Notes for a Radical Democratic Theater: Productive Crises and the Challenge of Indeterminacy." In *Staging Resistance: Essays on Political Theater*, edited by Jeanne Colleran and Jenny S. Spencer, 283–300. Ann Arbor: University of Michigan Press, 1998.

René, Leon, Otis René Jr., and Clarence Muse. Lyrics for "Sleepytime Down South." N.d. http://users.bart.nlo/ecduzit/billy/song/song261.html (accessed April 20, 2001).

Richards, Sandra L. "Writing the Absent Potential: Drama, Performance, and the Canon of African-American Literature." In *Performativity and Performance*, edited by Andrew Parker and Eve Kosofsky Sedgwick, 64–88. New York: Routledge, 1995.

Richardson, Laurel. *Writing Strategies: Reaching Diverse Audiences.* Sage University Paper Series on Qualitative Research Methods. Vol. 21. Newbury Park, CA: Sage, 1990.

Roach, Max. *We Insist! Freedom Now Suite.* With Abbey Lincoln, Coleman Hawkins, and Olatunji. Candid Records, 1958.

Robertson, William. *k.d. lang: Carrying the Torch.* Toronto: ECW Press, 1992.

Rubenstein, David. *Before the Suffragettes: Women's Emancipation in the 1890s.* Brighton: Harvester, 1986.

Sandoval, Chela. *Methodology of the Oppressed.* Foreword by Angela Y. Davis. Minneapolis: University of Minnesota Press, 2000.

———. "U.S. Third World Feminism: The Theory and Method of Oppositional Consciousness in the Postmodern World." *Genders* 10 (1991): 1–24.

"Sarah Vaughan." N.d. www.music.excite.com/artist/biography/24353 (accessed April 15, 2001).

"Sarah Vaughan, Biography." *DownBeat*, n.d. www.downbeat.com/default.asp?sect=artists (accessed June 3, 2005).

Sayre, Henry M. *The Object of Performance: The American Avant-Garde since 1970.* Chicago: University of Chicago Press, 1989.

Scarry, Elaine. *On Beauty and Being Just.* Princeton, NJ: Princeton University Press, 1999.

Schechner, Richard. "Performers and Spectators Transported and Transformed." *The New Kenyon Review*, New Series 3, no. 4 (1981): 83–113.

Scheflen, Albert E. *How Behavior Means.* Garden City, NY: Anchor, 1974.

Scheurer, Timothy E. "Goddesses and Golddiggers: Images of Women in Popular Music of the 1930s." *Journal of Popular Culture* 24, no. 1 (1990): 23–38.

Scott, James C. *Domination and the Arts of Resistance: Hidden Transcripts.* New Haven, CT: Yale University Press, 1990.

Sedgwick, Eve Kosofsky. "Teaching 'Experimental Critical Writing.'" In *The Ends of Performance*, edited by Peggy Phelan and Jill Lane, 104–15. New York: New York University Press, 1998.

Seiz, Janet. "An Interview with the 'Queen of Cool'—Patricia Barber." *Jazz Review*, May 2000. www.jazzreview.com (accessed April 15, 2001).

Showalter, Elaine. *The Female Malady: Women, Madness and English Culture 1830–1980.* New York: Pantheon, 1985.

Shugart, Helene A. "Postmodern Irony as Subversive Rhetorical Strategy." *Western Journal of Communication* 63, no. 4 (Fall 1999): 433–55.

Smith, Sidonie. *The Poetics of Women's Autobiography: Marginality and the Fictions of Self-Representation.* Bloomington: Indiana University Press, 1987.

Sontag, Susan. *Against Interpretation.* New York: Dell, 1966.

Sparkes, Andrew C. "Writing People: Reflections on the Dual Crises of Representation and Legitimation in Qualitative Inquiry." *Quest* 47 (1995): 158–95.

Stewart, Kathleen. "Cultural Poesis: The Generativity of Emergent Things." In *The Sage Handbook of Qualitative Research*, 3rd ed., edited by Norman K. Denzin and Yvonna S. Lincoln, 1027–42. Thousand Oaks, CA: Sage, 2005.

———. *A Space on the Side of the Road: Cultural Poetics in an "Other" America.* Princeton, NJ: Princeton University Press, 1996.

Stoller, Paul. *Sensuous Scholarship.* Philadelphia: University of Pennsylvania Press, 1997.

Streisand, Barbra. "My Man." Lyrics by Albert Willemetz and Jacques Charles. Music by Maurice Yvain. Translated by Channing Pollock. *Barbra Streisand: Just for the Record.* Columbia, 1991.

———. "The Way We Were." Lyrics by Marvin Hamlisch, Alan Bergman, and Marilyn Bergman. *Barbra Streisand: Just for the Record.* Columbia, 1991.

———. *My Name Is Barbra.* LP. Columbia, n.d.

"Susannah McCorkle, 55; Jazz-Pop Cabaret Singer and Writer." *Washington Post*, May 19, 2001. www.washingtonpost.com/wp-dyn/articles/A50453-2001May19.html (accessed May 19, 2001).

Tedlock, Barbra. "From Participant Observation to the Observation of Participation: The Emergence of Narrative Ethnography." *Journal of Anthropological Research* 47 (1991): 69–94.

"Transcendence." *The Random House Dictionary of the English Language.* 2nd ed. New York: Random House, 1987.

"Transcendent." *The Random House Dictionary of the English Language.* 2nd ed. New York: Random House, 1987.

Udovitch, Mim. "k.d. lang: How Did a Lesbian, Feminist, Vegetarian Canadian Win a Grammy and the Hearts of America?" In *Rock She Wrote: Women Write about Rock, Pop, and Rap,* edited by Evelyn McDonnell and Ann Powers, 330–39. New York: Delta, 1995.

Van Maanen, John. "An End to Innocence: The Ethnography of Ethnography." In *Representation in Ethnography,* edited by John Van Maanen (Thousand Oaks, CA: Sage, 1995).

Vaughan, Sarah. *All Time Favorites.* LP. Mercury, n.d.

———. "Lover, Come Back to Me." Lyrics by Oscar Hammerstein II and Sigmund Romberg. *Embraceable You.* Laserlight, 1996.

———. "My Man." Lyrics by Albert Willemetz and Jacques Charles. Music by Maurice Yvain. Translated by Channing Pollock. *Jazz 'Round Midnight.* Recorded Jan. 1967. Verve, 1992.

Visweswaran, Kamala. *Fictions of Feminist Ethnography.* Minneapolis: University of Minnesota Press, 1994.

Ward, Brian. *Just My Soul Responding: Rhythm and Blues, Black Consciousness, and Race Relations.* Berkeley: University of California Press, 1998.

*The Way We Were.* Videocassette. Directed by Sydney Pollock. Performed by Barbra Streisand and Robert Redford. Produced by Ray Stark. Raystar, 1973.

*Webster's New World Encyclopedia.* New York: Prentice Hall, 1992.

Weill, Kurt, and Bertolt Brecht. Lyrics for "Mack the Knife." BobbyDarin.net, n.d. www.bobbydarin.net/macklyrics.html (accessed June 6, 2005).

White, Hayden. "Writing in the Middle Voice." *Stanford Literature Review* 9, no. 2 (1992): 179–87.

Wilde, Alan. *Horizons of Assent: Modernism, Postmodernism, and the Ironic Imagination.* Baltimore: Johns Hopkins University Press, 1981.

Willemetz, Albert, and Jacques Charles. Lyrics for "My Man." Translated by Channing Pollock. Music by Maurice Yvain. In *The Great American Torch Song.* Miami: Warner Bros. Publications, 1996.

Williams, Raymond. *Keywords: A Vocabulary of Culture and Society.* Revised ed. New York: Oxford University Press, 1983.

———. *Marxism and Literature.* Oxford: Oxford University Press, 1977.

Wolf, Stacy. *A Problem Like Maria: Gender and Sexuality in the American Musical.* Ann Arbor: University of Michigan Press, 2002.

———. "Desire in Evidence." *Text and Performance Quarterly* 17 (1997): 343–351.

———. "Talking about Pornography, Talking about Theatre: Ethnography, Critical Pedagogy, and the Production of 'Educated' Audiences of 'Etta Jenks' in Madison." *Theatre Research International* 19, no. 1 (1994): 29–37. www.infotrac.com (accessed June 4, 2005).

Wrigley, Robert. "Torch Songs." In *The Jazz Poetry Anthology*, edited by Sascha Feinstein and Usef Komunyakaa, 242. Bloomington: Indiana University Press, 1991.

Zoglin, Richard. "The Way She Is." *Time*, May 16, 1994, 76–79.

# Index

# About the Author

**Stacy Holman Jones** is an assistant professor in the department of communication at the University of South Florida. She is the author of *Kaleidoscope Notes: Writing Women's Music and Organizational Culture*, which was also published as part of AltaMira's Ethnographic Alternatives series. She has published essays on women and music in journals including *Qualitative Inquiry* and *Text and Performance Quarterly*.